VICTORIAN LITERATURE AND FINANCE

Victorian Literature and Finance

Edited by
FRANCIS O'GORMAN

OXFORD
UNIVERSITY PRESS

OXFORD
UNIVERSITY PRESS

Great Clarendon Street, Oxford OX2 6DP

Oxford University Press is a department of the University of Oxford.
It furthers the University's objective of excellence in research, scholarship,
and education by publishing worldwide in

Oxford New York

Auckland Cape Town Dar es Salaam Hong Kong Karachi
Kuala Lumpur Madrid Melbourne Mexico City Nairobi
New Delhi Shanghai Taipei Toronto

With offices in

Argentina Austria Brazil Chile Czech Republic France Greece
Guatemala Hungary Italy Japan Poland Portugal Singapore
South Korea Switzerland Thailand Turkey Ukraine Vietnam

Oxford is a registered trade mark of Oxford University Press
in the UK and in certain other countries

Published in the United States
by Oxford University Press Inc., New York

British Library Cataloguing in Publication Data

Data available

Library of Congress Cataloging in Publication Data

Data available

Typeset by Laserwords Private Limited, Chennai, India
Printed in Great Britain
on acid-free paper by
Biddles Ltd., King's Lynn, Norfolk

ISBN 978-0-19-928192-3

1 3 5 7 9 10 8 6 4 2

For Katy Mullin, with love

Acknowledgements

Many thanks to a number of people with whom I have discussed this book and its aims especially Professor Bridget Bennett, Professor Dinah Birch, Dr Nancy Henry, Dr Audrey Jaffe, Andrew McNeillie, Professor Jane Moody, Dr Cristiano Ristuccia, Dr Matthew Rubery, Dr Richard Salmon, Professor Andrew Thompson, and Dr Jane Wright. Especial thanks to Dr Katy Mullin for careful reading, suggestions, and continually stimulating conversation. Thanks also to Professor Edward Larrissy for his generosity and to the final anonymous clearance reader for this book. I am grateful to the School of English at the University of Leeds for a semester's research leave in semester 1 2005–6, and to the Faculty of Arts Research Leave scheme for the following semester which enabled me to complete this book. I am grateful to Professor David Lindley, as Pro-Dean for Research in the Faculty of Arts, for his advice. I am incidentally pleased, looking back, to work in a School of English which was long the academic home of Professor Bonamy Dobrée (1891–1974), a scholar of English literature whose legacy is still apparent. His father was a banker; his grandfather (also Bonamy Dobrée (1794–1863)), was Governor of the Bank of England from 1859 to 1961.

Francis O'Gorman

Contents

Notes on Contributors

Gordon Bigelow teaches in the English Department at Rhodes College in Memphis, Tennessee, US. He is the author of *Fiction, Famine, and the Rise of Economics in Victorian Britain and Ireland* (2003).

Alison Chapman is an Associate Professor in English at the University of Victoria, Canada, and co-editor with Lisa Surridge of *Victorian Review*. She is the author of *The Afterlife of Christina Rossetti* (2000), the editor of *Victorian Women Poets* (2003), and the co-editor of *Unfolding the South: Nineteenth-Century British Women Writers and Artists in Italy* (2003) and *The Blackwell Companion to Victorian Poetry* (2002). *A Rossetti Family Chronology*, co-authored with Joanne Meacock, was published by Palgrave Macmillan in 2006.

Josephine M. Guy is Professor of Modern Literature at the University of Nottingham, UK. Her publications include a number of monographs on nineteenth-century literary history and culture and a study of Oscar Wilde's writing career co-authored with Ian Small. She is currently producing an edition of Wilde's critical writings for the Oxford English Texts Edition of *The Complete Works of Oscar Wilde*.

Nancy Henry, Associate Professor of English at the State University of New York at Binghamton, US, is the author of *George Eliot and the British Empire* (2002). She was co-editor of the *Victorian Studies* Special Issue on Victorian Investments (2002) and is working on a book about Victorian women and the cultures of investment.

Tara McGann is Visiting Assistant Professor in the Department of Literature at American University, Washington, DC. Having received her PhD in English and Comparative Literature from Columbia University in 2005, she is currently at work on a book, *Visible Hands: Narrating Finance in the Nineteenth-century Novel*.

Jane Moody is Professor in the Department of English and Related Literature at the University of York, UK. She is the author of *Illegitimate Theatre in London, 1770–1840* (2000), and co-editor of *Theatre and Celebrity in Britain, 1660–2000* (2005) and the *Cambridge Companion to British Theatre, 1730–1830* (2006).

Francis O'Gorman is Professor of Victorian Literature at the University of Leeds, UK. His books include *Late Ruskin: New Contexts* (2001); *Ruskin and Gender* (2002, ed. with Dinah Birch); *The Victorians and the Eighteenth Century: Reassessing the Tradition* (2004, ed. with Katherine Turner), and, most recently, an edition of Arthur Conan Doyle's *The Hound of the Baskervilles* (2006). He is writing a book about the Victorians and coming back from the dead.

Catherine Seville is Vice-Principal and Director of Studies in Law at Newnham College, Cambridge, UK. She is the author of *Literary Copyright Reform in Early Victorian England* (Cambridge University Press, 1999) and *The Internationalisation of Copyright Law: Books, Buccaneers and the Black Flag in the Nineteenth Century* (Cambridge University Press, 2006).

Nicholas Shrimpton teaches English at Lady Margaret Hall, Oxford, UK, where he is Thelma Herring Fellow and Vice-Principal. His recent publications include articles on Matthew Arnold, A. C. Bradley, William Empson, and the 'New Aestheticism'. He has served as his college's Treasurer and investment bursar, and between 1993 and 2001 was a director, and latterly chairman, of seven public companies, all of which traded profitably.

Hist! who comes next? The Wizard of Finance!
Whose spell on Budget Nights each bosom thrills
Beneath a charm that turns to bright romance
Bank Charters, Consols, and Exchequer Bills;

Edward Robert Bulwer-Lytton, first Earl
of Lytton (1831–91),
Glenaveril, or, The Metamorphoses (1885),
Canto III: ll. 393–6

Introduction

Francis O'Gorman

Nick Leeson, the rogue trader who brought down Barings Bank in 1995, was captured after fleeing Singapore and held temporarily in Höchst Prison, Germany. Later to be returned to Singapore, he was eventually sentenced to six and a half years in jail. While incarcerated in Höchst, Leeson searched the prison library for a book. There was scarcely anything except a damaged copy of Thomas Hardy's *Tess of the D'Urbervilles* (1891). 'Back in my cell', Leeson wrote in his 1996 autobiography,

> I was engrossed in the wretched tragedy of Tess, whose continual suffering as a milk-maid and potato-picker seemed roughly equivalent to mine as a futures trader. I read it without pause, well into Saturday night. But just after she had murdered the baddie and started to escape with her lover, with the police closing in on them in Stonehenge, the book finished because the last four pages were torn out. I lay there in shock: did she get away with it? Did she get caught? Was she executed for murder, or tried for a crime of passion? How much time did she serve?[1]

The novel speaks uncannily to his own situation: about pain and anxiety, calamity and *peripeteia*. Hardy's text plays out a drama in which Leeson seems a missing character. Tess, pursued by the constabulary for murder, stands in for the trader, captured by police in fleeing from a massive financial fraud. The lost pages clinch the connection: what will be the outcome of *Leeson's* crime? How much time will *he* serve? The futures trader, gambling for a living on how financial markets will behave next, finds himself speculating frustratedly on what will happen next in a nineteenth-century novel. Imagining the future holds him and the broken text together.

It is an unexpected connection between a Victorian novel and the contemporary world of high finance. *Victorian Literature and Finance* is about the connections between Victorian literature and the *Victorian* world of finance—its instruments, practices, theories, laws.[2] But Nick Leeson's curiosity is a hint

---

[1] Nick Leeson with Edward Whitley, *Rogue Trader* (London: Little, Brown, 1996), 327

[2] It is not possible to be absolute about these things but in matters of Victorian pronunciation *finance* was usual. Dr Johnson, as *OED* notes, stressed the first syllable and this pronunciation is

of what this book takes seriously because the essays here explore relationships between the two activities of high capitalism and Victorian literary imagining, and ponder their cross-over narratives, cognate forms of thought, and interrelationships of discourses. The collapse of Barings Bank was a late twentieth-century financial disaster, and the present book is interested in the past. But Leeson's observation is not inappropriate in this respect either because the Victorian financial world shaped the present British system of advanced capitalism. In analysing that history, the reader sees part of the genealogy of the contemporary and the narrative of secularization that leads to the networks of modern global capitalism.

Victorian literary critics are already familiar—rather over-familiar—with accounts of the relationship between literary writing and the capitalist economy of the nineteenth century. But that scholarship, and the polemic it included, has been focused differently from the present book's intentions. The familiarity is a legacy of Marxist literary criticism, drawn particularly to the social protests of nineteenth-century fiction. The emphasis of this tradition was typically on industrial capitalism and the economics of production: on the representation of industrial relations, the plight of the poor, the growth of union power, the abuses of employers, and on the divided allegiances of the middle-class novelist. Interest, in other words, was in societal divisions laid at the door of capitalism. Writing on 'Capitalism' in *Keywords* (1976), Raymond Williams observed that the capitalist could be defined 'as the useless but controlling intermediary between producers, or as the employer of labour, or, finally, as the owner of the means of production.' He went on to say that these definitions 'involved, eventually, and especially in Marx, a distinction of capital as a formal economic category from capitalism as a particular form of centralized ownership of the means of production, carrying with it the system of wage-labour.'[3] Underlining capitalism as a mode of the organization and funding of production, as the root force structuring labour and in turn class, Williams spoke for a range of critics from the 1960s to the early 1980s who were preoccupied with the economic foundation of industrial relations as it was represented in literature. Critical studies including David Craig's *The Real Foundations: Literature and Social Change* (1973), Williams's *The English Novel* (1970), P. J. Keating's *The Working Classes in Victorian Fiction* (1971), and Sheila Smith's *The Other Nation: The Poor in English Novels of the 1840s and 1850s* (1980) exemplified the results of such preoccupations.

Marxist criticism has relinquished its conspicuous place in the Anglo-American academy. Its emphasis on literature and the economics of production, and

by no means dead now. But nineteenth-century pronunciation guides accented the latter syllable. The first Earl of Lytton, who provides the motto quotation for this volume, accordingly rhymes 'Finance' with an iambic 'romance'; Elizabeth Barrett Browning, though less agreeably, rhymed it with (the iambic) 'a lance' in 'Napoleon III in Italy' (1860), ll. 375/377.

³ Raymond Williams, *Keywords: A Vocabulary of Culture and Society* (London: Fontana, 1976), 43.

particularly on the social-problem novel and literature between about 1830 and 1870, has been replaced, nevertheless, by the current, economically inspired interest among critics of different priorities. Chronologically, this new interest is in post-1870 Anglo-American writing, particularly the *fin de siècle*. Its key writers include Walter Pater, Oscar Wilde, George Gissing, Theodore Dreiser, and H. G. Wells, and other diverse discourses including music hall and advertising. Economically, it is the idea of consumption and its cultural reach which is of central interest. If the factory was the totemic capitalist structure for the earlier generation of writers, the equivalent for the new group of scholars considering the relationship of economics and culture—historians, literature scholars, cultural critics—is the department store, the shopping mall, and later the cinema.[4]

Walter Pater's definition of the aesthetic critic's business at the beginning of *The Renaissance* (1873) privileged the spectator of art as, though he did not use the word, a consumer. The 'objects with which aesthetic criticism deals', Pater said, are diverse, but the questions to be asked of them (music, poetry, painting), the same: 'What is this song or picture, this engaging personality presented in life or in a book, *to me*? What effect does it really produce on me? Does it give me pleasure? and if so, what sort or degree of pleasure?'[5] Pater's words were the clearest statement in English from the new Aesthetes about art as the consumption of pleasure in polite defiance of an earlier Ruskinian tradition that stressed the *production* of art by societies and its role as an index of their moral health. That the shy, indoors Walter Pater could have been speaking about shopping on the modern commercial High Street was, for recent critics, no accident. The new concern with the consumer has driven inquiries about art and capitalism in a fresh direction. Consumerism and the high art theories of the Aesthetes and the *fin de siècle*, the development of advertising and the probing of modern consumerist culture (prominent texts include George Gissing's *In the Year of Jubilee* (1894), Theodore Dreiser's *Sister Carrie* (1900), H. G. Wells's *Tono-Bungay* (1909)); the problems of maintaining artistic prestige or any sense of intrinsic value in a culture pre- occupied with utility and the (half-) satisfaction of consumers' desires—these are some of the topics of the current rewarding investigations.

Regenia Gagnier's work on the economist W. S. Jevons (1835–82) and the marginal revolution in theories of value offered an extensive account of how consumerist economics related to an understanding of art's worth in both the nineteenth and twentieth centuries. (There is, of course, a wider debate among literary critics and historians about precisely where and when consumerism may be coherently identified in British and North American culture,

---

[4] It is usually said that the Bon Marché store in Paris, founded in 1838 by Aristide Boucicault (1810–77), had become the first proper department store by 1852. Cf. Émile Zola, *Au bonheur des dames* (1883).

[5] Walter Pater, *The Renaissance: Studies in Art and Poetry* (Oxford: Oxford University Press, 1986), p. xxix. Italic original.

with recent work moving backward to locate its emergence in the eighteenth century, the seventeenth century, the Renaissance.)[6] Seeing the human subject as defined at the end of the nineteenth century by the 'insatiability of his desires',[7] Gagnier's *The Insatiability of Human Wants: Economics and Aesthetics in Market Society* (2000) argued for the cultural significance of Jevons's claim in his *The Theory of Political Economy* (1871) that the value of an item resided *only* in what price the market would pay for it, in what utility it was perceived to have to a customer. Gagnier's map of the cultural consequences of this emphasis was well received though dispute about how easily theories from the specialized discourse of the marginal revolution entered the broader culture remains. Other studies similarly interested in different shapes of consumerism, though not in Jevons, at the end of the century include—to take but three symptomatic instances from literary criticism and social history—Rachel Bowlby's *Just Looking: Consumer Culture in Dreiser, Gissing and Zola* (1985), Geoffrey Crossick and Serge Jaumain, eds, *Cathedrals of Consumption: The European Department Store, 1850–1939* (1998), and Erika Elaine Rappaport's *Shopping for Pleasure: Women in the Making of London's West End* (2000).

Prominent discussions of literature and economics in the Victorian period have explored the two fundamentals of traditional economic theory in relation to art and art theory. But the present book looks, broadly, at capitalism in the Victorian period from other angles because it moves beyond relations of production/consumption to the more complex structures of nineteenth-century advanced capitalism in its historical moment. Raymond Williams, defining the industrial nature of Victorian capitalism, found no place for the institutions and instruments of high finance in *Keywords*, remaining interested in relationships of a factory-dominated world. The structures and institutions that sustained the international economic power which Great Britain, by the end of the nineteenth century, had become were easily omitted. Such matters in which the present book is either explicitly interested, or which it implicitly offers more generally as legitimate for literary critics to consider, include the development of international banking and its systems of communication, currency, credit instruments, company law, insurance, intellectual property legislation, the stock market and financial trading, taxation, business cycle theories, the professionalization of accountancy, the national debt.

---

[6] See, for instance, John Brewer and Roy Porter (eds), *Consumption and the World of Goods* (London: Routledge, 1993); Cary Carson, Ronald Hoffman, and Peter J. Albert (eds), *Of Consuming Interests: The Style of Life in the Eighteenth Century* (Charlottesville: University Press of Virginia, for the United States Capitol Historical Society, 1994); Lorna Weatherill, *Consumer Behaviour and Material Culture in Britain, 1660–1760* (2nd edn, London: Routledge, 1996); Lisa Jardine, *Worldy Goods: A New History of the Renaissance* (London: Macmillan, 1996).

[7] Regenia Gagnier, *The Insatiability of Human Wants: Economics and Aesthetics in Market Society* (Chicago: University of Chicago Press, 2000), 94.

Recent recuperative work has begun to make some of these topics, which once might have seemed inaccessible, apparent to critics of culture. (Historians of economics and business have been interested in these themes for a while.) Some writers on literature included in the present volume have been instrumental in this, as have others. With her 2003 book on the British financial system in the nineteenth century, Mary Poovey made available for readers of Victorian literature and culture a sample of source texts from the business and periodical press. She remarked in her Introduction that the documents revealed the 'by-ways' of 'the world of nineteenth-century financial institutions' which were 'almost completely foreign to most modern readers'.[8] The volume was symptomatic of the willingness of a small group of Victorian humanities scholars to begin thinking seriously about complex manifestations of nineteenth-century financial life and, potentially, how those manifestations may have negotiated with cultural forms.

Other important discussions appeared before and after Poovey's. A special edition of *Victorian Studies* (2002), co-edited by Cannon Schmitt, Nancy Henry, and Anjali Arondekar brought an interdisciplinary expertise to questions specifically about Victorian investments including their relation to, and appearance in, aesthetic forms (see especially Audrey Jaffe's important essay, 'Trollope in the Stock Market: Irrational Exuberance and *The Prime Minister*'). This special edition, it should be added, forms the basis of an expanded collection forthcoming from Indiana University Press. Andrew Smith's special edition of the Canadian journal *Victorian Review* (volume 31.2, (2005)) on 'Literature and Money' moved the analysis of its topic beyond class issues and into currency's more diverse consequences on literary representations with an emphasis on sensation fiction, the correspondences between money and the meaning of the supernatural, and on women and money.[9] Yet with so much new data to present and interpret to a humanities readership, the current engagement with financial systems has not always been able to find space, despite good intentions, for much actual inquiry into actual literary writing, for detailed analysis of the relationships between finance and the imaginative textures of poetry, fiction, and drama.

Pierre Bourdieu's model of the field of cultural production—joined with the wider prevalence of theories of discoursal interrelation privileged also by New Historicists—has been notably influential in studies of literature and the

[8] Mary Poovey (ed), *The Financial System in Nineteenth-century Britain* (New York: Oxford University Press, 2003), p. ix.
[9] The contents are: Andrew Smith, 'Introduction: Literature and Money'; Mary Poovey, 'Discriminating Reading'; Andrew Smith, 'Dickens' Ghosts: Invisible Economies and Christmas'; Laurence Talairach-Vielmas 'Victorian Sensational Shoppers: Representing Transgressive Femininity in Wilkie Collins's *No Name*'; T. Silvia Wagner, 'The Miser's New Notes and the Victorian Sensation Novel: Plotting the Magic of Paper Money'; Dagni Bredesen, ' "What's a Woman to Do?": Managing Money and Manipulating Fictions in Trollope's *Can You Forgive Her?* and *The Eustace Diamonds*'.

marketplace.[10] Indeed, Bourdieu is the chief single theorist to have helped impel the present interest in Victorian studies in finance, a development given momentum by wider international events in very recent history and local developments in contemporary academe. The increasing and apparently successful expansion of capitalism into previously non-capitalist societies, a post-9/11 consciousness, despite that, of the insecurity of global financial systems and the fragility of the West's economic security are factors urging the present fascinations. More specifically for the university teacher, another has been the increasing pressure on academia to transforms itself in crucial ways along business lines in which making money through public grant income and Knowledge Transfer has encouraged researchers in the humanities to understand themselves anew as more obviously within, rather than wholly critically exterior to, a capitalist system and in part to re-conceptualize their work, with suggestive financial vocabulary, as situated within a 'knowledge economy'. Bourdieu's conception of the field of cultural production continues to provide an appealingly explanatory model of how material conditions, including publishing history, readership, and economic circumstances of marketing and presentation, assisted to produce cultural meaning for texts and shaped how they were and are read. Important studies including Peter D. McDonald's *British Literary Culture and Publishing Practice, 1880–1914* (1997) and Paul Delany's *Literature, Money and the Market from Trollope to Amis* (2002) have recently explored with authority Bourdieu's interpretive power for the period covered by the present book.[11] Bourdieu is not an explicit presence in the present collection. But a number of essays, including my own, implicitly examine his terms. Josephine Guy's essay is, certainly, an interrogation in part of his model, cannily exposing its limits for literary critics seeking to understand what aesthetic value might be.

Advanced studies of publishing and the material conditions of authorship since John Sutherland's *Victorian Novelists and Publishers* (1976) have, with and without Bourdieu's paradigms, provided invaluable documentary evidence about aspects of nineteenth-century culture's economic environment. Scholars interested in the subject area broadly denoted as the history of the book have included studies of reading, circulation, publishing, intellectual property, and advertising. Substantial contributions to knowledge about Victorian writing and its material circumstances include those particularly in the *fin de siècle,* woman's writing, working-class reading habits, and popular fiction. But the aim of the present book is as different from this group of scholars as it is from other recent discussions of Victorian financial life. *Victorian Literature and*

---

[10] See, for instance, Pierre Bourdieu, *Outline of a Theory of Practice*, trans. Richard Nice (Cambridge: Cambridge University Press, 1977) and *The Field of Cultural Production: Essays on Art and Literature*, ed. Randal Johnson (Cambridge: Polity Press, 1992).

[11] Largely outside Bourdieu's terms, a valuable new contribution to studies of Victorian literature and the material concerns of authorship is to be found in Daniel Hack, *The Material Interests of the Victorian Novel* (Charlottesville and London: University of Virginia Press, 2005).

Finance values a range of methodologies and it develops the current diverse interest in the actual specifics of Victorian financial life including—in Alison Chapman's, Josephine Guy's, and Catherine Seville's essays—the examination of publishing history. But its principal aims are not, as these essays in themselves make clear, the assemblage of quantitative data, or the narration of historical evidence about empirical developments in nineteenth-century capitalism, or the collecting of primary texts from the British financial system, or the explicit re-conceptualization of nineteenth-century economic theory. *Victorian Literature and Finance* has something to say directly and indirectly on all these subjects. Its first intention, however, is to bring recovered financial histories into direct contact with literary texts from the nineteenth century; to examine relationships, in different ways and with different theoretical bases, between a complex economic environment and—in a way so far not prominent among humanities scholars of British financial life—the imaginative, aesthetic substance of literary writing itself.

Many Victorian writers were connected in some direct or indirect way with the law, as John Sutherland demonstrated. But some were connected with financiers, too. Exceptionally Benjamin Disraeli, novelist, was Chancellor of the Exchequer[12]—but there were less high profile links. Robert Browning's father was a clerk in the Bank of England; *his* father a more senior official there; George Eliot married John Walter Cross, a banker. The father of Maria Beadnell, the young woman with whom Dickens fell in love, was a distinguished banker and Dickens himself, of course, knew the consequences of debt and laboured on matters of copyright and to secure the incomes of authorship. Alfred Tennyson was once an unsuccessful speculator but shrewd enough with later investments to leave £57,206 13s. 9d. on his death; William Stevenson, Elizabeth Gaskell's father, was an official at the Treasury. Matthew Arnold and his father were both actively engaged in copyright reform. The father of William Makepeace Thackeray was Secretary to the Board of Revenue in the East India Company in Calcutta; Edward Bulwer Lytton read political economy at Cambridge; Geraldine Jewsbury's father was an insurance agent; Amy Levy's a stockbroker. Oscar Wilde was related—with a grim irony—to a commissioner of bankruptcy and Arthur Hugh Clough to a banker. William Michael Rossetti worked for the Excise Office which became the Inland Revenue Board and left £26,580 3s. on his death; John Ruskin's father was a financially exceptionally successful sherry-importer and a wise investor; Gerard Manley Hopkins's father was an average adjuster in marine insurance; William Allingham worked as a banker and then in the Customs service; Henry James's grandfather had made one of the largest fortunes in the United States through banking and real estate (reputedly $3 m); William Morris was a successful businessman, leaving £54,117 11s. 7d.; Dinah Mulock Craik was married to an accountant.

12 February–December 1852; 1866–8.

Few European writers experienced Honoré de Balzac's ambivalence about whether to make his name by dedicating himself to literature or banking. Nonetheless, finance and its instruments were intriguingly available as potentially domesticated themes to a number of literary writers of Victoria's reign. But one did not need to be related to an accountant or a stockbroker to have access to financial discussion. Fiscal matters were analysed in print forms that readily circulated through Victorian culture in accessible ways including popular novels, periodical articles, newspapers, and advice manuals (such as Samuel Orchart Beeton's popular *Beeton's Guide Book to the Stock Exchange and Money Market: With Hints to Investors* (1870)). This circulation of financial knowledge prepared the way for our own culture's saturation with the vocabulary of advanced capitalism. High profile crashes—like the notorious fall of Overend and Gurney in 1866 that cost Samuel Beeton dearly—pitched debates about investment, banking, and financial regulation right into the heart of the public arena. While few literary writers may have literally studied W. S. Jevons on marginal utility or analysed in detail the updates of *Fenn's Compendium of the English and Foreign Funds: Debts, and Revenues of all Nations* (15th edn, 1893), the language of finance and the money markets was in evidence in educated culture far outside the confines of Lombard Street and Threadneedle Street.[13] For any of the largely middle-class writers with whom the present book is concerned who read the quarterlies, the journals and newspapers, let alone who possessed investments, a bank account, a copyright agreement, insurance, or stocks, such language was never remote.

Marxist criticism came, by definition, with a political position. In Victorian studies, it was the tendency of industrial fiction to protest against capitalism that formed the centre of critics' imaginative sympathies. Recently, Victorianist scholars have been more interested, in common with wider shifts away from apparently old canons and thematics, in the ways in which literary writers, especially women and popular fiction writers, have not so much criticized but profited from capitalism and made writing pay. Those who were able to manipulate their economic environment, chiefly systems of publishing, to secure advantageous deals and to exercise degrees of control over their own, and their work's, commodification and public circulation have been particularly privileged. Authors have included Oscar Wilde, sometimes imagined as loftily above the grubby world of markets and in firm opposition to bourgeois structures and values. Rather than discerning impatience with capitalism, such criticism has analysed the ways in which capitalism could function relatively successfully for producers of cultural artefacts. Recent work broadly in this spirit includes the studies by Paul Delany, David Finkelstein, Josephine M. Guy and Ian Small, Kate

---

[13] Lombard Street in London was named after Lombard bankers; in the Victorian period as now, it was shorthand for 'money markets' after the number of banks there; Threadneedle Street, since 1734, has been the location of the Bank of England.

Jackson, and Elizabeth James. The perceived trajectory of this critical writing prompted Jonathan Rose in *Victorian Studies* in 2004 controversially to describe a new manifestation of specifically 'capitalist criticism'[14] which was apparently the antonym of the old Marxism.

The texts admired by that Marxist generation, with their concentration on the relations of rich and poor, are suggestively absent from the present book: there is little or no discussion, for instance, of Benjamin Disraeli's *Sybil, or the Two Nations* (1845), Charlotte Brontë's *Shirley* (1849), Charles Kingsley's *Alton Locke* (1850), Charles Dickens's *Hard Times* (1854), or Elizabeth Gaskell's *North and South* (1854–5). This is not a matter of aesthetic preference but a result of deep conceptual re-orientations. Authors in this collection are working away from the cartography of social division and their financial themes are unhesitatingly centred on the concerns of the middle class. Jonathan Rose asked, provocatively, if, for a portion of modern critics of Victorian writing and economics, capitalism was now being recognized as 'good for Victorian literature'.[15] The present book does not make such a claim. It is neither in love with the market, nor hostile to it. But *Victorian Literature and Finance* does, taken as a whole, propose that readers understand the relationship between finance and literary practice in the nineteenth century as, at the very least, creative.[16]

When Tess Durbeyfield arrives at The Slopes, Mrs d'Urberville's country house, Hardy's narrator, regarding it from his heroine's point of view, remarks that 'Everything looked like money'.[17] Without making everything in Victorian literature look like money, this collection of essays proposes more imaginatively profitable transactions between literature and the domains of high finance, the complex world of advanced capitalism, than have customarily been allowed. Whether it is a consideration of how a literary narrative could place desire in an understanding of value, how a modern notion of risk might influence the representational strategies of the stage, the ways in which Victorian writing responded to philosophical arguments about the nature of currency, the presence of conflicting contemporary theories of financial collapse in Trollope's fiction, or the culture of jeopardy in which Rider Haggard constructed his adventures, the subjects of chapters in this volume mark a new stage in the analysis not of capitalism's deleterious effects on the aesthetic life of a nation—but of its literary suggestibility

Prose fiction features significantly. It is central to Nicholas Shrimpton's essay on money, Gordon Bigelow's discussion of Isaac Butt, Tara McGann's of Trollope, and my essay on Rider Haggard. Naturally, the Victorian novel, with its social responsiveness, is a particularly rich location of ideas in a study of this

---

[14] Jonathan Rose, 'Was Capitalism Good for Victorian Literature', *Victorian Studies*, 46 (2004), 489–501, 489.

[15] See the title of Rose's article.

[16] Cf. ibid. 501. Nancy Henry continues this debate, below, 111–31.

[17] Thomas Hardy, *Tess of the D'Urbervilles* (Harmondsworth: Penguin, 1978), 77.

kind. But the emphasis is not an exclusive one, and the realist text is not the only form of prose fiction admitted. Shrimpton ranges widely across different forms of prose writing; McGann's interest is precisely in the faultlines of one definition of the much-contested term 'realism'; Gordon Bigelow considers the non-fiction of Thomas De Quincey; Catherine Seville examines Edward Bulwer Lytton's drama; Jane Moody looks at financial danger on the stage across the period; Alison Chapman analyses the politics behind making money from poetry in periodicals; I contemplate a successful form of adventure fiction which seems, *prima facie*, far from realist concerns; and Josephine Guy considers Oscar Wilde's drama and non-fictional prose at the *fin de siècle*. The presence of only one chapter on poetry should not, though, be taken as an indication of the editor's belief in verse's general separation from issues considered in this volume.[18]

Nicholas Shrimpton's opening essay provides a broad frame, and is a reminder from the beginning of the empirical, technical histories literary critics cannot do without. New Historicism has had, of course, a significant influence on studies of economics in post-Medieval literature including in the Victorian period. A number of essays in this collection work broadly with its assumptions, implicitly offering a model of literature's relationship with finance as one in which the two societal practices constitute overlapping discursive fields. For such critics, narrative patterns, imaginative shapes, the contours of ideas and thought can be related, brought into contact with each other, across different manifestations of a culture's discourses and activities. Shrimpton's chapter draws its authority from a different kind of historicism. Examining Victorian literature's explicit response to—its public, open statements about—money across the whole century, Shrimpton seeks to place those textual occasions in the context of a recuperated empirical history of the nineteenth-century financial debate, intersecting with the philosophical and theological. His essay examines the technical arguments about money as they figured in the modern world of Victorian finance, and the theological language often mobilized by literary writers in the earlier part of the period to understand the proper realm, the moral force, of wealth, and what 'doing well' might mean. It is a secular notion of money that this chapter perceives struggling to establish itself during the nineteenth century—and that movement towards secularization is a theme throughout the volume; indeed, a master-theme.

Martha Woodmansee and Mark Osteen's crucial edited volume *The New Economic Criticism: Studies at the Intersection of Literature and Economics* (1999) argued that the benefits arising from a better dialogue between literary critics

---

[18] Rewarding recent work on Victorian poetry and economics includes two essays by Gerhard Joseph: 'Producing the "Far-off Interest of Tears": Tennyson, Freud, and the Economics of Mourning', *Victorian Poetry*, 36 (1998), 123–33 and 'Commodifying Tennyson: The Historical Transformations of "brand loyalty"', in Martha Woodmansee and Mark Osteen (eds), *The New Economic Criticism: Studies at the Intersection of Literature and Economics* (London: Routledge, 1999), 307–20.

and economists were not only to be found in more nuanced theories of culture, better understandings of literature's relationship to shifting forms of economic life. Improved exchange might also promote greater self-questioning by academic *economists* in the Anglo-American academy working apparently unselfconsciously with neoclassical paradigms of economic behaviour, 'mathematization, objectivity, free rational choice, exogenous tastes, etc'.[19] Gordon Bigelow, in the present volume, interrogates neoclassical assumptions in the modern academy and constructs, in the process, an intriguing case for the significance of post-Romantic literature addressing itself to desires and feeling in the formation of the new economic subject in the nineteenth century. Considering the *Chapters of College Romance* by the Irish politician, lawyer, and writer on economics Isaac Butt (1813–79), together with some of Thomas De Quincey's economic writing, Bigelow argues that Butt's 'romantic' narratives offer a model of human subjectivity which requires the re-orientation of traditional economic analysis. That model involves rejecting a theory of the market based on rational calculation to insist on an emotional and spiritual principle at work in economic life. It is literary writing, particularly the gothic and supernatural, which suggestively emerges from this account of the genealogy of the nineteenth-century economic subject as the peculiarly serviceable cultural form for the construction of an economic identity defined by desire.

No consideration of the relationship between literature and the structures of high capitalism in the nineteenth century could bypass questions of intellectual property. Recent work on authorship in the period has developed further understanding of the competing ways in which literary authorship was configured and disputed in the post-Romantic nineteenth century. Clare Pettitt's *Patent Inventions: Intellectual Property and the Victorian Novel* (2004), for instance, examined patent law and legal arguments surrounding new technology as they related to—belonged in the same discursive frame as—a shifting definition of what *work* an author did, and what he or she actually *produced*. Catherine Seville's *Literary Copyright Reform in Early Victorian England* (1999) had earlier considered the specific legal debates leading to the 1842 Copyright Act and, from that perspective, cognate disagreements about what the literary work was, what kind of labour it involved. Central to such criticism is the tension between a notion given new force by Romanticism of the author as gifted creator, and one as workman, entitled to the same rewards for his labour as any other producer.[20] Within the discussions is the distinctively post-Romantic anxiety

---

[19] Martha Woodmansee and Mark Osteen, 'Taking Account of the New Economic Criticism: An Historical Introduction' in *The New Economic Criticism*, 3–50, 22.

[20] Works recently adapting or challenging the model of authorial genius in the Romantic period include Jack Stillinger, *Multiple Authorship and the Myth of Solitary Genius* (Oxford: Clarendon Press, 1991); Lucy Newlyn, *Reading, Writing, and Romanticism: The Anxiety of Reception* (Oxford: Oxford University Press, 2000), and Andrew Bennett, *Romantic Poets and the Culture of Posterity* (Cambridge: Cambridge University Press, 1999).

about how literary writing is rewarded, and whether a professionalized system of payment including extended copyright law demeaned the aesthetic value of that which should be produced not for cash but by some inner necessity driven by other-worldly inspiration. In the present volume, Catherine Seville looks at the involvement of one hugely successful mid-century writer, Edward Bulwer Lytton (1803–73), in disputes about copyright, both national and international. She presents for the first time a detailed survey of the intersections between financial and literary forms of value in his legal dealings and public articulations of the nature of modern authorship, and maintains a sense of how these debates were echoed in Lytton's dramas.

The question of literature's value and its measurement, such as that which Lytton pondered, is of sustained significance for the present volume. *Is* there an uncomfortable inverse relationship between a book's worth and the money it makes? Balzac did not represent British writers in his self-proclaimed ability to take up international finance. But his decision, early in his career, to write hack works in order to create time for the serious business of what became *La comédie humaine* (written 1827–47) emblematizes the perceived division between work that was paid well and that which was aesthetically valuable which haunted writers across the Channel. Writing for money—despite Dr Johnson's misgivings in the previous century—was a spectre of literary debasement for many in the period, even if Anthony Trollope's *An Autobiography* (1883) represented a remarkable repudiation of the connection. Alison Chapman's essay on Elizabeth Barrett Browning (1806–61) considers the matter of what made literary writing valuable—and how money could be involved without compromising aesthetic significance—from an unusual angle. Her starting point is a specific, local question: why did Elizabeth Barrett Browning agree to publish thirteen poems in the American periodical, *The Independent*, between March 1860 and November 1861 when she had been previously suspicious of printing her work in serials? She was well paid for them, but she was not in the habit of simply writing for money. Chapman explores how Barrett Browning's political commitment to the unification of Italy was expressed financially and she argues that profits from *The Independent* need to be seen in the context of her support for the *Risorgimento*. Making money from serious poetry in the serial press remained a challenging issue in general terms. But international politics licensed a different viewpoint at this moment of Barrett Browning's involvement with a modern media culture whose borders were not merely national ones.

Neither, in the expanding world of international capitalism, were the borders of the British stage. Dion Boucicault's *The Poor of New York* (1857) was played in North America and across England, and it created a sensation. The drama caught the mood of panic that followed the collapse of the New York branch of the Ohio Life Insurance and Trust Company in 1857 with liabilities of $7m. It was a disaster that created financial disarray in both the Old and New World, and Boucicault deftly transformed the resulting sense of capital's insecurity into stage spectacle. In doing so, he made a financial calamity profitable. Jane Moody's chapter examines Victorian drama and its dealings with risk and liability. She proposes *The Poor of New York* as a striking example of a wider issue: the dramatization of scenes from advanced capitalism, particularly the transformation of financial danger into theatrical display, which occurred diversely on the Victorian stage. Analysing interwoven financial relationships, Moody establishes the common elements of trust, illusion, and deceit that bound capital and drama together and which were knowingly exploited to produce what she names the 'capitalist aesthetics of Victorian sensation culture'. The cultural form of nineteenth-century drama is uncannily like capital itself because it is 'built on appearances, characterized by insoluble contradiction, and defined by extreme forms of distortion': in the age of high capitalism, Moody suggests, drama accordingly acquired a peculiar diagnostic power.

The languages of high capital, the discourses of finance in the nineteenth century, were almost exclusively middle class—and also mostly male. Indeed, the present book implicitly makes a case for the recovery, as a matter of overlooked aesthetic and intellectual significance, of discourses of prosperity that are largely white, male, metropolitan, and middle class in distinction from the contemporary academy's present interests in other, often opposite, terms of identity. Yet the pitch is not crudely political because it is made from a belief that historical and literary analyses are in places losing their full amplitude and depth as a consequence of the academy's current marginalization of certain forms of once high-profile discourses, genres, and protagonists. The argumentative consensus of chapters here lies not in an agreed ideological position but in the book's overall claim about, simply, the significance of finance for the literary imagination understood as widely as possible. Nancy Henry's essay reminds us, nonetheless, that if finance was a 'white, male, metropolitan, and middle-class' discourse, then it was not uniformly so. Thinking specifically about matters of female influence in the public world, Henry argues that one of the consequences of literary critics' preoccupation with censuring capitalism is the failure to consider those Victorian women who made the most of financial opportunities available to them. Specifically, those who benefited from and helped develop what Henry calls the 'Victorian culture of investment'. It may be that the figure of Catherine Vernon in Margaret Oliphant's *Hester: A Story of Contemporary Life* (1883), the head of the family bank, is unusual. But Henry looks at women in fiction and in real life who, if not running financial institutions, made a significant contribution by investing in business. They acquired, in turn, financial responsibility and power in what might easily seem a male world. Was capitalism good for literature? Nancy Henry recovers one of the ways in which, certainly, some of capitalism's profits for women were not merely illusory.

Victorian literature in the first part of the period habitually associated financial reward with moral virtue: that was the symptomatic logic of Dickens's *Oliver Twist* (1837–9) and of Ruskin's only foray into prose fiction, *The King of the*

Golden River (1851); the link underlay the financial probity of the hero of Dinah Mulock Craik's *John Halifax, Gentleman* (1856). As part of this rather Protestant form of economics went the natural corollary: a suspicion that only the morally corrupt could financially fail, or, at least, fail spectacularly. *That* was the logic of *The King of the Golden River* too and Dickens's *Little Dorrit* (1855–7). It is also the assumption behind the repeated trope of the crooked financier such as Bulstrode in George Eliot's *Middlemarch* (1871–2), Lopez in Trollope's *The Prime Minister* (1875–6), and, much later, the dubious men behind the 'Sahara Limited' scheme of H. Rider Haggard's *The Yellow God* (1909). Parenthetically, it might be observed that one of the oblique ways in which Nick Leeson's *Rogue Trader* draws its imaginative substance from the Victorian period is in the re-animation of such a figure. And the appropriateness is enhanced by the fact that Barings had experienced earlier grave financial calamity in 1890 thanks, it was widely known, to the reckless fiscal actions of Edward Charles Baring, first Baron Revelstoke (1828–97). In Chapter 7 of the present book, Tara McGann considers not indifference to the wellbeing of financial institutions but another fictional instance of the nineteenth-century financial rogue—and asks if he really was one. Augustus Melmotte, the financier of Trollope's *The Way We Live Now* (1875), has an occasional hint of Jewishness, adding a racial stereotype to the financial.[21] McGann argues, however, that the novel is in fact divided between replaying an all-too familiar stereotype of the fraudulent financier (Jewish or otherwise) and acknowledging a modern economic idea. The emerging business cycle theory fundamentally divorced morality from financial crash: it was part of the secularization of money described by Nicholas Shrimpton. Business cycle theory proposed that business cycles—movements from peak to trough, boom to bust—were not comprehensible in terms of moral judgement, moral reward, or individual financial impropriety but were, simply, *cyclical*, a natural part of the economic life of modern capitalism, of the way we live now. Melmotte's ruin and suicide, in this reading, exposes a division in Trollope's realism (with 'realism' meaning here an empirical faithfulness to the shape of modern thought). The representation of the financier is caught between an old and new understanding of financial panic, between the restatement of a moralized trope of villainy which had dominated previous fiction and a new kind of 'realism' about business that acknowledged Melmotte's failure was nothing to do with the nature of his soul but with the indifferent rhythms of complex financial life which were—*indifferent*.

My own essay finds another set of finance-related divisions behind a novelist's representations and proposes a fresh relationship between an aesthetic practice and the money markets. Henry Rider Haggard's work, I begin by arguing, is

---

[21] The most convincing account of the compound, shifting nature of Melmotte's identity is the chapter 'Is Melmotte Jewish?' in John Sutherland's *Is Heathcliff a Murderer?: Great Puzzles in Nineteenth-century Fiction* (Oxford: Oxford University Press, 1996), 156–62.

revealingly divided in its presentation of reward. Heroes of the romances often stand to acquire extensive fortunes, yet Haggard infrequently allows money to be their first motive or their noblest. The division speaks of Haggard himself, a romance writer hoping both for financial success and, against popular perceptions of his craft, to produce works of literary value. A range of tropes and imaginative habits in the fiction subtly reveal divisions between money and markers of cultural value, specifically longevity, which seemed problematic to Haggard. In the second half of the essay, I observe that Haggard's works are connected with a further form of financial life in that his heroes are exceptional risk takers. They correspond in this respect with the financial adventurers about whom Haggard also wrote, the speculator and venture capitalist *avant la lettre* who was struggling to articulate his position at the end of the nineteenth century as a legitimate agent of economic progress. While literally reproducing the moralized trope of the speculator-villain (the same with which Trollope wrestled), Haggard's fiction was also enthralled by the chance-taker and his pleasures, the rewards of risk, the proceeds of danger. Plotting the profits of jeopardy, Haggard's fiction was in a more divided relationship with the conflictual discourses of the adventurer than his financial villains suggest. My essay proposes that these divisions suggest a conflict in late Victorian understandings of speculation and its relation to economic progress itself.

Josephine M. Guy, in the final essay of this collection, returns to other tensions about financial value to make a forceful point about contemporary historians of culture. Oscar Wilde's relationship with capitalism, Guy notes, was no simple matter of privileging high art over the demands of bourgeois values. Wilde may have appeared, with the mantra of *l'art pour l'art*, to have revived a Romantic distaste for associating the aesthetic with the financial. But he was also, of course, a writer needing to shape his work to suit the requirements of the market in which he published. Guy, using Wilde, contemplates the hidden assumption of some critics working on the publishing history of the *fin de siècle* that understanding the material environment of a writer's work is enough. She suggests that there is a tendency in such studies either to assume that the disinterment of details about a material environment is sufficient to make the author significant, or such studies are over-confident in transferring answers about a writer's material situation to specifically aesthetic questions. Guy maintains that the contemporary scholar of publishing history must always recognize limits to what an increased knowledge of an author's dealings with the market reveals. Without such recognition, important matters about form, authorial intention, and literary value are left unanswered.

'Finance' as a noun is customarily judged to have its roots in the Old French *finer*, to end, to settle a dispute, or pay off a debt. To finance, in this sense, is an act of conclusion, a closing of an account. The financial domains of advanced Victorian capitalism considered in this book are about opening up prospects and prosperity, initiating accounts rather than closing them, aspiring increase not closure, growth not ending. Similarly, the intentions of this book are to open up connections between literary texts and the economic, to explore creative relations, to develop not close off speculation.

Such exploitation of etymology has a natural pleasure, and so have verbal quibbles, puns, and homophones. But in the business of thinking about literature and finance the reader must be, as indeed in many other realms, suspicious. It is easy to believe that in borrowing the language of finance to describe literary texts the critic has demonstrated something more credible/creditable than a pleasing adaptability of a word's meaning. 'Narrative reward', 'literary value', 'aesthetic credit', the 'promise of fiction', the 'reader's wager', the 'debt to the past'—it is superficially tempting to think such terms carry within them some greater hidden truth about the relations between literary discourse and the world of money than that provided by simple verbal aptness. This is a temptation to be resisted, even when the stylistic profit of those metaphors, the credit of writing about finance with wit, remains. Fiscal vocabulary is used in this volume with self-consciousness and self-scrutiny. The connections examined here are understood in a variety of ways. But just as the essays move beyond the well-recognized place of imagining and dreaming, of the fictive itself, in understanding the place of the economic in human society (the Victorians themselves were commentators on this), so they critique the mere portability of economic vocabulary.

Opening *Lombard Street* (1873), his influential study of money markets, Walter Bagehot (1826–77) declared the solidity of his purposes and with gratifying coincidence accidentally described the spirit of the present book's investigation into the literary imagination and economic history. 'I venture to call this Essay "Lombard Street,"' Bagehot said, 'and not the "Money Market," or any such phrase, because I wish to deal, and to show that I mean to deal, with concrete realities.' A 'notion prevails', he went on, 'that the Money Market is something so impalpable that it can only be spoken of in very abstract words, and that therefore books on it must always be exceedingly difficult: But I maintain that the Money Market *is* as concrete and real as anything else[.]'[22]

It *is* indeed.

---

[22] Walter Bagehot, *Lombard Street: A Description of the Money Market* (1873; London: Murray, 1915), 1.

1

'Even these metallic problems have their melodramatic side': Money in Victorian Literature

Nicholas Shrimpton

' "Papa! what's money?" ' Paul Dombey made his memorable enquiry in the third part-issue of Dickens's novel *Dealings with the Firm of Dombey and Son, Wholesale, Retail and for Exportation*, first published in December 1846. 'The abrupt question', we are told, 'had such immediate reference to the subject of Mr. Dombey's thoughts, that Mr. Dombey was quite disconcerted. "What is money, Paul?" he answered. "Money?" "Yes," said the child, laying his hands upon the elbows of his little chair, and turning the old face up towards Mr. Dombey's: "what is money?" '

With the possible exception of Mr Micawber's definition of happiness in *David Copperfield* ('Annual income twenty pounds, annual expenditure nineteen nine six, result happiness. Annual income twenty pounds, annual expenditure twenty pounds ought and six, result misery'),[1] Paul Dombey's question is the most celebrated encounter with the topic of money in Victorian literature. It plunges his father into 'a difficulty':

He would have liked to give him some explanation involving the terms circulating-medium, currency, depreciation of currency, paper, bullion, rates of exchange, value of precious metals in the market, and so forth; but looking down at the little chair, and seeing what a long way down it was, he answered: 'Gold, and silver, and copper. Guineas, shillings, half-pence. You know what they are?'

'Oh yes, I know what they are,' said Paul. 'I don't mean that, Papa. I mean, what's money after all ... what can it do?'

Money, Mr Dombey replies, ' "can do anything" '. But his prematurely wise son is not content with this careless overstatement: ' "Why didn't money save me my Mama?" returned the child. "It isn't cruel, is it?" ' Dombey, as a leading London import-export merchant, is shocked by this suggestion. He is,

---

[1] Charles Dickens, *David Copperfield* (Oxford: Oxford University Press, 1981), 150.

nonetheless, obliged to concede his son's point. Though 'a very potent spirit, never to be disparaged on any account whatever,' money 'could not keep people alive whose time was come to die'.[2] Life, health and human affection are all beyond its powers.

Despite its mercantile title, *Dombey and Son* actually develops into a study of pride and patriarchy rather than of Mammonism. The cover-design for the part-issues includes a cheque book, a bundle of scrip, a cash box, and a ledger, and monetary metaphors occur frequently in the early chapters: Florence Dombey is 'merely a piece of base coin that couldn't be invested'; Mr Dombey is 'glossy and crisp like new bank notes'; Susan Nipper 'holds that childhood, like money, must be shaken and rattled and jostled about a good deal to keep it bright'.[3] But these pecuniary images soon disappear, and Dombey takes less and less interest in the running of his business. Instead, Dickens gives us a social and psychological account of the humbling of a disagreeably proud man and a study of family relationships: Dombey and Son proves, of course, to be Dombey and daughter after all.

The brief enquiry into the nature of money in Chapter 8 is, none the less, a valuable introduction to the treatment of the topic in Victorian literature. It is so because of its ambiguous or dyadic quality. On the one hand it invokes the complex technical issues which the concept of money had, by the mid-nineteenth century, come to involve ('circulating medium, currency, depreciation of currency, paper, bullion, rates of exchange, value of precious metals in the market, and so forth'). On the other, it points to the more traditional—and moralistic—understanding ('the love of money,' in the words of St Paul's first Epistle to Timothy, 'is the root of all evil')[4] which would characterize so much of the literary treatment of finance.

Dickens's immediate purpose in using the technical vocabulary of monetary theory was almost certainly to make a joke. There is, obviously, a ludicrous incongruity in a conversation about money between a prominent businessman and a four-year-old. But the passage does also reflect the serious concerns of its era. Commentators sometimes suggest that Dickens's interest in money was prompted by the struggle to raise finance for the *Daily News*. Bradbury and Evans were willing to put up half the capital (£22,500, or £1,782,000 in 2004 values) but the failure of 'a Great Broker in the City' in November 1845 scared off other potential investors.[5] Despite the need to get the newspaper into print, the share issue was not fully subscribed until the end of the year. This anxious

[2] Charles Dickens, *Dombey and Son* (Oxford: Oxford University Press, 1974), 93–5.

[3] *Dombey and Son*, 3, 19, 28.   [4] 1 Timothy 6: 10.

[5] *The Letters of Charles Dickens: The Pilgrim Edition*, ed. Madeline House, Graham Storey, Kathleen Tillotson, 12 vols (Oxford: Clarendon Press, 1965–2002), iv. 424 (letter of 4 November 1845). The 'Great Broker' was the stockbroker S. F. Stallard. Throughout this chapter I use the Bank of England's CDKO (the serial code of the retail price index) long-term indicator of prices of consumer goods and services 1800–1974, kindly updated to 2004 for me by Mark Robson.

encounter with high finance may have sharpened Dickens's concern with money. But Dombey's attempt to define it in fact reflects something less narrowly personal—an intense debate about the nature, status, and proper management of money which ran through the entire first half of the nineteenth century, reaching its climax in 1844.

Philosophical discussion of the nature of money was not, of course, a new phenomenon. Aristotle considered it in the *Nicomachean Ethics*, insisting even then that money was a measuring or signifying system and, as such, clearly distinct from wealth:

all commodities exchanged must be able to be compared in some way. It is to meet this requirement that men have introduced money; money constitutes in a manner a middle term, for it is a measure of all things ... It is necessary ... that all commodities shall be measured by some one standard ... And this standard is in reality demand ... But demand has come to be conventionally represented by money; this is why money is called *nomisma* (customary currency), because it does not exist by nature but by custom (*nomos*), and can be altered and rendered useless at will.[6]

The two key notions that money is a measure of value and a medium of exchange are already present here, and the parallel between money and language would become a commonplace. Juvenal, in his *Satires*, spoke of the 'real poet ... whose pieces are struck from no common mint', punning as he did so on the word for mint ('moneta'—from which the English word 'money' derives) since it was in the Temple of Moneta (Mnemosyne or the Mother of the Muses) that Roman money was coined.[7]

This analogy between money and literature was reinforced in the age of print, since coins had been the earliest form of reproductively printed text. David Hume, in his essay 'Of Interest', in 1752, reiterated Aristotle's point that money had 'chiefly a fictitious value'.[8] Adam Smith, in *The Wealth of Nations* (1776), strengthened the ancient distinction between money and wealth by redefining the latter as what we would now call Gross National Product (GNP) rather than as bullion. He also provided a series of metaphors for the way in which money functioned. It was 'the great wheel of circulation, the great instrument of commerce'. The 'gold and silver money which circulates in any country may ... be compared to a highway, which, while it circulates and carries to market all the grass and corn of the country, produces itself not a single pile of either'. Bank notes, on the other hand, were 'a sort of waggon-way through the air'. Commerce and industry, 'though they may be somewhat augmented, cannot be altogether so secure, when they are, thus, as it were, suspended upon the Daedalian wings

[6] Aristotle, *Nicomachean Ethics*, trans. H. Rackham, Loeb Classical Library (London: Heinemann, 1968), 283–5.

[7] *Juvenal and Persius*, trans. G. G. Ramsay, Loeb Classical Library (London: Heinemann, 1918), 141–2 (Satire 7, ll. 53–5).

[8] David Hume, *Essays and Treatises on Several Subjects*, 2 vols (London: Cadell, 1793), i. 294.

of paper money'.[9] The narrator's vision, in Tennyson's 'Locksley Hall' (1842), of a future in which

> the heavens fill with commerce, argosies of magic sails,
> Pilots of the purple twilight, dropping down with costly bales;[10]

stands, chronologically, half-way between the literal advent of commercial air transport and Smith's figurative account of the operation of a paper currency. For Hume, in his essay 'Of Money', the conventional conception of it as a wheel of trade was not subtle enough: 'It is none of the wheels of trade: It is the oil which renders the motion of the wheels more smooth and easy.'[11]

The tendency to see money as something more substantial than merely an Aristotlean 'middle term' was not easily eradicated. Richard Whately, in the appendix 'On certain terms which are peculiarly liable to be used ambiguously' which he added to his *Elements of Logic* (1826), deplored the continuing tendency to use the words wealth and money 'as synonymous'.[12] But by 1875, in *Money and the Mechanism of Exchange*, W. S. Jevons could confidently identify the four roles of money as a medium of exchange, a measure of value, a standard of value from time to time, and a store of value. He added a famous list of the key qualities of money—utility and value, portability, indestructibility, homogeneity, divisibility, stability of value, and cognizability—which summed up the theoretical enquiries of the previous hundred years.[13]

Though this suggests a high degree of agreement about money in the abstract, its practical identity proved more troubling. If money was a signifying system, it seemed a remarkably unstable signifier. Britain moved from bimetallism (a currency backed by both gold and silver) to the gold standard in 1774, when silver ceased to be legal tender for sums in excess of £25. Following Sir Isaac Newton's fixing of the gold price in 1717 at £3 17s. 10½d. an ounce, banks would exchange coins and paper currency at this rate, with a deduction for the cost of coining.[14] But in 1797, during the war with France, convertibility into gold was suspended. Britain was left, for almost a quarter of a century, with a 'paper pound'. It was soon noticed that Bank of England notes were depreciating against foreign currencies and precious metals (the 'agio', or premium for gold, rose to 36 per cent at the peak in 1813). This inflationary effect prompted a

---

[9] Adam Smith, *An Inquiry into the Nature and Causes of the Wealth of Nations*, ed. R. H. Campbell, A. S. Skinner, and W. B. Todd, 2 vols (Oxford: Oxford University Press, 1976), i. 291 and 321.

[10] *The Poems of Tennyson*, ed. Christopher Ricks, 3 vols (2nd edn, Harlow: Longman, 1987), ii. 126.

[11] Hume, *Essays and Treatises*, i. 279.

[12] Richard Whately, *Elements of Logic* (9th edn, London: Longman, 1864), 232.

[13] W. Stanley Jevons, *Money and the Mechanism of Exchange* (2nd edn, London: King, 1876), 13–16 and 31.

[14] The mint par value of the pound sterling was thus 123.25 grains of 22 carat (i.e. 11/12ths fine) gold. The rate used at the Bank after coinage costs was £3 17s. 6d. in 1774, rising to £3 17s. 9d. in 1836 after Nathan Rothschild sought to deal directly with the Mint at full price.

committee of investigation: the Bullion Committee, chaired by Francis Horner. It also prompted a fierce theoretical controversy between rigid Bullionists (such as David Ricardo), moderate Bullionists (Horner, Henry Thornton, William Huskisson, and T. R. Malthus), and anti-Bullionists—who were for the most part bankers and businessmen, less troubled by inflation than by an inconvenient limitation of the money supply. The Bullion Report was published in 1810 and debated by parliament the following year. Horner's committee concluded that the depreciation had been caused by the creation of excessive credit, chiefly through the over-issue of notes by the Bank of England. Their suggested solution was to return to full convertibility after two years. The moderate Bullionists, in the judgement of D. P. O'Brien, 'had ... laid the foundations for modern monetary theory'.[15] Politicians, however, found the recommendations too risky and it took another fierce debate to pass, in 1819, the Act for the Resumption of Cash Payment ('Peel's Act') which took effect in 1821.

Once again, very different views were expressed about how to define and operate a currency. Should money, as the anti-Bullionists continued to believe, be simply a local convenience, created endogenously by the needs of trade, and guaranteed by the goods whose sale and purchase it funded (the so-called 'Real Bills' doctrine)? Or did sound money need to be exogenously created by a central authority, and backed by reserves with intrinsic rather than merely concrete value? Even those who took the latter view could disagree about the particular means to be adopted. The banker Alexander Baring (later Lord Ashburton and the uncle of Rosa Baring, the model for Tennyson's Maud) initially recommended the use of silver rather than gold. William Cobbett hated paper currency and celebrated sound money as the 'cement of civil society,' the 'life-blood of the nation', and the thing which, 'next to the very air we breathe, is necessary to our existence in civil society'. But he bitterly opposed repaying a National Debt incurred in inflated currency with money backed by gold: 'making the Bank pay in specie, without first reducing the interest of the Debt ... *must* spread ruin and famine over the kingdom.'[16]

In the event, the deflationary effects of a return to the gold standard at £3 17s. $10\frac{1}{2}$d. in 1821 were very mild, and the monetary problem of the 1820s proved to be a rather different one. A delayed post-war boom led to a frenzy of speculative company promotion and a wild expansion of credit. The boom peaked and crashed in 1825. More than sixty banks failed in a disaster which, as Norman Russell has shown, haunted the British imagination for the rest of the nineteenth century.[17]

[15] D. P. O'Brien, *The Classical Economists* (Oxford: Clarendon Press, 1975), 151.

[16] *Cobbett's Weekly Political Register*, 34, no. 25 (13 March 1819), 771; no. 8 (10 October 1818), 226; no. 26 (20 March 1819), 800.

[17] See Norman Russell, *The Novelist and Mammon: Literary Responses to the World of Commerce in the Nineteenth Century* (Oxford: Clarendon Press, 1986), 43–59.

The most famous literary consequence of the commercial crisis of the mid-1820s was the ruin of Sir Walter Scott. But, both at the time and later, these extraordinary financial events also provided material for literature. Russell points to Disraeli's *The Voyage of Captain Popanilla* (1828), Dickens's *Nicholas Nickleby* (1838), Thackeray's *The Great Hoggarty Diamond* (1841), Bulwer Lytton's *The Caxtons* (1849), Dinah Mulock's *John Halifax, Gentleman* (1856), and Charles Reade's *Hard Cash* (1863). All of these are set in, or to some degree reflect, 'the year 1825,' when, in Reade's words, 'it was not one bubble but a thousand; mines by the score ... companies by the hundred; loans to every nation or tribe ... in short, a fever of speculation, and the whole nation raging with it'.[18]

The specifically monetary background to this crisis was the discovery that convertibility was a necessary but not sufficient condition of financial stability. In theory, bank notes were convertible into gold on demand. But since country banks issued their own notes, without limit, and kept only a fractional reserve on their own premises, there was no guarantee that gold could be supplied in time to avert a sudden 'run'. In the technical language of Glyn Davies, 'Convertibility merely carried the micro-economic advantage of guaranteeing ... the ability of changing paper money into gold at a fixed price ... convertibility could not also carry any macro-economic guarantee of supplying the country with the optimum quantity of money.'[19]

Paper money, in other words, was still a problem and writers were quick to say so. Tom Moore published his *Cash, Corn, and Catholics* volume in 1828 with its wry 'Dialogue between a [gold] Sovereign and a One-Pound Note':

> Said a Sov'reign to a Note,
> In the pocket of my coat,
> Where they met in a neat purse of leather,
> 'How happens it, I prithee,
> That although I'm wedded *with* thee,
> Fair Pound, we can never live together?[20]

Peacock wrote his *Paper Money Lyrics* in the winter of 1825–6 though, afraid that they might offend his boss James Mill, he did not publish them until 1837. The opening poem, 'Pan in Town', is an account, spoken by the Greek god, of the commercial panic of 1825:

> The Country banks are breaking:
> The London banks are shaking:
> Suspicion is awaking:
> E'en quakers now are quaking:
> Experience seems to settle,

---

[18] Charles Reade, *Hard Cash: A Matter-of-Fact Romance*, 3 vols (London: Sampson Low, 1863), i. 188–9.

[19] Glyn Davies, *A History of Money* (Cardiff: University of Wales Press, 2002), 305.

[20] *The Poetical Works of Thomas Moore*, ed. Charles Kent (London: Routledge, n.d.), 424.

That paper is not metal,
And promises of payment
Are neither food nor raiment[21]

Subsequent lyrics parodied contemporary writers, including Wordsworth, who, as Distributor of Stamps for Westmoreland (the collector, that is, on a 4 per cent commission, of the stamp duty charged on legal documents, newspapers, and insurance policies), was deemed to be directly implicated in the paper money system:

I have a pleasant little nook secured from colds and damps,
From whence to paper money men I serve out many stamps;
From thence a fair percentage gilds my dwelling in the glen;
And therefore do I sympathise with the paper money men.[22]

Peacock's preface, dated 20 July 1837, made it clear that the problem of giving substance to a paper currency had not gone away in the interval between composition and publication:

these little ballads are as applicable now as they were twelve years ago. They will be applicable to every time and place, in which public credulity shall have given temporary support to the safe and economical currency, which consists of a series of paper promises, made with the deliberate purpose, that the promise shall always be a payment, and the payment shall always be a promise.[23]

Attempts had been made, since 1826, to make the currency more reliable. Two Bank Acts, in 1826 and 1833, prohibited the issue of notes of less than £5, encouraged the foundation of joint-stock banks, made Bank of England notes legal tender, and removed short term bills of exchange from the ambit of the usury laws (thus introducing the possibility of a variable 'bank rate'). But there had, none the less, been another business crisis, in 1836, when the Northern and Central Bank failed, and in 1839 there would be yet another. The Bank of England on this occasion was obliged to borrow £2.9 m (£196 m) from Paris and Hamburg to avoid collapse, and, for the first time, breached the limit set by the usury laws by raising the bank rate to 6 per cent.[24]

A Committee on Joint Stock Banks met in 1836 and was succeeded by a Committee on Banks of Issue in 1840. Both before these committees and outside them, in a stream of books and pamphlets, the quarrel about money between Bullionists and anti-Bullionists was revived as a dispute between the Currency and Banking Schools. The Currency School, led by S. J. Loyd (later Lord Overstone) and Robert Torrens, argued that the paper currency should be

---

21 *The Works of Thomas Love Peacock*, ed. H. F. B. Brett and C. E. Jones, 10 vols (London: Constable, 1924–34), vii. 101.

22 Ibid. vii. 113.   23 Ibid. vii. 99–100.

24 When the medieval prohibition of usury was relaxed in 1545 a maximum rate of interest was set at 10%. This was reduced to 5% in 1713. The Usury Act was repealed in August 1854.

strictly limited and substantially backed with gold. The Banking School believed that paper money should be created in proportion to the needs of trade, at the discretion of individual bankers, and that the informal 'Palmer Rule' (whereby the Bank sought to have a bullion reserve equal to one-third of its total liabilities) was a sufficient guarantee of stability. Loyd's *Remarks on the Management of the Currency* (1840) and *Thoughts on the Separation of the Departments of the Bank of England* (privately printed 1840, published 1844) carried the day for the Currency School. The Bank Charter Act was passed, on the lines which they had suggested, in July 1844.

Sir Robert Peel's speech presenting the Bill to the House of Commons on 6 May 1844 made it clear that money remained a contentious matter:

I advert at the outset to the great principles which govern, or ought to govern, the Measure of Value, and the Medium of Exchange ... I fear there is not a general agreement on those fundamental principles—that there is still a very material difference of opinion ... My first question, therefore, is what constitutes this Measure of Value? What is the significance of that word a 'Pound,' with which we are all familiar? ... If a 'Pound' is a mere visionary abstraction, a something which does not exist either in law or in practice, in that case one class of measures relating to paper Currency may be adopted; but if the word 'Pound,' the common denomination of value, signifies something more than a mere fiction—if a 'Pound' means a quantity of the precious metals of a certain weight and certain fitness ... in that case another class of measure ... will be requisite.[25]

Peel's definition of a Pound was, of course, the latter one: 'a certain definite quantity of gold with a mark upon it to determine its weight and fineness', and he went on to insist on the need for a strict limit on the size of the fiduciary (that is, not backed by gold) issue of Bank of England notes, and for a gradual abolition of the notes printed by country banks. But when he returned to the problem of defining money he acknowledged the existence of an alternative view—not reflected in the Bill—that the 'currency' also included such things as bank deposits and bills of exchange

in using the word money, I mean to designate by that word the coin of the Realm and promissory notes payable to the bearer on demand. In using the words paper currency, I mean only such promissory notes. I do not include in those terms bills of exchange, or drafts on bankers, or other forms of paper credit. I will not weary the House with a discussion as to the precise nature of deposits, or whether they constitute a part of the currency of the country.[26]

In a subsequent debate, Charles Buller would claim that the £38 million of British paper money envisaged by the Act (£16 million of Bank of England notes backed by gold, plus a fixed 'fiduciary' issue of £14 million of Bank of England notes, plus

[25] *Hansard's Parliamentary Debates* (London: Longman, 1844), 3rd series, vol. 74, col. 723.
[26] *Hansard*, vol. 74, col. 733.

the £8 million of notes issued by joint-stock and country banks)[27] was actually dwarfed by the £132 million worth of bills of exchange currently in circulation.[28]

This unacknowledged additional liquidity damaged the intellectual reputation of the Bank Charter Act but probably contributed to its long-term success. In modern terms, the restriction on the issue of primary money inhibited inflation while the existence of so much secondary money—managed with increasing skill as the century wore on by the use of the bank rate—encouraged growth. Despite the need for suspensions in 1847, 1857, and 1866 ('Black Friday', when bank rate rose to 10 per cent after the Overend and Gurney crash), the Act established a basis for the remarkable financial stability of the second half of the nineteenth century, 'helping', in Glyn Davies's words, 'to secure real, non-inflationary growth over most of the following seventy years'.[29]

By the 1870s, with other countries belatedly following Britain's example in shifting from bimetallism to the gold standard, it was possible to feel less anxious about money. The Old Lady of Threadneedle Street ruled serenely over the world's financial system and issued a remarkably trustworthy currency. The so-called 'Great Depression' of the 1870s and 1880s (which hit agricultural but not industrial or commercial incomes) was accompanied by a disinflationary rise in the real value of money. Goods, in other words, got cheaper. Real wages rose by over a quarter between 1870 and 1886, and by 1896 retail prices were at their lowest level for two centuries. The pound sterling, which in 2004 values had been worth £73 in 1868, was worth £86 in 1896.

Not surprisingly, novels whose plots involve bank failures (like Elizabeth Gaskell's *Cranford* (1853), or Reade's *Hard Cash* (1863), or Margaret Oliphant's *Hester* (1883)) tend in the second half of the century to be set back, wholly or partly, into the pre-1844 past. Oliphant's novel, in which a woman—contrary to Mr Dombey's assumptions about daughters—is the manager of a country bank, is sub-titled 'A Story of Contemporary Life'. But we are told in the third chapter that the near-failure of the bank with which the book opens, 'happened a great number of years before the beginning of this history'.[30] The second crisis takes place at least thirty years later (since Catherine Vernon is, by then, retired) and involves theft by the manager, not a conventional 'run'. Reade, similarly, records distinct phases in the history of a country bank. The first is the panic of 1825, the second the railway share mania of the 1840s. Richard Hardie, the manager, handles both of these with honesty and good judgement. But he is gradually

[27] Peel's figures (*Hansard*, vol. 74, col. 1332). The currency also included actual gold, silver, and copper coins.

[28] *Hansard*, vol. 74, col. 1845.

[29] Davies, *History of Money*, 314. Compare Jevons, *Money and the Mechanism of Exchange*, 312: 'Since 1844 ... currency theorists have been unanimous in attributing all kinds of evils to a settlement of our currency, which I believe to be a monument of sound and skilful financial legislation.'

[30] Margaret Oliphant, *Hester* (Oxford: Oxford University Press, 2003), 23.

corrupted and his eventual failure is a consequence of speculation and fraud. His clerk, Mr Skinner, turns 'mole-catcher' and confronts him with the truth:

you had only to take the money of a lot of fools that fancy they can't keep it themselves; invest it in Consols and Exchequer bills, live on half the profits, put by the rest, and roll in wealth. But this was too slow, and too sure, for you; you must be Rothschild in a day; so you went into blind speculation ... And now for the last eight months you have been doctoring the ledger.[31]

The problem, in other words, was no longer systemic but individual. Like Dickens's Merdle (in *Little Dorrit* (1855–7)) and Trollope's Melmotte (in *The Way We Live Now* (1874–5)), though on a smaller scale, Hardie is a fraudulent speculator. Dishonest or injudicious financiers were a recurrent feature of the second half of the nineteenth century: George Hudson 'the Railway King' failed in 1849, John Sadleir in 1856, Baron Albert Grant in 1879. Baring Brothers, the bank which dominated the London bill-acceptance market, almost collapsed in 1890 when its loans in Argentina were frozen by a revolution in Buenos Aires.[32] But money itself, in Reade's novel, is genuinely capable of being 'Hard Cash'—so much so that when David Dodd's ship is attacked by pirates as he returns home with his savings (the 'Hard Cash' of the title) he is saved from a bullet by the £14,000 (£982,000) of bank notes in his wallet.[33]

This is not to say the technical and practical worries about money entirely disappeared. Walter Bagehot, in *Lombard Street* (1873), celebrated the London money market as 'by far the greatest combination of economical power and economical delicacy that the world has ever seen'. But he refused to involve himself in what he still saw, almost thirty years later, as a 'fierce controversy' about the Bank Charter Act.[34] And in British India, where the rupee (like the currencies of China and Japan) was backed by silver rather than gold, there were serious monetary problems. In 1873 a fall in the price of silver (partly brought about by the drop in demand for silver after European countries abandoned bimetallism) caused the rupee to slide from an exchange value of 2s. to only 1s. 3d. by 1893. In that year the situation seemed so serious that the Government of India closed the mints. 'Such a fall in the value of the legal and undebased coinage of a large group of countries comprising more than half the world's population was', Glyn Davies observes, ' without precedent'.[35] This was a

---

[31] Reade, *Hard Cash*, ii. 19 and 24. *Hard Cash* contains one illustration: a facsimile of the receipt issued by Hardie for Dodd's money (facing ii. 32).

[32] On Hudson, Sadleir, and Grant see Russell, *Novelist and Mammon*. On the Baring crisis see Charles P. Kindleberger, *A Financial History of Western Europe* (London: Allen & Unwin, 1984), 92, and Davies, *History of Money*, 346–50.

[33] See Reade, *Hard Cash*, i. 282

[34] Walter Bagehot, *Lombard Street: A Description of the Money Market* (14th edn, London: Murray, 1920), 3.

[35] Davies, *History of Money*, 625. See also Marc Flandreau, *The Glitter of Gold: France, Bimetallism and the Emergence of the International Gold Standard, 1848–1873* (Oxford: Oxford University Press,

sufficiently pressing concern for Wilde to reflect it in *The Importance of Being Earnest* (1895). 'The chapter on the Fall of the Rupee', Miss Prism remarks to Cecily as she leaves her with her Political Economy textbook, 'you may omit. It is somewhat too sensational. Even these metallic problems have their melodramatic side.'[36]

Both in theory and in practice, in other words, 'money' was an uncertain matter in Victorian Britain. The theoretical disagreements peaked in 1844, shortly before Dickens began work on *Dombey and Son*, and thereafter the anxieties were less acute. But the underlying concern was an enduring one (in the 1850s, for example, the flood of bullion from California and Australia threatened to undermine the gold standard)[37] and this technical suspicion reinforced the moral and religious hostility to money. Aristotle had identified money in the *Nicomachean Ethics* as a mere system of measurement. But even in that text he noted that the gods do not use it ('it would be absurd to suppose that they actually have a coinage or currency of some sort!')[38] and in the *Politics* he both attacked usury as unnatural and distinguished economics (or the management of a household) from chrematistics (or money-making).[39]

Jesus insisted that 'Ye cannot serve God and mammon.'[40] St Paul saw 'the love of money', rather than of wealth, as 'the root of all evil'.[41] And, despite what is often seen as a change of attitude to the achievement of worldly success in the Protestant (and especially Calvinist) tradition, Bunyan deplored Christian's encounter, in *The Pilgrim's Progress* (1678), with 'Mr Money-love' and depicted the latter's fatal fall into the silver mine on a 'little hill called Lucre'.[42]

Paul Dombey's concern that money might be 'cruel' had more immediate precedents in Romantic writing. 'Getting and spending, we lay waste our powers,' Wordsworth observed in his 'The world is too much with us' sonnet.[43] For Shelley, in the *Defence of Poetry* (written in 1821 but not published until 1840), 'Poetry, and the principle of Self, of which Money is the visible incarnation, are

2004), 243 for a table of gold–silver exchange ratio variations (units of silver per one unit of gold) which shows a drop in the value of silver from 15.33 in 1853 to 26.49 in 1893.

[36] Oscar Wilde, *The Importance of Being Earnest* ed. R. Jackson, (London: Black, 1990), 45.

[37] See R. A. Church, *The Great Victorian Boom, 1850–1873* (London: Macmillan, 1975), esp. 16–20. The world's gold stock increased by 30% between 1848 and 1857; the Bank responded by cutting interest rates and increasing discounts. In 2004 values, a pound was worth £91 in 1852, £70 in 1855 (recovering to £82 by 1859 as the boom increased output).

[38] Aristotle, *Nicomachean Ethics*, 623.   [39] See Aristotle's *Politics*, Bk 1, chs 8–10.

[40] Matthew 6: 24.

[41] The word in the Greek Testament is *philarguria, arguria* being cognate with the words *argurion* (money, piece of money) and *arguros* (silver). Recent scholarship suggests that the Epistles to Timothy may be by a follower of St Paul. I am grateful to Professor John Day for his advice on these matters.

[42] John Bunyan, *The Pilgrim's Progress* (Oxford: Oxford University Press, 1928), 107–15.

[43] *The Poetical Works of William Wordsworth*, ed. E. de Selincourt and H. Darbishire, iii (2nd edn, Oxford: Oxford University Press, 1954), 18.

the God and Mammon of the world.'[44] This attitude was an enduring one, as was the reluctance to desynonymize money and wealth.

Carlyle did have a sense of the role of money as a medium. In *Chartism* (1839) he listed 'coined-money' and 'exchange-bills', together with 'railway trains … laws, books, war-fleets, spinning-jennies, warehouses and West-India Docks', as the most astonishing creations of the modern (Anglo-Saxon) mind, and remarked that 'Cash is a great miracle.'[45] 'Money is miraculous,' he insisted in *Past and Present* (1843), 'What miraculous facilities has it yielded'. These formulations, however, were invariably the first clause of a rhetorical contradiction:

What miraculous facilities has it yielded … but also what never-imagined confusions, obscurations has it brought in; down almost to total extinction of the moral-sense in large masses of mankind! 'Protection of property,' of what is '*mine*,' means with most men protection of money,—the thing which, had I a thousand padlocks over it, is least of all *mine*; is, in a manner, scarcely worth calling mine! The symbol shall be held sacred … the thing signified shall be composedly cast to the dogs. A human being who has worked with human beings clears all scores with them, cuts himself with triumphant completeness forever loose from them, by paying down certain shillings and pounds.[46]

There is an explicit understanding here of the difference between money as a 'symbol' and wealth as 'the thing signified'. But it is money which remains the immediate object of Carlyle's attack on what he sees as the materialism (both philosophical and practical) of the modern age. We worship in 'Mammon's Temple' and follow the doctrines of a 'Mammon-Gospel'.[47] 'I know Mammon too,' Carlyle declared in *Past and Present*: 'Banks-of-England, Credit-Systems, world-wide possibilities of work and traffic; and applaud and admire them.' But 'Mammon is like Fire; the usefulest of all servants, if the frightfulest of all masters!'[48] If money was dangerously powerful, it could also be disappointingly impotent. Directly anticipating the account of the limitations of money in Chapter 8 of *Dombey and Son*, Carlyle argued in *Chartism* that:

Cash is a great miracle; yet it has not all power in Heaven, not even on Earth. 'Supply and demand' we will honour also; and yet how many 'demands' are there, entirely indispensable, which have to go elsewhere than to the shops, and produce quite other than cash, before they can get their supply![49]

Like Dickens, Ruskin would become, in matters of social analysis, a disciple of Carlyle. But his first attack on Mammonism was written in 1841, several years before he became an admirer of his fellow-Sage. *The King of the Golden*

---

[44] *The Complete Works of Percy Bysshe Shelley*, ed. R. Ingpen and W. E. Peck 10 vols (London: Benn, 1927–30), vii. 134.
[45] *The Centenary Edition of the Works of Thomas Carlyle*, ed. H. D. Traill, 30 vols (London: Chapman & Hall, 1897–99), xxix. 171 and 169.
[46] Carlyle, *Works* x. 194.   [47] Ibid. x. 209 and 183.   [48] Ibid. x. 289.
[49] Ibid. xxix. 169.

River identified wealth (like the eighteenth-century Physiocratic economists) not with gold but with agricultural fertility, and linked such fertility consequentially to altruistic behaviour. In *The Stones of Venice* (1851–3) this ethical stress continued but was presented as a social and historical problem. Since agriculture was impossible for a city built in the sea, Venice was (as Britain would increasingly become) a commercial economy. Yet medieval Venice provided, in Ruskin's judgement, an ideal model of the just society. How could these things be reconciled? As long as 'the vitality of religion in private life' was able to purify the operations of the market, Ruskin argued, Venice remained admirable. In medieval St Mark's:

Men met … from all countries of the earth, for traffic or for pleasure; but, above the crowd swaying for ever to and fro in the restlessness of avarice or thirst of delight, was seen perpetually the glory of the temple, attesting to them … that there was one treasure which the merchantman might buy without a price … in the word and the statutes of God.[50]

This search for a model of righteous commerce continued in a more analytical way in the books on political economy which Ruskin wrote between 1857 and 1867. Here he was obliged to acknowledge the technical distinction between money and wealth, and in the 'Definitions' chapter of *Munera Pulveris* he gave a relatively conventional account of it. Money is distinguished from both 'Wealth' and 'Riches', and explained as 'not wealth, but a documentary claim to wealth':

Money has been inaccurately spoken of as merely a means of exchange. But it is far more than this. It is a documentary expression of legal claim … If the wealth increases, but not the money, the worth of the money increases; if the money increases, but not the wealth, the worth of the money diminishes … The use of substances of intrinsic value as the materials of a currency, is a barbarism … It is, however, still necessary, partly as a mechanical check on arbitrary issues.[51]

This is an account of money as a medium of exchange and a store of value, accompanied by a quantity theory of its operation and a reluctant endorsement of the gold standard. But it does not include the other key conventional quality of money: that is, as a measure of value. This is because Ruskin's economic theory omits, or belittles, the concept of demand. Goods, in his view, have an absolute or intrinsic worth. Such worth is established, partly by Divine or Natural authority, and partly by the labour theory of value which he, like Marx, took selectively from the complex attempts to establish the relative roles of supply and demand in the price theory of Classical Economics. There is, in a phrase used in *Unto This Last*, 'NO WEALTH BUT LIFE', and 'The Veins of Wealth' are punningly reinterpreted to contain, not gold ore but blood.[52] Accordingly,

[50] *The Works of John Ruskin*, ed. E. T. Cook and A. Wedderburn, 39 vols (London: Allen, 1903–12), x. 140.

[51] Ibid. xvii, 157–9. *Munera Pulveris* (1872) appeared as 'Essays on Political Economy' in *Fraser's Magazine* June 1862 to April 1863.

[52] Ruskin, *Works* xvii. 105. The capital letters are Ruskin's.

in *Munera Pulveris*, 'Store-Keeping', or the management of real wealth ('an intrinsic value developed by a vital power')[53], is sharply distinguished from mere 'Coin-Keeping'. In his lecture 'Traffic' (1864), Ruskin, in his most Carlylean manner, represented the Mammonism of the modern age as a statue of 'The Britannia of the Market' with 'her corslet, of leather, folded over her heart in the shape of a purse, with thirty slits in it, for a piece of money to go in at, on each day of the month'.[54] It was Shakespeare, however, who provided Ruskin with his positive image of a just economy, and once again the context was a Venetian one. *The Merchant of Venice* suggested the idea of a 'merces' (market: literally wages or merchandise) informed by the quality of 'mercy' (charity).[55] This Medievalist model of altruistic commerce was important because money was also, in another of Ruskin's definitions, 'power over men'.[56]

    That notion has precedents in classical value theory. 'Wealth, as Mr Hobbes says, is power,' Smith writes in *The Wealth of Nations*, 'a certain command over all the labour ... which is then in the market'.[57] But it has obvious parallels with the Marxian view, also developing at this date, of money as an oppressive force. In the first volume of *Capital* (1867) Marx argued that 'the money-form of an object is not an inseparable part of that object but is simply the form under which certain social relations manifest themselves'.[58] For Max Weber money would be 'a weapon' in 'the struggle for economic existence'.[59] William Morris's *News from Nowhere* (1890) depicts a post-revolutionary society where there is no money, in a fable which combines Marxism with the literary Medievalism of Keats and Ruskin (as early as 1820, Keats's poem 'Robin Hood' had expressed Maid Marion's surprise that in later centuries, 'honey | Can't be got without hard money!').[60] Morris's narrator attempts to pay for a pipe and some tobacco. The gesture is dismissed as an 'exhibition of extinct commercial morality'.[61]

    These hostile accounts are, however, only one extreme of the views of money taken in Victorian literature. At the other pole lies the unembarrassed enthusiasm of such writers as Henry Buckle and Thomas Macaulay. Buckle, in the first volume of his *History of Civilization in England* (1857) argued that 'of all the great social improvements the accumulation of wealth must be the first, because without it there can be neither taste nor leisure for that acquisition of knowledge on which ... the progress of civilisation depends'. In his second volume (1861) he delivered a stinging rebuke to the denouncers of Mammonism. 'We constantly hear', he wrote,

---

[53] Ruskin, *Works* xvii. 164.   [54] Ibid. xviii. 450–1.   [55] Ibid. xvii. 224.
[56] Ibid. xvii. 46.   [57] Smith, *Wealth of Nations*, i. 48.
[58] Karl Marx, *Selected Writings in Sociology and Social Philosophy*, ed. T. B. Bottomore and M. Rubel (Harmondsworth: Penguin, 1967), 184.
[59] Max Weber, *Economy and Society* (Berkeley: University of California Press, 1978), 108, quoted in Geoffrey Ingham, *The Nature of Money* (Cambridge: Polity, 2004), 67. Weber's *Wirtschaft und Gesellschaft* was first published in 1922.
[60] John Keats, *The Complete Poems*, ed. John Barnard (Harmondsworth: Penguin, 1973), 225.
[61] William Morris, *News From Nowhere* (Oxford: Oxford University Press, 2003), 32.

of the evils of wealth, and of the sinfulness of loving money; although it is certain that, after the love of knowledge, there is no one passion which has done so much good to mankind as the love of money. It is to the love of money that we owe all trade and commerce ... Trade and commerce have made us familiar with the productions of many lands, have awakened curiosity, have widened our ideas by bringing us in contact with nations of various manners, speech, and thought, have supplied an outlet for energies which would otherwise have been pent up and wasted, have accustomed men to habits of enterprise, forethought and calculation, have, moreover, communicated to us many arts of great utility, and have put us in possession of some of the most valuable remedies with which we are acquainted, either to save life or to lessen pain. These things we owe to the love of money. If theologians could succeed in their desire to destroy that love, all these things would cease, and we should relapse into comparative barbarism. The love of money, like all our appetites, is liable to abuse; but to declaim against it as evil in itself ... is to betray an ignorance, natural perhaps, in former ages, but shameful in our time.[62]

Macaulay, in the last two volumes of his *History of England* (1855) gave an exhilarating account of the growth of banking, the creation of the National Debt and the Bank of England, and the recoinage of 1696. These were the foundations, in Macaulay's account, of what others called the capitalist system, and of Britain's economic predominance. His account of the recoinage celebrates it as a combination of philosophical distinction and practical success, in a passage which makes witty metaphorical use of the vocabulary of the mint:

The state of the currency had during some time occupied the serious attention of four eminent men ... Two of them were politicians who had never, in the midst of official and parliamentary business, ceased to love and honour philosophy; and two were philosophers, in whom habits of abstruse meditation had not impaired the homely good sense without which even genius is mischievous in politics ... never had the world seen the highest practical and the highest speculative abilities united in an alliance so close, so harmonious, and so honourable as that which bound Somers and Montague to Locke and Newton.

It is much to be lamented that we have not a minute history of the conferences of the men to whom England owed the restoration of her currency and the long series of prosperous years which dates from that restoration. It would be interesting to see how the pure gold of scientific truth found by the two philosophers was mingled by the two statesmen with just that quantity of alloy which was necessary for the working. It would be curious to study the many plans which were propounded, discussed and rejected ... till at length a plan was devised of which the wisdom was proved by the best evidence, complete success.[63]

Whig politicians and empirical philosophers have combined (or 'mingled'), Macaulay suggests, to create the necessary preconditions for the market economy in which we are fortunate enough to live.

Most treatments of money in Victorian literature operated in the intellectual territory between these extremes. At one level the response consisted simply of

---

[62] H. T. Buckle, *History of Civilization in England*, 3 vols (Oxford: Oxford University Press, 1936), i. 33 and iii. 273–4.

[63] Thomas Babington Macaulay, *The History of England*, 4 vols (London: Longman, 1849–55), iv. 629–30.

an attempt to register the experience of living in what was, to an ever greater extent, a money economy. Gustav Schmoller, reviewing Georg Simmel's *The Philosophy of Money* in 1901, observed that in Simmel's analysis of contemporary society, 'Money appears ... as the focal point, the key, the quintessence of modern economic life and pursuits.'[64] This meant that it was appropriate for writers, in the Age of Realism, to be specific about prices and incomes. Such specificity was inevitable in texts explicitly concerned with money. John Davidson's poem 'Thirty Bob A Week' (1894) is an expression of evolutionary determinism which gives a grimly resigned account of poverty (30s. a week is £6,600 a year in 2004 prices).[65] Samuel Warren's novel *Ten Thousand A-year* (1839–41) is a black comedy in which a crooked lawyer enables a shop assistant, Tittlebat Titmouse, to inherit a fortune (£675,000 a year in 2004 prices), and then blackmails him. The account of Titmouse's financial circumstances is minutely precise. At the beginning of the book he earns £35 a year (£2,360) and, 'On Friday night, the 28th July 18—, the state of Mr Titmouse's affairs was this: he owed his landlady £1, 9s.; his washerwoman, 6s.; his tailor, £1, 8s.—in all, three guineas; besides 10s. to Huckaback ... and a weekly accruing rent of 7s. to his landlady.'[66] But this pecuniary precision was also found in writing of other kinds. Dickens, in 1849, is painfully specific about David Copperfield's financial circumstances in Murdstone and Grinby's warehouse: 'a salary ... of six shillings a week' (6s. in 1824, where this episode is set, would be £22 in 2004) plus, it would seem, his rent. From his 6s. of disposable income, he spends 2d. a day for breakfast, 2d. for supper, and between 4d. and 6d. on 'dinner' (modern lunch).[67]

In Charlotte Brontë's *Villette* (1853), Lucy Snowe embarks on her career with just 'fifteen pounds' of savings (£1,200 in 1853, £1,100 in the early 1840s). In Chapter 6 she over-tips a waiter and is overcharged by a waterman: 'Three times that afternoon I had given crowns where I should have given shillings'.[68] When Margaret Hale, in Elizabeth Gaskell's *North and South* (1854–5), offers Mr Thornton her fortune to recapitalise his business, we are told not only how much it is but also what rate of interest it is earning: 'eighteen thousand and fifty-seven pounds, lying just at this moment unused in the bank, and bringing me in only two and a half per cent' (or £1,266,000, earning £32,000 a year).[69]

[64] G. Schmoller, *Jahrbuch für Gesetzgebung, Vermaltung und Volkswirtschaft*, 25 (1901), 800, here quoted from the introduction to Georg Simmel, *The Philosophy of Money*, ed. D. Frisby; trans. T. Bottomore, D. Frisby, and K. Mengelberg (2nd edn, London: Routledge, 1990), 8. Simmel's *Philosophie des Geldes* was first published in 1900; English trans. is of the rev. 2nd edn (1907).

[65] *The Poems of John Davidson*, ed. Andrew Turnbull, 2 vols (Edinburgh: Scottish Academic Press, 1973), i. 63 (first published in the *Yellow Book* (July 1894)).

[66] Samuel Warren, *Ten Thousand A-year*, 2 vols (Edinburgh: Blackwood, 1854), i. 77.

[67] *David Copperfield*, 135–7.

[68] Charlotte Brontë, *Villette* (Oxford: Oxford University Press, 1984), 56 and 69.

[69] Elizabeth Gaskell, *North and South* (Oxford: Oxford University Press, 1973), 435. The sum increased from £1,857 to £18,057 between the first and second book editions of 1855. As Easson notes, the original figure was 'clearly inadequate for Thornton's purposes'.

Trollope's novels are full of financial detail. *The Warden* (1855) is outwardly a scene of clerical life but inwardly a narrative where everything hangs on the rightness or wrongness of paying a salary of £800 (£57,000) to the Warden of Hiram's Hospital. Lily Dale's suitors in *The Small House at Allington* (1862–4), Johnny Eames and Augustus Crosbie, are both what we would now call civil servants. What distinguishes them is money. Crosbie is a senior clerk with 'seven hundred a year' (£56,000). Eames has 'a clerkship in the Income-tax Office, with eighty pounds a year' (£6,330).[70] George Eliot was less lavish with precise numbers than Trollope. In *Middlemarch* (1871–2), for example, we are told that Casaubon is rich, but not how rich. We are, however, given the exact figure for Dorothea Brooke's income. She and Celia have 'seven hundred a-year each' (£52,000 each in the early 1830s, where the book is set, £54,000 in 1871).[71] This would be the product, in 4 per cent Consols, of a joint fortune of £35,000 (or £2.6 m).

Also at a relatively simple level, money provided a new repertoire of plots. Love, ambition, and moral salvation or damnation remained the staples. But money could both give a fresh twist to familiar stories and provide new ones. In *Middlemarch* it is the financial provisions of Casaubon's will which present Dorothea with her agonizing choice between philanthropy and private happiness. In Trollope's *Framley Parsonage* (1860–1) the plot hangs on Mark Roberts's agreement to endorse a bill. This is not a wicked act. But Roberts's inability to refuse a request which creates a potential liability of £500 (£40,000) is a financial misjudgement which amounts to moral weakness. The self-help narrative of a strenuous rise from penury to prosperity was frequently used. This could be deployed either positively, as with the Brontë protagonists who begin as governesses, companions, or clerks but end up running their own schools, or negatively, as with Hardy's *Mayor of Casterbridge* (1886). Henchard's fall is a modern tragedy because it is so specifically commercial.

Douglas Jerrold's novel *A Man Made of Money* (1848–9) is a Magic Realist story *avant la lettre* in which a man wishes he were 'made of money' only to find his wish come terribly true: Solomon Jericho can reach inside his jacket and draw out banknotes, not from his wallet but from his breast. As he (literally) expends himself he shrinks until 'his whole body bent and swayed like a piece of paper, moved by the air'.[72] Though this is an untypically fantastical plot, it does contain an interesting account of the role of money in nineteenth-century narrative:

In the old poetic time the same fairy that would lead men astray for the sake of the mischief, would, by way of recompense, churn the butter and trim up the house, while the household snored. Now, money is the prose fairy of our mechanical generation.[73]

---

[70] Anthony Trollope, *The Small House at Allington* (London: Dent, 1970), 11 and 9.

[71] George Eliot, *Middlemarch* (Oxford: Oxford University Press, 1986), 9. Eliot's first thought, in manuscript, was £600.

[72] *The Works of Douglas Jerrold*, ed. W. Blanchard Jerrold, 4 vols (London: Bradbury and Evans, 1864), iv. 194.

[73] Ibid. 81.

Monetary plots and monetary details, operating in conjunction, create fictions in which, in the words used by Robert Louis Stevenson and Lloyd Osborne in their novel *The Wrecker* (1892), 'there is scarce a page in which the dollars do not jingle'.[74]

But Georg Simmel's point about the money economy amounts to rather more than this. Money, in his account, both expresses and determines relationship.[75] Adam Smith had implied this in *The Wealth of Nations* when he suggested that the ethic of sympathy developed in his *Theory of Moral Sentiments* (1759) operated only within the circle of one's own family and friends. Outside that circle the world was a marketplace. Man has 'almost constant occasion' for the help of his fellow citizens but 'it is in vain for him to expect it from their benevolence only ... It is not from the benevolence of the butcher, the brewer, or the baker, that we expect our dinner, but from their regard to their own interest'.[76] Carlyle developed that thought into the claim, made first in *Chartism* and repeated in *Past and Present*, that '*Cash Payment* had ... grown to be the universal sole nexus of man to man'.[77] Marx and Engels, in turn, drew directly on Carlyle for their claim, in the *Communist Manifesto* (1848), that the bourgeoisie 'has put an end to all feudal, patriarchal, idyllic relations' and 'left remaining no other nexus between man and man than ... callous "cash payment" '.[78]

Simmel was critical of some of Marx's views on this topic—he thought, for example, that the idea of 'the elimination of use-value in favour of exchange value in a society based upon commodity production' was only really true of money itself.[79] But he did believe that money economies were characteristic of decentralised and individualistic social systems. Quoting Macaulay on the way in which English constitutional life preferred 'expediency' to 'symmetry', Simmel argued that,

money itself is completely formless ... It is significant that we term money in circulation 'liquid' money: like a liquid it lacks internal limits and accepts without reserve external limits that are offered by any solid surroundings. Thus, money is the most decisive and completely indifferent means for transporting the supra-individual rhythm in the conditions of life into the harmony and stability that allow a freer, more individual and more objective confirmation of our personal energies and interests.[80]

If that sounds positive, Simmel was anxious to stress the ways in which money created distance as well as connection, or separated people as much as it linked them:

---

[74] Robert Louis Stevenson and Lloyd Osbourne, *The Wrecker* (London: Cassell, 1892), 425.

[75] See Simmel, *Philosophy of Money*, 128: 'Money is a reification of the general form of existence according to which things derive their significance from the relationship to each other.'

[76] Smith, *Wealth of Nations*, i, 26–7.

[77] Carlyle, *Works*, xxix, 162 (*Chartism*) and x, 33 (*Past and Present*).

[78] K. Marx and F. Engels, *Manifesto of the Communist Party* trans. Samuel Moore (Moscow: Progress, 1967), 44. Engels had reviewed *Past and Present* in the *Deutsch-Französische Jahrbücher* in February 1844.

[79] Simmel, *Philosophy of Money*, 130.   [80] Ibid. 495.

Modern man's relationship to his environment usually develops in such a way that he becomes more removed from the groups closest to him in order to come closer to those more remote from him. The growing dissolution of family ties ... the increasing emphasis upon individuality ... goes hand in hand with the formation of relationships with what is most remote.[81]

In Victorian literature these concerns present themselves as a question, or persistent enquiry. *Has* cash payment 'grown to be the universal sole nexus of man to man', or not? If not, what other links survive, and to what extent? Is the greater individuality of modern life a good thing or a bad one? Is money our friend or our enemy? Poets do sometimes address these issues. Tennyson's *Maud* (1855) echoes Carlyle's distinction between the selfish individualism of the modern age and a medieval spirit of self-sacrifice which survives only in warfare. But the novel, with its characteristically interpersonal and social concerns, considers the question much more frequently.

George Eliot's account of Mr Tulliver's bankruptcy in *The Mill on the Floss* (1860), and of the response to it by his extended family, is an almost textbook examination of the social function of money. Personal and monetary relationships jostle uncomfortably throughout the central chapters of the book. Marrying for money was another obvious context in which human and financial connection could be compared. Gwendolen Harleth's marriage to Mr Grandcourt in *Daniel Deronda* (1876) is perhaps the supreme example. When Grandcourt sends the engagement ring he encloses a cheque for £500 (£37,500). 'How very kind and delicate!' Gwendolen's mother remarks.[82] Edith Granger's relationship with Mr Dombey is equally significant, providing the chief focus for the money theme in the second half of that novel. Not all accounts of the place of money in matrimony were negative. Clara Douglas, in Bulwer Lytton's play *Money* (1840), makes an eloquent attack (in the spirit of Jane Austen) on the foolishness of marrying without means.[83]

These texts directly juxtapose familial or erotic relationship with monetary relationship. Most literary encounters with money took the simpler form of asking whether it was, in general, a good thing or a bad one. The answers given can often seem indecisive. The traditional moral contrast between the merits of 'land' and the defects of 'money' weakened in the 1840s, during the debate over the Repeal of the Corn Laws, as the landed interest began to be seen as the enemy of cheap food. But money, in itself, remained a problem. That problem frequently expressed itself paradoxically—in an inconsistency between the criticism of materialism in the body of the text and a celebration of it in the conclusion. Having denounced money, in other words,

[81] Ibid. 476.
[82] George Eliot, *Daniel Deronda* (Oxford: Oxford University Press, 1984), 286.
[83] See M. R. Booth (ed.), *English Plays of the Nineteenth Century*, 5 vols (Oxford: Oxford University Press, 1973), iii. 232.

authors went on to make their heroes rich. The most notorious case here is Dickens's *Our Mutual Friend* (1864–5). The hero simulates poverty to test the moral worth of his potential wife, and wealth is spectacularly figured as dirt in the lucrative dustheaps. But, in the happy ending, Mr and Mrs John Harmon are living in luxury: 'on Bella's exquisite toilette table was an ivory casket, and in the casket were jewels the like of which she had never dreamed of'.[84]

There is, as Raymond Williams disapprovingly noted, a similar effect in *Dombey and Son*.[85] In Chapter 8 money was condemned as 'cruel' and impotent. Yet at the end of the book we are given the cheering news that 'Mr. Gills's money has begun to turn itself, and ... is turning itself over and over pretty briskly.'[86] That is not all. In Chapter 58, when Dombey's bankruptcy is declared, Dickens uses the ancient analogy between money and texts of other kinds to defend money:

The world was very busy now, in sooth, and had a deal to say. It was an innocently credulous, and a much ill used world. It was a world in which there was no other sort of bankruptcy whatever. There were no conspicuous people in it, trading far and wide on rotten banks of religion, patriotism, virtue, honour. There was no amount worth mentioning of mere paper in circulation, on which anybody lived pretty handsomely, promising to pay great sums of goodness with no effects. There were no short-comings anywhere, in anything but money.

Later in the same chapter Dombey's specifically merchant virtues are celebrated when we are told that he will 'clear the House' by 'payment to the last farthing of his means.' 'His pride,' Mr Morfin remarks, 'shows well in this.'[87]

Very occasionally a text will address the moral problem of money in a more consistent way. Dickens's *Great Expectations* (1860–1) deconstructs the distinction between inherited money (traditionally the best or 'cleanest' kind) and criminal money (traditionally the worst). The one, it seems, is as bad as the other, and in the final chapter Dickens attempts a positive definition of what monetary wealth might, in a good sense, be. 'You live abroad still?' Estella asks Pip, who by then is a partner in Clarriker and Co., 'And do well, I am sure?' 'I work pretty hard for a sufficient living,' Pip replies, 'and therefore—Yes, I do well.'[88] This, however, is exceptional. Elsewhere, the attempts to find a golden mean are more awkward. Greed and mammon-worship are figured on the satirical or denunciatory surface of Victorian texts. The usefulness of money is inscribed, much more deeply, in their plots. Even Trollope's *The Way We Live Now* (1874–5), with its savage attack on the mercenary spirit of the age, ends

[84] Charles Dickens, *Our Mutual Friend* (Oxford: Oxford University Press, 1952), 778.

[85] See Williams's introduction to Charles Dickens, *Dombey and Son* ed. P. Fairclough (Harmondsworth: Penguin, 1970), 30.

[86] *Dombey and Son* (Oxford: Oxford University Press, 1974), 830.   [87] Ibid. 773–4 and 778.

[88] Charles Dickens, *Great Expectations* (Oxford: Oxford University Press, 1993), 479.

with Roger Carbury's making Paul and Hetta Montagu the heirs to his large estate in Suffolk, and with talk of 'the amount of the income'.[89]

Critics tend to see this inconsistency as muddle, or bad faith, or (in the case of Marxist critics) as an expression of the inherent flaws of capitalism. Cedric Watts concludes his book *Literature and Money* (1990) with the claim that 'the main paraphrasable story about money has been a story of contradiction'. This is because, 'the monetary system, which prevails because it facilitates the exchange and distribution of commodities, also impedes social justice'.[90] In Macherey's more theoretical terms, such 'contradiction' would constitute a 'fissure' or 'gap' in the text which reveals the discord between 'the historical reality' and its '*dominant* representation'.[91]

The truth, I suspect, is rather more complex. Theological views of the absolute goodness or badness of money were, in the nineteenth century, gradually giving way (like the Usury Act) to subtler and more technical understandings. In these circumstances writers were endeavouring, with greater or lesser degrees of sophistication, to find an acceptable definition of what Dickens called 'doing well'. Julia Dodd, in Reade's *Hard Cash*, momentarily expresses a fierce rejection of money: ' "If anybody settles any of their trash on *me*, I'll beat them, and throw it in the fire," said I; "and I hated money." ' Her brother Edward has no patience with this view: 'did I hate clothes and food, and charity to the poor, and cleanliness, and decency? Then I didn't hate money, "for none of these things can exist without money, you little romantic humbug; you shut up!" '.[92] But just how much of it was 'sufficient'?

Ruskin did not sympathize with the movement away from medieval assumptions about wealth. But he was acute enough to observe that it was the rediscovery of 'Plato, Aristotle and Cicero' and the pagan virtues of 'Prudence, Justice, Courage and Temperance' which had caused the change.[93] In the same text in which he identified money as a medium of exchange, the *Nicomachean Ethics*, Aristotle argued that, 'In respect of pleasures and pains ... the observance of the mean is Temperance, the excess Profligacy ... In regard to giving and getting money, the observance of the mean is Liberality; the excess and deficiency are Prodigality and Meanness'.[94] Victorian texts figure 'Prodigality' as greed or conspicuous consumption, and 'Meanness' as improvidence, bankruptcy, and miserliness. The golden mean between them—adequacy, prudence, comfort,

---

[89] Anthony Trollope, *The Way We Live Now* (Oxford: Oxford University Press, 1982), 473. For more on *The Way We Live Now*, see Tara McGann, 'Literary Realism in the Wake of Business Cycle Theory: *The Way We Live Now* (1875)', below, 133–56.

[90] Cedric Watts, *Literature and Money: Financial Myth and Literary Truth* (Hemel Hempstead: Harvester Wheatsheaf, 1990), 199–200.

[91] Pierre Macherey, *A Theory of Literary Production*, trans. G. Wall (London: Routledge & Kegan Paul, 1978), 238.

[92] Reade, *Hard Cash*, ii. 167–8.

[93] Ruskin, *Works*, x. 370–1 (*The Stones of Venice*, vol. 2, ch. 8).

[94] Aristotle, *Nicomachean Ethics*, 99.

respectability, or even, perhaps, the normative income-band which would be suggested by twentieth-century redistributive taxation—is harder to describe. But it is implied by the very inconsistency between rhetorical denunciation ('Mammonism') and narrative conclusion ('Yes, I do well') which we find so troublesome. However contradictory their texts may sometimes seem, it was a new, secular ideal of money, like Aristotle's 'Liberality', which Victorian authors were struggling to establish.

2

Inside Out: Value and Display in Thomas De Quincey and Isaac Butt

Gordon Bigelow

In November 1833, there appeared in the *Dublin University Magazine* the first in an occasional series of mildly sensational tales called *Chapters of College Romance*. Printed under the name Edward O'Brien, the stories were much later collected into a single volume and attributed to their real author, Isaac Butt. In 1833 Butt was 21 years old, an undergraduate at Trinity College, and one of a group of students and recent graduates who together had launched the *Dublin University Magazine* earlier that same year. His series opens as follows: ' "Chapters of College Romance!" Do not, reader, be startled at these words.'[1] This reassurance, however unnecessary, seems directed against a popular view of Trinity College as a decidedly unromantic place. 'Do not imagine', he goes on, 'that within these courts dedicated to learning there is no place for "romance" ' (*CR*, 1). 'There is romance', he continues,

wherever there is a deviation from the modes of acting or of thought that are common among men; there is romance wherever there is a disinterested act; wherever there is a high and ardent spirit to break through, by one eccentric effusion of its native generosity, the dull monotony of the selfishness of ordinary life. There is romance wherever interest is sacrificed to feeling. (*CR*, 2)

Butt draws on the broadest sense of the word 'romance' in the period to suggest anything wildly imaginative or patently unreal, in the manner of tales in the old *romanz* vernacular. But the usage also signals something more specific here, for romance is set up not simply in opposition to reason, but to a specific sort of economic reason: to self-interest, to 'the selfishness of ordinary life'. Romance is a 'native' capacity, accessed through 'feeling', but potentially obscured or ruined by self-interested calculation. Romance is a 'spirit' which exists on an ethically superior plane, elevated above the cruder dictates of the material world.

Isaac Butt is known primarily for his later political career as a moderate nationalist, for his legal oratory, and for his work as a political economist. He

---

[1] Isaac Butt, *Chapters of College Romance* (London: Skeet, 1863), 1. All references are to this one-volume edition and will be cited within the text as *CR*.

held a chair in political economy at Trinity from 1836 to 1841, and published a series of lectures delivered in these years. His brief attempt at gothic fiction has been of interest to few. However, what is evident in these stories is a sustained consideration of questions at the heart of Butt's political economy. These questions overlap significantly with those treated in a series of essays on Ricardo written between 1823 and 1844 by Thomas De Quincey. What I will argue here is that in the work of these two writers we can see the beginning of a total reorientation of economic analysis. It is, in Butt's terms, a 'romantic' reorientation, which rejects a theory of the market based on rational calculation, and insists on an emotional and spiritual principle at work within economic life. By the close of the nineteenth century, the dominant theory of the market will rely centrally on this emotional or spiritual principle that Butt calls 'romance'. As a result, imaginative literature, particularly in the gothic or supernatural mode, seems to provide an especially receptive medium in which to cultivate ideas about economic subjectivity. The view of the human subject developed in these texts by Butt and De Quincey works according to a particular logic of visibility and display, and it produces a theory of the market ready for the age of the consumer.

COLLEGE AND ROMANCE

The opposition between 'romance' and rationality operates throughout Butt's stories in a number of registers. One is the battle between self-interest and altruism indicated in the passages above from the stories' introduction. Generous and spontaneous characters, motivated by the power of their affections, are practised upon by cynics and speculators, and Butt's sympathies lie solidly on the romantic side of the equation. The 'romance' characters, those with authentic and generous hearts, are pitted against schemers and social climbers, with Butt's narrator, in a typical passage, celebrating 'young hearts over whom the world has not yet thrown its deadening spell, to wither up all their feelings into the sear insensibility of what the world calls prudence' (CR, 2). It is the encounter of 'romance' with rationality that we find encapsulated in the title of Butt's collection, 'Chapters of College Romance': 'College' as a dry and pitiless scholarship, plus 'romance' as feeling, passion, spirit. The 'College Romance' formula is set forward prominently in the central novella of the collection, a piece of 150 pages called 'The Billiard Table'. Here early on the narrator comments that there are 'two great principles that set all life in motion, and actuate the generous or the prudent deeds of man ... selfishness and feeling—romance and prudence' (CR, 25).

The opposition works throughout the text as a master trope, a scale on which the book charts characters and situations. In 'The Billiard Table' all the characters are described in these terms: original, authentic, and generous hearts *versus* artificial masks of 'deadened' self-interest. The main character, Edmund Connor, a young student and heir to a large estate, meets the narrator's young cousin Letitia Jephson. The Jephsons are described as 'people of the world' (*CR*, 13), and while their daughter Letitia, we are told, 'had naturally some feeling', she had been raised by her mother, described as 'an excellent manager' (*CR*, 14), to 'bec[o]me ... cold-hearted and fashionable' (*CR*, 20). Under her mother's 'management', she has been focused entirely toward what the novel calls 'a speculation in the matrimonial market' (*CR*, 19). The calculating world forces Letitia to repress her natural romance in favour of the false and self-interested show of 'fashion'. In the terms of Butt's introduction, the world has 'thrown its deadening spell' over Letitia's original 'romance' of character.

Edmund Connor is also characterized in the terms of the same opposition:

[He] had much of enthusiasm in his disposition, perhaps more than was consistent with steadiness of conduct, [or with] prudence. He had mixed little ... in the world; and there was about Letitia Jephson an affectation of fashionable refinement, that exterior deportment which women call polish, which always has its fascinations for the inexperienced. (*CR*, 21–2)

Too full of enthusiasm, Edmund is all 'heart' and no 'art'. His inexperience shows in the way he accepts the outward surfaces of Letitia's worldly presentation as an indication of some inner truth. He acknowledges a highly constructed image of femininity as if a great and spontaneous natural event.

Given its rejection of an increasingly powerful discourse of domestic femininity in the 1830s, the symbolic vocabulary of gender here is well worth noticing. Its most suggestive reference point would be Edmund Burke's *Reflections on the Revolution in France* (1790), a defining work of political conservatism for Butt's generation. Here Burke contrasts a 'manly' love of liberty—characteristic of British Parliamentary government—with the 'effeminate' excesses of the hyper-rationalist French Ideologues. Femininity is thus a 'deadening' or killing intellect, an unchecked application of political reason.[2] Letitia Jephson's self-interested calculations in the marriage market, similarly, associate the feminine with rational calculation. Excessive rationality is the death of the 'masculine' heart. Burke is an especially important intellectual ancestor for the founders of the *Dublin University Magazine*, who consciously evoked him both as an ideological authority and a fellow countryman;[3] I will return to the subject of his influence below.

The formula of 'College + Romance' that structures these characterizations results in a specific psychological model of human experience, a model the

---

[2] Seamus Deane's reading of the *Reflections* is especially useful in linking this metaphor of sexual difference with the logic of value. Deane shows that, in Burke's text, both the political violence and the disastrous financial insolvency of the Revolutionary government stem from a 'feminized' principle of pure calculation. See the chapter 'Phantasmal France, Unreal Ireland' in his *Strange Country: Modernity and Nationhood in Irish Writing since 1790* (Oxford: Oxford University Press, 1997).

[3] On Burke and the intellectual background of the *Dublin University Magazine*, see Wayne Hall, *Dialogues in the Margin: A Study of the Dublin University Magazine* (Washington, DC: Catholic University of America Press, 1999), 3–6; and Seamus Deane, *Celtic Revivals: Essays in Modern Irish Literature, 1880–1980* (1985), (paper edn, Winston-Salem, NC: Wake Forest University Press, 1987), 98.

book posits at every turn. Feelings, according to this view, are an a priori force, associated with nature, pre-dating the encounter with the social world. This aboriginal 'romance', supposedly at the core of the human, and indicated in the metaphor of 'the heart', is overlaid with the deceptive appearances and false masks of social life. The book stresses the primary vitality of the inner world, the experience of an inner subjectivity, the impulses of 'the heart'. This focus on what J. S. Mill would call 'the internal culture of the individual,' in the well known passage from his autobiography,[4] will turn out in fact to be the crucial force in economic theory in the nineteenth century.

But the opposition between romance and rationality operates in other ways as well, beyond the stories' mode of characterization. A different eruption of the 'romantic' into the rational world can be found in the gothic conventions on which a number of the tales rely. In the story 'Reading for Honours', an ambitious and sedulous student, studying for a prize exam, finds himself consumed with jealousy for another more talented competitor. He begins at this point to dream of a gigantic scorpion, which threatens to draw the blood from his heart. This little castration fantasy appears absolutely real to him, and he is convinced that the scorpion exists and will kill him. He explains to his friend O'Brien, the narrator of the collection, 'why should not our souls in sleep as naturally see the future, as in our waking hours they do the past?' (159). The formulation resembles the Swedenborgian doctrine of inner sight on which Sheridan Le Fanu's stories so frequently turn. And indeed Le Fanu's first published tales—collected later as *The Purcell Papers*—were prepared for the *Dublin University Magazine* while Butt acted as general editor between 1834 and 1838.[5]

In another of Butt's pieces, called 'The Murdered Fellow', a young student, Brown, is persuaded by a charismatic older boy, named Williams, to assassinate a Fellow of the College who has threatened Brown with expulsion. Once the crime has been accomplished, Williams laughs and declares, rather bluntly, 'the Evil one is my master and I was to get for him your soul. Mark me you are damned' (*CR*, 286). Williams disappears, but Brown remains haunted—perhaps literally—by his corrosive spirit. Brown is convinced that Williams will return to claim his soul; Brown dies shortly afterward, under mysterious circumstances. Dreams and 'romantic' imaginings have a lethal weight here, exerting a superior force over the material world.

But the clearest infusion of 'romance' into the rational world—and the most evident clue to the story's economic designs—works through the motif of gambling. It is a form of gambling that is alluded to in the title of the story I discussed above, 'The Billiard Table', and betting on games of chance is viewed

[4] John Stuart Mill, *Autobiography* (1873), ed. Jack Stillinger (Boston: Houghton Mifflin, 1969), 86.
[5] The best discussion of Swedenborgian doctrine in Le Fanu's work is W. J. McCormack, *Sheridan Le Fanu and Victorian Ireland* (Oxford: Clarendon Press, 1980). See pp. 54–6 for a description of Le Fanu's early relationship with Butt.

in the tale as analogous to speculation in the 'matrimonial market'. Just as Edmund is dazzled by the dress and manners of Letitia Jephson, he is lured into an obsession with billiards through another false friend, a Trinity student name Wilson. Knowing of the fortune Edmund will inherit, Wilson steers Edmund into the world of gambling to win his money. But he dupes Edmund by teaching him billiards purely as an exercise in mechanics and physics: Edmund later tells the narrator that 'the principles of the game [are] strictly scientific: the rules that determine the impulse and rebound of the balls [are] all matters of mathematical investigation' (*CR* 28). While Edmund is introduced to billiards as a game of empirical reason, his attachment to it is soon one of pure passion, as he becomes helplessly addicted to the excitement of the betting.

This irrational and all-consuming passion, within the supposedly scientific game, is highlighted in the description of the gambling hall Edmund frequents, on a night when he has dragged the narrator along with him for a billiards lesson:

> As we passed down the stone steps ... our attention was caught by a curious ... and well-concealed passage, which led from behind the steps under the building. With a natural curiosity, we determined to explore it. It was flagged and vaulted overhead something like those subterranean caverns which you may read of as belonging to old castles in romance, or see in the cellars of a wine merchant. (*CR*, 44–5)

They follow this passageway, marked here without much subtlety as a kind of gateway to 'romance,' and find that it leads to a door directly underneath the billiard room:

> There was no key-hole ... the door fitted so exactly that its separation from the flags was scarcely marked by a line of red light. We heard, however, the confused sound of voices within ... There seemed, to my mind, something unnatural, at least unearthly, in the sound. I could not help thinking of all the tales I had read of fiends feasting; and I almost expected that the door would open and disclose to us their infernal rites. (*CR*, 45–6)

The trope is familiar now from countless horror films: beneath the placid surface of ordinary life, we discover a dark passageway to hell. Here the scene of gambling springs from this satanic sub-basement, a place where, the narrator affirms, 'I heard the rattling of dice, and now and then ... the bitter and yet fierce intonations of a voice that spoke all the bad passions of the human heart' (*CR*, 46–7).

Gambling works here not via mechanics or mathematics, but through a theological force of evil, and we should see in these descriptions the contours of the same rhetorical landscape Butt has inhabited throughout the text. While gambling looks like a morally neutral realm of numbers and measurable impulses (i.e. the domain of 'college'), it is in fact shot through with an atavistic force of romantic horror. Edmund finally realizes his gambling friends are cheating him, and he ends up renouncing his faith in everything but money:

> he became cold, heartless, and sneering. He went to the bar, where he was for some time doing little; he was distinguished for nothing but a bitter savageness of disposition, and

a mocking at all the feelings of mankind. Once or twice he came forward on the liberal side in politics. (*CR*, 146)

With this last turn, on the question of liberal politics, we can see the full implications of Butt's gothic mode in these stories. It is a mode best understood, again, in reference to Burke.

In an important pamphlet on the gothic in Ireland, Luke Gibbons writes, 'Not least of Edmund Burke's rhetorical achievements in the *Reflections* ... was to launch a powerful counter-offensive against the conventional Gothic, shifting the locus of terror from the ancient to the modern, from Jacobite to Jacobin.'[6] The repressed that returns in the gothic is typically associated with a pre-enlightenment vision of politics: an arbitrary despotic power, sowing violence and terror through the institutions of the Catholic Church or the feudal state. This dangerously irrational power is figuratively masculine, a predatory force that needs to be destroyed. Burke twists this formula, locating horror in the ruthless progressivism of modernity itself. This is the gothic mode of the *Chapters of College Romance*, which exalt the terrors of Enlightenment materialism and feminized images of rational self-interest. The ghost that plagues the tales is not from a Catholic past but the future of a liberal state, that is, a state where citizenship is conceived terms of the self-interest of individuals.

In this anti-liberal stance, Butt is responding to pressures particular to Anglo-Irish intellectual life in the 1830s, and his response is inseparable from the vision of Irish society and Irish history offered within the pages of the *Dublin University Magazine*. Under threat of liberal reform, represented by the limited extension of Catholic civil rights in 1829 and the Reform Act of 1832, the small Protestant land-owning class to which Butt belonged needed to demonstrate the limits of liberal politics. This was the project of the *Dublin University Magazine*: to forge an alternate vision of social progress and sectarian cooperation in Ireland, avoiding the liberal path of secularization and suffrage, which would have led to the political marginalization of Butt's class.

POLITICAL ECONOMY IN THE 1830s

Isaac Butt's fiction infuses the supposed rationality of college life with the 'romance' of the gothic. His political economy works likewise to infuse the supposed rationality of the capitalist marketplace—as it was described in liberal political economy—with the romance of human feeling, subjective perception, and desire.

---

[6] Luke Gibbons, *Gaelic Gothic: Race, Colonialism, and Irish Culture*, Research Papers in Irish Studies (Galway: Arlen House, 2004), 14. Gibbons is drawing here from his study *Edmund Burke and Ireland: Aesthetics, Politics and the Colonial Sublime* (Cambridge: Cambridge University Press, 2003).

During the worst years of the Irish Famine, in 1846 and 1847, Butt wrote a series of ferocious articles attacking the rigid free trade policies of the British treasury and demanding vigorous state intervention to bring cheap foodstuffs to collapsing Irish markets. He later reflected 'I am not one of those who believe that grievances which may be called "sentimental" are therefore no grievances at all.'[7] In a recent discussion of Butt's economic writings, Terry Eagleton emphasizes Butt's 'sensitivity to custom and sentiment,' and he remarks that Butt was 'a romantic to the core'.[8] Eagleton is surely right in this. But if it is the case that Butt's revision of classical political economy is a romantic one, it is also necessary that we see modern economic thought from this time forward as a discipline formed by and resting on these same romantic principles.

This romantic economics emerges through Butt's argument on the theory of value. Rejecting the classical connection of value with labour or land, Butt, among others in the 1820s and 1830s, worked to understand value in relation to utility. The rise of a utility theory of value was a gradual one, and it would be fully realized only with the work of William Stanley Jevons (1835–82) in the 1870s. One prominent early writer in this tradition, however, was Butt's mentor at Trinity, Mountifort Longfield (1802–84). Longfield was Trinity's first Professor of Political Economy, appointed in 1832 to the newly created Whately Chair, a rotating five-year endowed appointment sponsored by Archbishop of Dublin, Richard Whately (1787–1863). Before accepting this post in the (Anglican) Church of Ireland, Whately held a chair in political economy at Oxford and there worked with Nassau Senior (1790–1864) to move the study of wealth and poverty in new directions.

Both at Oxford and in his new involvement at Trinity, Whately was an avowed opponent of Ricardo, whose views he found inimical to Christian doctrine. Ricardo's work suggested that in some circumstances the growth of capitalist markets and investment practices could benefit the rich at the expense of the poor. This potential for class antagonism in Ricardo's theory was seized on by critics of capitalism in the 1820s and 1830s—the so-called Ricardian Socialists—and used to argue the injustice of free trade policy. For Whately, Ricardo's suggestion of class antagonism, like Malthus's theory of population, was fundamentally unchristian, since it questioned the justice of God's will as enacted on earth. Given this particular theodicy, which viewed the present system of resource distribution as an expression of divinely ordained natural law, it was crucially necessary for political economy to reconcile the interests of the classes, to prove that capital growth produced mutual benefits and a harmony of interests for all.[9]

---

[7] Isaac Butt, *The Irish People and the Irish Land* (Dublin: Falconer, 1867), quoted in Terry Eagleton, *Scholars and Rebels in Nineteenth-century Ireland* (Oxford: Blackwell, 1999), 104.

[8] Eagleton, *Scholars and Rebels*, 103.

[9] Laurence S. Moss, *Mountifort Longfield: Ireland's First Professor of Political Economy* (Ottawa, IL: Green Hill, 1976), 14–16; Thomas A. Boylan and Timothy P. Foley, *Political Economy and*

Marx argued that this phase of British economic thought witnessed a significant transition away from the philosophical spirit of Adam Smith and toward an undisguised political advocacy. 'In place of disinterested inquirers,' he remarks, 'there stepped hired prize-fighters; in place of genuine scientific research, the bad conscience and evil intent of apologetics.'[10] Whether one reads the writing of Whately, Longfield, and Butt as bad faith interventions into the debate over the progress of capital, it is clear that their understanding of wealth and poverty grew from a historical experience of tremendous ideological pressure. As hand-picked winners of the Whately Chair in Political Economy, Longfield and Butt would seem to have appealed to Whately's sense of a divine logic in the marketplace. What is clear irregardless is that their work on value pushed economic theory in the direction of its dominant modern form.

Longfield's work disputed the link between labour and value by focusing on the problem of wage rates, that is, on the fluctuating value of labour itself. Wage rates could only be understood, he argues, if analysed in terms of the utility a given worker provided to a given employer. The usefulness of a particular kind of labour, as judged by the purchaser or consumer of that labour: this was the true factor in determining market wages.[11]

Butt adapts and expands his teacher's work, though in his brief, haphazard career as a political economist he does not completely develop the ideas he offers. His contribution is clearest in an 1837 lecture called 'Rent, Profits, and Labour.' Here he begins by establishing utility as the central defining characteristic of all human economic activity:

We ... perceive that it is in the power of man so to modify things as to make them subservient to his uses: that is, to create utility that did not exist before. This creation of utility we call production. Wherever throughout this lecture I use the expression 'the product,' you will understand me to speak of the utility created by the operation of any agent.[12]

Even with all this talk of utility, however, we seem still to be in the world of labour and production. In fact Butt goes on to argue that 'articles produced by an equal quantity of the same kind of labour will exchange for one another',[13] which makes it seem as if value is a calculus of labour. He resolves this seeming

Colonial Ireland: The Propagation and Ideological Function of Economic Discourse in the Nineteenth Century (London: Routledge, 1992), 67–9.

[10] Karl Marx, *Capital: A Critique of Political Economy*, i, trans. Ben Fowkes (New York: Vintage, 1977), 96, quoted in Ronald Meek, 'The Decline of Ricardian Economics in England' in *Economics and Ideology and Other Essays: Studies in the Development of Economic Thought* (London: Chapman & Hall, 1967), 51. Mark Blaug essentially confirms Marx's diagnosis, arguing that the utility theory of value in the 1830s developed as 'a more or less conscious effort to counter the spread of socialism' (*Ricardian Economics: A Historical Study* (New Haven: Yale University Press, 1958), 140.)

[11] Moss, *Longfield*, 90–4.

[12] Isaac Butt, *Rent, Profits, and Labour: A Lecture Delivered before the University of Dublin in Michaelmas Term, 1837* (Dublin: Curry, 1838), 14.

[13] Ibid. 20.

contradiction as he continues, for it turns out that not just labour, but all factors of production contribute proportionally to the creation of value. Just as with labour, all 'things produced by an equal expenditure of the powers of capital will exchange for each other'.[14] And the same holds for raw materials, or for land in agricultural production.

Now if all production is a matter of the creation of utility, as Butt affirmed at the outset, then labour functions simply as one among many useful things, one commodity among others, which are combined to create an ultimately useful product. The value of the product would be a matter of the utility of each element of its production. Historian Laurence Moss sums up Butt's argument in this way:

Despite the deficiencies of Butt's attempt to sketch an explanation of relative commodity prices in terms of 'utility created,' the analysis does represent one of the earliest attempts to discover how the utility created by factors of production employed in combination can be imputed to each separately.[15]

The idea that value can be understood through some measurement of the end utility of finished goods, or the intermediate utility of raw materials, represents a major shift in economic thought. Where classical political economy had emphasized the broadly social dimensions of commodity production, comparing different forms of labour, working to understand the relation between food prices, wages, and manufactured goods, here the whole theory hinges not on any idea of the social whole but solely on the perceptions of individual purchasers acting in the marketplace. To argue that a thing's value is equal to its utility is to say already that there exists someone to judge that utility, a potential purchaser, a consumer. With the utility theory of value, political economy moves away from its Enlightenment origins as a rational analysis of human productive powers and takes on a romantic view of inner subjectivity, basing its conclusions on psychological and philosophical assumptions about how human perception works.

In the terms of early nineteenth-century politics, political economy was the territory of liberals. It offered a view of the market as self-regulating machine, an arena of social life drained of all metaphysical significance. In terms of policy, liberal political economy was associated primarily with the opposition to all poor relief—since it interfered with the natural functioning of the labour market—and the repeal of barriers to free trade. From Butt's point of view, liberal political economy sees the marketplace in the same way that Edmund O'Connor sees the billiard table: a series of objects and vectors, understandable in purely material terms. In Butt's story, gambling represents the fatal error of this mechanistic view. Seeing the billiard table as a field of merely physical phenomena, Edmund blinds himself to the emotional and spiritual power, the

---

[14] Ibid. 20–1.
[15] Laurence S. Moss, 'Isaac Butt and the Early Development of the Marginal Utility Theory of Imputation', *History of Political Economy*, 5. 2 (1973), 335.

'romance', of the game, and he thus exposes himself to spiritual ruin. In this way Butt associates mechanistic philosophy with the work of the devil. In this backlash against Enlightenment materialism, Butt stands for the spiritual authority of the (Anglican) Church of Ireland, for the allegiances of honour and tradition. When Edmund in 'The Billiard Table' deserts the entrenched colonial order of Trinity Protestant Toryism, and runs for office as a liberal, he embraces the gambler's error, seeing a world where value flows according to its own mechanical laws, without regard to human feeling.

What Butt's work does is to point in the direction of an anti-liberal political economy, a science of value that accounts for what Dickens once called 'the romantic side of familiar things'.[16] Butt's stories, all composed while he was in his early twenties, anticipate his work in economic theory and the course of economic thought in the modern era more generally. From his paradoxical and narrow position within the world of the Irish Protestant ascendancy, he begins to shape an economics that insists on the mysterious contours of individual subjective experience. It is this mystic interiority which, in modern economic theory, drives the market in its constant motion.

THOMAS DE QUINCEY

Because of the economic fascinations in Butt's gothic tales—speculation, calculation, gambling, self-interest—he seems most powerfully linked not with his Dublin colleague Le Fanu, but with that other supremely gothic figure, Thomas De Quincey. De Quincey's obsession with the power of the mind's own representations is evident enough in the *Confessions*, as is his interest in political economy. Indeed his primary intellectual work during the painful phase of his opium addiction seems to have been a Kantian reading of Ricardo. Having rejected earlier work in political economy as logically unsound, De Quincey is delighted with Ricardo's *Principles of Political Economy and Taxation* (1817), and he describes Ricardo's achievement in precise Kantian terms:

Mr. Ricardo had deduced, *à priori*, from the understanding itself, laws which first gave a ray of light into the unwieldy chaos of materials, and had constructed what had been but a collection of tentative discussions into a science of regular proportions, now first standing on an eternal basis.[17]

In this way De Quincey applied a certain vision of German idealist philosophy, one of the backdrops for literary Romanticism in Britain, to Ricardo's theory of

---

[16] Charles Dickens, *Bleak House* (Harmondsworth: Penguin, 1971), 7; see also Robert Newsom's analysis of the phrase in his book *Dickens on the Romantic Side of Familiar Things: Bleak House and the Novel Tradition* (rpr. edn, Santa Cruz, CA: The Dickens Project, 1988).

[17] Thomas De Quincey, *Confessions of an English Opium Eater* (1821), ed. Althea Hayter (Harmondsworth: Penguin, 1986), 101.

the market, and what he produces is his own kind of Romantic economics. De Quincey's earliest critiques of Ricardo's work, published in the 1820s, reportedly inspired Samuel Bailey's 1826 *Dissertation on the Nature, Measure, and Causes of Value*, along with Longfield's work one of the early arguments for a utility theory of value.[18]

Unlike Isaac Butt's literary pursuits, De Quincey's political economy has attracted a certain amount of scholarly attention. Joseph Schumpeter devoted a page of his *History of Economic Analysis* to De Quincey, if only to conclude that, even with his 'delight in refined logic', De Quincey 'touched economics only peripherally'.[19] Josephine McDonagh, in her excellent *De Quincey's Disciplines*, seeks to correct this received view of De Quincey as an oddball dilettante, hovering at the margins of nineteenth-century intellectual history. McDonagh emphasizes De Quincey's influence on Bailey, and thus on the central trend in the nineteenth century toward a consumer-centred theory of value.[20] De Quincey collected and revised his early work on Ricardo in his 1844 book, *The Logic of Political Economy*; in 1854 the book was reissued, published together with work by Butt's Dublin patron, Archbishop Whately, and called *Chapters of Political Economy*.

I have discussed *The Logic* in some detail elsewhere.[21] The point I am interested in here is that De Quincey takes the same position on the question of value that we have seen in the work of Isaac Butt. *The Logic of Political Economy* asserts that debates on the question of value have been confused because political economists were never clearly aware of the difference between what he calls the 'measure' and the 'ground' of value.[22] For De Quincey, universal attempts to measure value are fruitless because it will never be possible to find a reliable standard of measurement. He argues that this longed-for 'standard'—a value that will '*stand still when all other objects are moving*—' does not exist since no single value 'can be privileged from change affecting itself'.[23] What political economy must find is the 'ground' of value, its 'principium essendi', the essential principle that causes or creates value.[24]

According to De Quincey, the essence of value is the 'strong affirmative attraction of the article concerned; in a positive adaptation of this article to each individual buyer's individual purposes'.[25] That is, value is determined by an object's 'intrinsic serviceableness',[26] the particular adaptation that makes it

[18] Josephine McDonagh, *De Quincey's Disciplines* (Oxford: Clarendon Press, 1994), 48. De Quincey later mentions this circumstance in *The Logic of Political Economy*, *The Works of Thomas De Quincey*, xiv, ed. John Whale (London: Pickering & Chatto, 2001), 189 and 213.

[19] Joseph A. Schumpeter, *History of Economic Analysis*, ed. Elizabeth Boody Schumpeter (New York: Oxford University Press, 1954), 477. For further discussion see Gordon Bigelow, *Fiction, Famine, and the Rise of Economics in Victorian Britain and Ireland* (Cambridge: Cambridge University Press, 2003), 202–3.

[20] McDonagh, *De Quincey's Disciplines*, 60. [21] Bigelow, *Fiction, Famine*, 100–3.
[22] De Quincey, *Logic of Political Economy*, 212. [23] Ibid. 214, emphasis original.
[24] Ibid. [25] Ibid. 215. [26] Ibid. 212.

helpful or pleasurable to possess. This essential utility will provoke greater or lesser degrees of desire felt by consumers, and consumers will pay according to the guide of these inner feelings.

In this formulation the precise value of any good or service is accurately shown, at any given time, by its price in the market. But to arrive at this seemingly straightforward result, the theory relies on an elaborate estimation of the internal lives of consumers. While De Quincey begins by searching for the essence of commodities, his attention shifts rapidly to the essence of the purchaser. Inherent qualities of objects disappear, retreating in polite Kantian fashion, as *noumena* whose existence we theoretically affirm but for which we can never account directly. Thus while value starts as an essential quality of things, it turns out that the qualities of things do not really matter in this system, since they are not available in any reliable way. What matters is the subjective desire for things, and this desire, according to De Quincey's careful reasoning, is the only 'standard' in an otherwise unstable world. What De Quincey suggests here, in such openly metaphysical terms, will become the central principle of modern economic thought: commodities have value only to the extent that they command a market.

Like Isaac Butt, De Quincey is a conservative writing against a largely liberal field. His early essays display the loyalty to Ricardo which he describes in the *Confessions*. But by the time of the *Logic*, his most systematic work on political economy, he has rejected central features of Ricardo's work. As McDonagh puts it, 'Ricardo served De Quincey as a frame on which to hang certain High Tory opinions and around which he might weave his gothic imaginings.'[27] Thus political economy provides the occasion for political and literary speculation. John Whale also emphasizes the literary dimension of De Quincey's economic writings. De Quincey, he writes, 'sees Ricardo's economics as a form of the sublime', and he suggests that De Quincey's interest in Ricardo is largely aesthetic.[28] Of these two writers, De Quincey and Butt, De Quincey looks ahead more clearly toward a theory of value based on consumer desire. Butt still links the internal world of the economic agent with a Burkean-Coleridgean 'heart', imbued with loyalty, piety, and (in that always already masculine term) virtue. In this sense Butt's political economy would be closer in overall terms to Ruskin's, in *Unto this Last* (1860) than to De Quincey's. Ruskin's insistence that 'social affections' be counted among the forces of economic life,[29] matches Butt's emphasis on 'sentiment' in his work during the Famine. However Butt and De Quincey both hold that the value of commodities can be understood on an individual, not a social basis. And the individual each starts with is not

---

[27] McDonagh, *De Quincey's Disciplines*, 53.

[28] John Whale, Headnote for *The Logic of Political Economy*, in *Works of Thomas De Quincey*, XIV 4. 187.

[29] John Ruskin, *Unto this Last and Other Writings*, ed. Clive Wilmer (rev. edn, Harmondsworth: Penguin, 1997), 167.

the clear-headed young *homo-economicus*—to paraphrase feminist economist Susan Feiner—but a rather nervous character, prone to ghostly imaginings and metaphysical pressures.[30]

INSIDE OUT

Another way to sum up the findings of these gothic economists from the 1830s is to say that each develops a new logic of visibility, where objects exist primarily not in themselves, but as visible manifestations of some inner truth. This inner truth belongs not to the object but to the perceiving agent, always estimating the utility of the thing, judging the degree of ease, pleasure, satisfaction, or productivity the object will yield up. To see a thing is not to take its measure, but to measure your hidden desire, and to see the hidden desire of another consuming viewer. This understanding of the market is founded on what we might call the occult theory of value. Value is occult, i.e. hidden, lodged in the interior of the consumer, but it is also in some way mystified, located where positive methods of analysis cannot reach. These hidden truths of the consumer are embodied in the commodities he or she chooses. Commodities here have no concrete status, since none will 'stand' still, in De Quincey's terms, to reveal its inner qualities. The truth belongs to the consumer alone, but this truth is itself hidden, occult, traceable only through the purchases which form its visible correlative.

We find in this occult consumer, theorized by De Quincey and Butt, the kind of figure whom Jonathan Crary has called 'the observer'. Crary shows that in this same period, starting in the 1820s and 1830s, optical physiology developed techniques for leading the eye into error, for producing images that had no objective existence, beyond the nerve impulses from the retina itself. The eye, Crary writes, was 'shown to be defective, inconsistent, prey to illusion, and, in a crucial manner, susceptible to external procedures of manipulation and stimulation that have the essential capacity to produce experience for the subject'.[31] In looking through a stereoscope, or watching the little moving images produced by toys like the phenakistiscope, the subject sees a world that exists only as a mental representation. 'Light', Crary suggests, 'loses its ontological privilege' here, as vision seems to provide an increasingly unreliable access to truth.[32] The regime of the observer produces a kind of 'visual nihilism',[33] where all retinal images have an equivalent status, regardless of their relationship to things outside the mind. And since the truth of objects is annihilated, the truth is available

---

[30] Susan Feiner, 'A Portrait of *Homo Economicus* as a Young Man', in *The New Economic Criticism: Studies at the Intersection of Literature and Economics*, ed. Martha Woodmansee and Mark Osteen (London: Routledge, 1999), 193–209.

[31] Jonathan Crary, *Techniques of the Observer: On Vision and Modernity in the Nineteenth Century* (Cambridge, MA: MIT Press, 1990), 92.

[32] Ibid. 88.   [33] Ibid. 14.

through sense data itself, the retinal image projected within the interior space of the subject. The world of objects becomes a system of images.

What De Quincey and Butt's work seems to mark is the transition toward an economics centred on such an observer. Is the scorpion real or is it a product of the mind's own capacity to construct images? Is Williams, in 'The Murdered Fellow', truly an agent of supernatural evil, or is he just a really, really mean guy? We do not know, and more importantly it does not matter. Whether the spirit is guest or host, its image produces felt experience for the characters in question, and its power is deadly. From this point, political economy begins its own Kantian 'Copernican revolution'. Just as the world has certain existence only in the excitation of the sensorium, the true nature of worldly things can be known only through the impulse of desire registered by the consumer. Crary's work has met with objections from scholars arguing that the range of Victorian reactions to new visual technologies was far more diverse than Crary acknowledges: these critics suggest that Crary's claim of a major epistemological crisis in the middle nineteenth century is overblown.[34] However, while these challenges offer important supplements to Crary's work,

---

[34] John Jordan and Carol Christ, for example, point out that the Victorians Crary sees in the throes of 'visual nihilism' were also interested in the claims of photography and physical optics to provide clearer access to objective knowledge (*Victorian Literature and the Victorian Visual Imagination* (Berkeley: University of California Press, 1995), pp. xxi–xxii). Kate Flint also suggests that Crary is too sweeping in his account, arguing that the 'particularities of spectatorship' in the period were more diverse (*The Victorians and the Visual Imagination* (Cambridge: Cambridge University Press, 2000), 22).

The most thorough-going critique of Crary appears in a somewhat unexpected place, though one with curious relevance to the gothic economics we have looked at here. This is Simon During's book *Modern Enchantments: A Cultural History of Secular Magic* (Cambridge, MA: Harvard University Press, 2000). Given that Crary touches on optical tricks and magic-lantern shows, his story crosses During's, and During comments extensively on Crary in the culminating chapter of the book. Like Jordan, Christ, and Flint, During argues that Crary's account leaves out important elements of visual culture in the nineteenth century; for During the most crucial of these is the rise of the commercial magic show. While Crary sees the optical tricks of the period as hallmarks of a relatively sudden crisis of perception, During sees them as part of a centuries-long tradition of illusionism. He calls this tradition 'secular magic', since audiences and performers were never under any impression that the tricks drew on real supernatural power. The nineteenth century simply forms the last phase of a long transition, wherein the fading belief in a supernatural reality is 'channeled for the most part into show business and literature' (27). In this modern commercial form, magic is 'self-consciously illusory' (ibid.). Audiences for 'secular magic' shows were already thoroughly disenchanted: glad to be diverted by dazzling new optical illusions, but not racked with doubt as to the status of the eye. Where Crary sees dissolving bonds of an earlier material and spiritual reality, During sees a wised-up and thoroughly realist popular culture.

During concludes that 'the visual controls' of the magic business (the optical tricks and technologies) 'could work to very different effects from the modernity described by Crary' (286). Still, During's emphasis on the rise of optical tricks as consumer goods—in magic shows and ultimately in film—seems to emphasize the importance of Crary's account for understanding modern views of value in the marketplace. Indeed in During's hands these magical entertainments and engineered hallucinations seem to provide the paradigmatic form of consumer experience in modern economics: every purchase is akin to paying to watch an optical trick, since you pay for what you perceive, and what you perceive truly exists only inside your own head. Crary's brief and ambitious book needs to be read with the corrections proposed by these critics. But what confirms the viability of his broader narrative—his sense of an increasing subjectivism in the modern understanding of perception—seems to be confirmed when we place it alongside the major trend in nineteenth-century economic thought. The gradual shift toward a theory of value based on utility indicates that the social field came to be viewed increasingly as a field of 'observers' in Crary's sense, or what I have called 'occult consumers': actors who create value through their hidden desires.

But if value is equal to the desire of the purchaser, then the commodity functions as a perfect and exactly adequate expression of that desire. Within this theory, the commodity puts on display the inner, subjective truth of a shopper turned inside out. The choice of purchases is the expression of that romantic core of individual being, and thus in the increasingly elaborate displays of goods, from the Crystal Palace to the Department store, to the continuum of shopping mall that seems now to be the United States, we find a visual array of potential subjective experience, a ghostly lexicon of self-expression. In Butt and De Quincey value is a ghostly thing, like an ocular effect, verifiable only in that it exists in the mind of the consumer. This is the metaphysical structure of modern economic thought, solidified at the close of the nineteenth century in the theory of marginal utility, and persisting yet in the neoclassical theory that dominates the economics departments of universities around the world.

This narrowing of the significance of things, until they seem to exist only as perceptions, dreams of identification, is of course what Marx described as fetishism. In the market, the commodity is an apparition, a ghost you have dreamed up, but which haunts you nonetheless. Yet to pass beyond this idealist view of the matter of life, it is not adequate simply to ruin the projector, to stop the whirring phenakistiscope, and show a bewildered world the plain truth behind the illusion. It is this point that Derrida set out to explore in *Specters of Marx*.[35] For Derrida here, indeed, it is the ghostly quality of objects, what he calls their 'spectrality', that might crack open the hermetic logic of globalization, of a neoliberal world order, where the ethics of freedom seem to be equated totally with the freedom to trade. The ghost, the *revenant*, revisits us from the past, speaking of hidden crimes, forgotten injustices, and unsettling the triumphant rhetoric of the present. The ghostly aspect of value cannot be exorcised for value is a collective and socially nuanced mode of signification.

Meanwhile, the situation of contemporary economic discourse, academic and popular, seems to correspond to that described by Victoria Nelson in her book *The Secret Life of Puppets* (2001). In this study of idols and dolls, from late antiquity to the present, Nelson argues that while the scientific revolution of

the significance of his argument is its success in describing how modern culture uses the market to understand the phenomenal world.

35 Jacques Derrida, *Specters of Marx: The State of the Debt, the Work of Mourning, and the New International*, trans. Peggy Kamuf (London: Routledge, 1994).

the seventeenth century drove the magic out of the phenomenal world, popular culture in Europe and the US has continued to dream of supernatural powers, non-material forces that could make the ventriloquist's puppet rise and walk, and animate the cold circuitry of the cyborg. Nelson writes, 'having exiled spirit not just from matter but from our entire worldview, we backers of [empirical reason] no longer see the many strands of influence that still stretch back to the early history of our culture.'[36] It is this sort of lingering influence that these gothic economists of the 1830s can help us to see: a metaphysical premise within a modern science of value. Today economics calculates things as pure quantities, pure measurements of exchange value, while all the time its notion of value posits a deep and secret plane of psychic life.

Understanding the modern science of capitalism in this way can help to explain why the subjective theory of value we have seen in the work of Butt and De Quincey should appear, first of all, so early in the nineteenth century, and second, within the sphere of literature. Part of the answer for Isaac Butt has to do with the particular demands of Anglo-Irish intellectual life. Under threat of liberal reform, the Anglo-Irish ascendancy needed to demonstrate the limits of the liberal view. But given the importance of an extreme subjectivism for the later development of neoclassical economics, it may be also that literature in the nineteenth century offered a particularly advantageous way to debate questions at the centre of economic theory. With their focus on ambiguous mental events and dubious visions, the *Chapters of College Romance* present an implicit commentary on questions of choice, desire, and rationality. In doing so, they draw on the now diverse resources represented by an evolving literary Romanticism, and a reconfigured set of gothic conventions. De Quincey's economic writings are also, in their own way, chapters of romance, for they enlist a version of the German idealist tradition in effort to establish the laws of political economy on an 'eternal' footing, and to ground these laws within the structure of human perception itself. In a century that moves from 'natural supernaturalism' to psychological realism, literary discourse deals with the micro-social sphere of human interiority, and hence implicitly with the micro-economic question of the consumer.[37]

[36] Victoria Nelson, *The Secret Life of Puppets* (Cambridge, MA: Harvard University Press, 2001), 29.

[37] I presented parts of this paper in several venues and benefited from insightful responses in each. In particular, I am grateful to the Centre for Irish Studies, NUI, Galway, which sponsored a period of research leave in 2004. Thanks also to the English department at Vanderbilt University and the Dickens Project, University of California, Santa Cruz.

3

Edward Bulwer Lytton Dreams of Copyright: 'It might make me a rich man'

Catherine Seville

Giving judgment in the most famous copyright case of the eighteenth century, and holding that copyright had become a creature of statute rather than the common law, Lord Camden observed:

> Glory is the reward of science, and those who deserve it, scorn all meaner views: I speak not of scribblers for bread, who teaze the press with their wretched productions; fourteen years is too long a privilege for their perishable trash. It was not for gain, that Bacon, Newton, Milton, Locke, instructed and delighted the world; it would be unworthy such men to traffic with a dirty bookseller for so much a sheet of a letter press. When the bookseller offered Milton five pounds for his Paradise Lost, he did not reject it, and commit his poem to the flames, nor did he accept the miserable pittance as the reward of his labour; he knew that the real price of his work was immortality, and that posterity would pay it.[1]

Edward Bulwer Lytton (1803–73) longed for such immortal glory. Yet he also sought present recognition of his genius; from his peers, from the public, and from his publishers. His sense of self-worth was in some ways closely tied to his artistic standing—which was considerable. However, he was extraordinarily sensitive to criticism; paranoid in his swiftness to discern unfairness or bias in his political and literary reception. He therefore looked to financial reward as an additional means of measuring the world's esteem.

Taking the market as an index, Lytton's success was extraordinary—rivalling that of Dickens in terms of sales and earnings. Yet whatever he achieved, still he felt undervalued. Longing to be respected and lauded as he felt an artist should be, he instead felt slighted and misunderstood. These tensions led him to demand greater legal protection for literary work, and his influence on the development of copyright law was far from insignificant. But these campaigns were greeted with some ambivalence by his contemporaries. While the idea of 'securing to the

---

[1] *The cases of the appellants and respondents in the cause of literary property before the House of Lords* (1774). *Donaldson* v. *Becket* (1774) 2 Bro. PC 129.

labourer his hard-earned hire for the most toilsome and precarious of all mental exertions' was appealing, there were many who felt, with Lord Camden, that excessive pursuit of lucre spoke to a lack of true artistic worth.[2] When the Court of Exchequer Chamber held that foreigners could obtain British copyright simply by first publication there, Lytton argued at a public meeting that the law should be changed to deny Americans copyright until America was prepared to grant reciprocal rights to British writers. The literary set reacted with disapproval. *The Athenaeum* was highly critical, observing that retaliation was no remedy for the admitted problem, and that to set a noble example was the better course.[3] James Fenimore Cooper made the same point privately to the publisher George Putnam:

as for the decision of the Barons of the Exchequer, I never doubted what it would be, and I am greatly surprised that Sir Edward Lytton does not see the poor figure he is making in the course he is pursuing ... It is miserable policy for England to do that which is wrong because [America] has done so.[4]

Lytton would have perceived this disapproval, and felt it keenly. He believed that the world owed authors a debt which it did not adequately acknowledge, and he chafed in frustration at the unfairness. In *Ernest Maltravers* he charts the development of an high-born, moneyed author, imbued with apparently conventional heroic qualities. Yet much of the character's interest lies in his unflinching efforts to realize these virtues in the fickle and undiscerning contemporary world. Maltravers 'had called the PEOPLE of his own and other countries to be his audience and his judges; and all the coteries in the world could have not injured him'. In the preface to the edition of 1840 Lytton rightly chided readers who 'lazily ... confound the Author-in-the-Book with the Author-of-the-Book', but his own experience must have informed the acute descriptions of the author fighting in hostile conditions to maintain his integrity and balance: Maltravers 'was like the member for an immense constituency, who may offend individuals, so long as he keep his footing with the body at large'. Maltravers survives by making literature 'his glorious and divine profession'. Injuries to his person are injuries suffered in a meritorious cause. Enduring aims obliterate thoughts of short-term gain: Maltravers 'loved Literature the more, because her distinctions were not those of the world—because she had neither ribbands, nor stars, nor high places at her command. A name in the deep gratitude and hereditary delight of men—this was the title she bestowed.' There is no need to insist on a facile identification of Lytton with Maltravers to appreciate the tensions and discomforts of the Victorian authorial profession being outlined here.[5] Although

[2] Dramatic Authors' Society (2nd circular, 1833). *Lytton Papers* (Hertfordshire Archives and Local Studies) D/EK W102/24. Published with permission.
    [3] *The Athenaeum* 5 July 1851. For more criticism see *The Examiner* (5 July 1851), *Literary Gazette* (5 July 1851); *Art Journal* (1 Sept. 1851), 240–1.
    [4] 23 July 1851: *The Letters and Journals of James Fenimore Cooper*, ed. James Franklin Beard, 6 vols (Cambridge, MA: Harvard University Press, 1960–8), vi. 279.
    [5] *Ernest Maltravers*, Bk 5, ch. 6; Bk 8, ch. 6.

nothing would ever compensate Lytton for his own sense of isolation and rejection, he seemed compelled to continue the search for a remedy—in the concrete forms of public statute and private contract.

Lord Lytton (as he became),[6] enjoyed the distinction of having a copyright law named after him when he was only 30—the Dramatic Copyright Act of 1833 was commonly known as 'Bulwer-Lytton's Act'. Lytton became an MP in 1831, by which time he was already known for his Radical sympathies. Thinking major political change inevitable, he was a supporter of Parliamentary reform, and spoke in favour of the Great Reform Act. However, he feared that unchecked political liberty could lead to revolution, favouring wider public access to information and literature as an antidote. His opposition to the stamp duties on newspapers and advertisements—the so-called Taxes on Knowledge—was based on this belief. Since stamped newspapers were beyond the means of working-class buyers, unstamped literature also circulated, including, inevitably, quantities of radical political material. Lytton argued that all people needed respectable reading. He eventually engineered the reduction of the newspaper tax to a penny, although he faced criticism for having compromised short of abolition. But Lytton was not a diehard Radical. He was in many ways aristocratic in temperament, and there was much about popular politics that he found distasteful, leaving him stranded between the Whig and Radical camps. A poor Parliamentary performer, who dreaded speaking and did so very inadequately, his profile in the House was low. Lytton did speak on major issues such as electoral reform, slavery, and the Corn Laws. But a significant proportion of the few speeches which he did make were linked to his career as a writer.

Status—his own, and that of writers generally—preoccupied Lytton throughout his life. Authors' organizations had been tried as early as 1735, when the Society for the Encouragement of Learning was founded with the intention of giving authors a rightful share of the profits of their books. Opposition from booksellers put paid to this ambition. The Royal Literary Fund (1790) and the Royal Society of Literature (1820) followed, but both provoked criticism because they dispensed charity and patronage, rather than working to advance authors' rights. There was further adverse publicity in 1831 when William IV refused to maintain his financial support for the Royal Society of Literature's pensions, which were abruptly withdrawn from their beneficiaries. Coleridge was one of those affected.[7] Writing about the incident in the *New Monthly*, Lytton warned that since readers took their morals and ideas from their national

---

[6] Born Edward George Earle Lytton Bulwer on 25 May 1803, he was created a baronet in 1838. On succeeding to the Knebworth estate in 1843 he added Lytton to his surname, under the terms of his mother's will, and was known thereafter as Sir Edward Bulwer-Lytton. In 1866 he was raised to the peerage as Baron Lytton of Knebworth, and consequently was addressed as Lord Lytton. To avoid distracting changes in the text, he will be referred to as Lytton throughout this article.

[7] For more on these early authors' organizations, see Catherine Seville, *Literary Copyright Reform in Early Victorian England* (Cambridge: Cambridge University Press, 1999), 149–52.

literature, achieving a good standard was worth some attention and investment. As a consequence of the political changes wrought by Reform, he saw men of letters as being 'in a painful state of transition'. Although no longer the servants of the aristocracy, the 'great public' was not yet willing to offer protection and respect:

in England, the word *author* draws after it a kind of lenient and good-natured obloquy, more detrimental than even hate to the respectability and interests of the tribe.

The following year Lytton sketched his own plan for a Literary Union, which would have been a highly political body: 'the Abolition of all Taxes on Knowledge, the necessity of universal Education, are the first articles of the creed.' Any man who had written a work above ten pages would be eligible to join, with subscriptions according to means. 'Motto of the Society—"The People."' Lytton freely admitted that linking the Society with the politics of popular interest would deter many eminent literary men from membership, and also confessed that he himself had neither leisure nor enthusiasm to establish such a scheme.[8]

Lytton showed more resolve when helping to found the Guild of Literature and Art in 1851. The aim was to provide salaries and residences to 'professional' writers and artists of distinction who, though worthy and prudent, had nevertheless fallen on hard times. Much of the inspiration and enthusiasm seems to have been Lytton's. He offered Dickens's amateur theatrical company a new comedy, *Not So Bad As We Seem*, to be performed in London and the provinces, in order to fund the Guild's initial endowment. A substantial sum was raised. Lytton also gave a considerable piece of land at Knebworth, on which cottages for Guild members were eventually built. The Guild's grants were certainly intended as a mark of fraternal honour. But it became just another benevolent fund. The model of authorship funded by patronage was now considered a tainted one, although its power was immensely hard to shake off.[9] With its very public profile, Guild membership left its intended beneficiaries vulnerable to jibes about their imprudence and lack of worldliness. Thackeray, never able to resist a dig at Lytton, reportedly described the Knebworth project as 'a literary Soup-Kitchen; Sir Edward walking up and down with a silver ladle in his well-gloved hands tasting the soup by way of trial.'[10] Leading authors did not wish to be associated

---

[8] 'Literature as a Profession' *New Monthly Magazine*, 32 (Sept. 1831), 227–32, 232. 'Proposals for a Literary Union', *New Monthly Magazine*, 35 (Nov. 1832), 418–21. All men 'connected by literature with any newspaper or other periodical' were to be eligible for membership, also. It is unclear whether unpublished works would have sufficed, but presumably so. Publication was to be a primary aim of the Union, Lytton regarding the power of the public press as one of its underlying drivers.

[9] See Helen Small, 'The Debt to Society: Dickens, Fielding, and the Genealogy of Independence' in Francis O'Gorman and Katherine Turner (eds), *The Victorians and the Eighteenth Century: Reassessing the Tradition* (Aldershot and Burlington, VT: Ashgate, 2004) esp. 34–6.

[10] *The Critic* (15 March 1852).

with this sort of charity. Unable to fulfil its high purposes, the Guild was eventually wound up.

In the absence of other provision, members of the literary establishment were often ready to dip into their own pockets to support needy writers and their dependants, although this was usually done very discreetly. Lytton himself offered significant personal support, both financial and moral, to certain literary figures; although his most devoted efforts were reserved for those unlikely to eclipse him. What continued to rankle was the public's low esteem for the literary profession, which he felt flowed, at least in part, from the State's reluctance to reward literary talent adequately.[11] However, given competing demands on the public purse, it was hard to persuade governments that the needs of authors—either for honours or pensions—represented a priority. Those affected instead sought to improve their economic rewards by securing increased legislative protection. Lytton was closely involved in a number of these legal initiatives.

Lytton's efforts towards dramatic copyright dated from his time as a political radical. There were close thematic links to the campaign against Taxes on Knowledge. At this time only the two 'patent' theatres at Covent Garden and Drury Lane were licensed for performance of 'legitimate' drama. Other theatres—so-called minor theatres—flourished in London, but were restricted to the lighter dramatic forms; burlettas, musical farces, singing, dancing, rope-walking, melodramas, animal shows, and so on. It was a matter of continued complaint that this lowered the standard of the unlicensed theatre unnecessarily, without raising the standard of dramas played at the patent theatres—which began to trespass into the minor theatres' territory of spectacle in order to attract audiences. One difficulty the patent theatres faced was the lack of high-quality legitimate drama. But for any leading author considering writing a dramatic work, the absence of performing rights was a serious disincentive.

Before 1833, once a drama had been disclosed in public, either in print or by performance, there was nothing to prevent anyone from performing it. Literary copyright prevented only a rival publication of the text. Theatre managers were free to stage an author's work in any form, without acknowledgement or recompense. Within London, plays enjoyed some informal protection; theatre managers tended not to play each other's dramas without making some arrangement. However, this was based on mutual entrepreneurial self-interest, and was of little advantage to the playwright. Authors had traditionally been paid via benefit nights. Contracts for fixed sums gradually displaced the benefit system, but it was virtually impossible to secure any reward from the provincial theatres, which would stage successful plays as soon as they could. This had the effect of making serious dramatic writing unattractive to established authors, because they

---

[11] See Lytton's 'Letters to Lord John Russell' (*c*.1846), intended for publication but never completed: *Speeches of Edward, Lord Lytton: now first collected with some of his political writings hitherto unpublished and a prefatory memoir*, 2 vols (London: Blackwood, 1874), esp. i, pp. xxxii–xliv.

knew their work would be instantly exploited by others, in situations over which they had no control.[12] It also placed a downward pressure on the rates offered by London theatre managers.

Another hazard facing playwrights was the system of dramatic censorship, which required all new plays to be submitted to the Lord Chamberlain before they could be put on in public. The Examiner of Plays exacted a fee, and the cuts required could seem capricious. The potential political censorship was particularly objectionable to radicals. Lytton entered into the lists with zeal. In February 1832 he presided at a meeting at the City of London Tavern, to memorialize Parliament 'against the system of oppression which has so long fettered and discouraged dramatic authors'. His piece in the *New Monthly* publicized the cause.[13] In May he secured the appointment of a Select Committee to inquire into the laws affecting dramatic literature.[14] Lytton chaired the committee, which sat over two months and took a great deal of conflicting evidence, to the amusement and exasperation of the periodicals:

Thus, it will be seen, that twelve days have been expended by a grave Committee of the House of Commons, in examining nearly forty gentlemen, whose opinions no one person connected with theatricals could have found difficulty in detailing in one half hour. The only one point on which there is an unanimity of opinion, is respecting the great value of Mr Knowles's play of the 'Hunchback'.[15]

The committee's recommendations were simple and comparatively moderate. A more streamlined licensing system was proposed, allowing all licensed theatres to present 'legitimate' drama if they chose. There was a strong recommendation that dramatic works should not be exhibited without the express consent of the author. But there was no proposal to abolish the office of censor.

Lytton introduced two bills in the following session, one concerned with licensing and the extension of legitimate drama, the other with dramatic authorship. The issue of censorship had to be dropped. The dramatic authorship bill was relatively uncontroversial, and was given the Royal Assent in June. The licensing issue proved more troublesome. The much despised Alfred Bunn became the sole lessee of *both* patent theatres during this time, re-awakening antagonism to the monopoly. Although the bill passed the House of Commons in July, there was resistance in the House of Lords, where it was rejected by a majority of four. Lytton presided over a lively public meeting at the Crown and Anchor Tavern, to consider the bill's future prospects. A petition was drafted, and a fund started, to defray the expenses of any minor theatre facing legal action. Lytton subscribed

---

[12] See Byron's fruitless efforts to prevent the performance of his play *Mario Faliero*, published, but intended only for private reading. Elliston put a much cut version on at Drury Lane, without authorization, outraging both author and publisher: *Murray* v. *Elliston* (1822) 5 B & Ald. 657.

[13] 'The State of the Drama', *New Monthly Magazine* 34 (Feb. 1832), 131–5.

[14] *Hansard*, Parliamentary Debates (series 3), vol. 13, cols 239–47 (31 May 1832).

[15] *The Athenaeum* (3 Nov. 1832), 713–14.

a handsome 35 guineas to the cause.[16] In fact the patent monopoly was to last another ten years. Nevertheless, Lytton had managed to obtain a 'stage right' for dramatists, and this was a noteworthy achievement. The Dramatic Authors' Society was set up in the same year, as a collecting society to enforce the new right. An agent was appointed, and theatre managers were circularised (in the politest terms) to encourage them to use the Society's convenient services.[17]

* * *

Lytton's own dramatic writing was yet to come,[18] although his novels—particularly *Pelham* and *Paul Clifford*—were already highly successful. Following the 1833 Act, dramatists could perform their work with security. However, the patent theatre's continuing monopoly of legitimate drama lessened demand, and made the writing of such plays a speculative business. Nevertheless, the movement to regenerate the English drama carried a good deal of literary prestige. A cluster of figures associated with the renowned actor Macready sought to raise dramatic standards, although their efforts met with a mixed public reception. Browning's first drama *Strafford*, for instance, was taken off after only four nights at Covent Garden. Macready took a leading role in Lytton's first play, *The Duchess de la Vallière*, performed at Covent Garden in January 1837. It was not a success, even when extensively reworked, and played only eight days. Osbaldiston, the theatre's manager, had paid a sum which reflected Lytton's previous literary success, and sought (unsuccessfully) to have the terms of the contract varied. However, when Macready himself took over as manager at Covent Garden, later in that year, Lytton offered him his second play, *The Lady of Lyons*, for nothing. It was sufficiently popular for Macready to volunteer a cheque for £210 for the first fourteen nights, which Lytton returned.[19] But his third play, *Richlieu*, (Covent Garden, 1839) made him the most successful playwright of the late 1830s, and Macready offered him £600 for a forty-night run. Similar fees were paid by Ben Webster at the Haymarket for *The Sea Captain* (1839) and *Money* (1840). High though these figures were in the dramatic world, Lytton was already considerably better paid for his novels, and *Money* was his last staged play.

---

[16] *True Sun* (14 and 15 Aug. 1832).

[17] Dramatic Authors' Society (2nd circular): D/EK W102/24. Paradoxically, Lytton always resented paying the Society's 10% fee.

[18] One can only surmise that the success and security offered by novel writing made dramatic writing less tempting. At their first meeting in 1834 Macready urged Lytton to write a play. Lytton replied that he had written one, now lost, on the death of Cromwell. It was to Macready that Lytton took *The Duchess de la Vallière*, early in 1836. The leading role was designed for Macready, and the play was dedicated to him. In response to Bunn's proposal on payment, Lytton demanded an additional £200 down, £5 a night for the two following seasons, after which the copyright was to revert to him. Macready though this 'rather a hard bargain', and did not think that Bunn would concede it. William Charles Macready, *Macready's reminiscences and selections from his diaries and letters*, ed. Sir F. Pollock, 2 vols (London: Macmillan, 1875), ii. 10.

[19] C. H. Shattuck, *Bulwer and Macready* (University of Illinois Press: Urbana, 1958), 76.

Another dramatist in the same circle was Talfourd, whose *Ion* was the hit of the season at Covent Garden in 1836, with Macready in the title role. Lytton's *Lady of Lyons* was dedicated to Talfourd. Talfourd, who was a lawyer and an MP, as well as a dramatist, brought in an ambitious copyright bill in 1837. He sought to introduce provision for international copyright agreements, and to consolidate domestic copyright law, requesting a substantial increase in copyright term. Lytton supported the bill, and presented a petition in its favour. Many prominent literary figures, notably Wordsworth, campaigned for the bill. However, concerted opposition from the publishing and printing trades brought repeated defeat, forcing Talfourd to curtail his ambitions. In 1841 success was confidently predicted, when a powerful if idiosyncratic speech from Macaulay in the House of Commons unexpectedly brought a further humiliating defeat, much to the frustration of the bill's supporters. Fonblanque, editor of the *Examiner*, wanted Lytton to write an article countering Macaulay's points. The message came via Forster, who was furious with all parties,

For heaven's sake put in a word for real interest at stake. As the head of literary men of the day, say one word on their behalf. Expose the absurdity of Talfourd as well as Macaulay, and show how the whole thing has failed.[20]

Lytton performed the hatchet job on these two as asked, though he sheltered under the cloak of anonymity, asking Forster to return the manuscript and burn the covering letter.[21] The article was an authoritative and high-profile defence of the principles underlying the copyright bill, and did much to neutralize Macaulay. But Talfourd was mortified by this ruthless public criticism, as he noted in his diary.[22] Like Lytton, Talfourd was acutely sensitive regarding his literary and personal reputation. One wonders if Talfourd's minor dramatic successes helped to sharpen Lytton's rivalrous pen.

A copyright bill did pass the following year, giving a significant extension to the domestic term. The international situation remained unsatisfactory, however. The 1838 International Copyright Act had given a power to grant copyright to foreign authors, on condition that the foreign state granted reciprocal privileges to British authors. Lytton had written forcefully in its support.[23] But the measure was unfruitful, for various reasons. The meagre package of benefits available

---

[20] Forster to Lytton (? Feb. 1841): D/EK C14.

[21] Fortunately, Forster did not do so. 'I hasten to send you an article on the Copyright which I think settles the question ... Be sure not to breath a syllable to a soul upon the author's life—I have not spared either Macready or Talfourd. It would be highly unpleasant to have myself even suspected as author.' Lytton to Forster (? February 1841), D/EK C27. 'The Defeated Copyright Bill', *The Examiner* (28 Feb. 1841), 130–1.

[22] 'For five years I have worked the Copyright Bill in the House of Commons—to see it thrown out in one night by Macaulay—to read in my friend the Examiner that if I had made one business like speech the measure would have been committed.': *Memoranda for 1842*, 6 Jan.: *Berkshire Record Office* D/EX 1410/2/1/3.

[23] *Monthly Chronicle*, 1 (April 1838), 163–8.

seemed an unattractive exchange for those countries which offered generous copyright provision to their own citizens. At the other end of the spectrum were countries who were hostile to the very idea of international copyright. As far as British authors were concerned, America was the foremost 'pirate'. Huge numbers of British works were reprinted there and distributed in their thousands to the massive American market. Local publishers were under no legal obligation to provide any recompense whatsoever, whether to the original author or publisher. Competition between publishers was fierce, though, and there was a great advantage to being first in the market. As a result, the most popular British writers—of whom Lytton was one—were able to command sums for sales of advance sheets.

Lytton's early novels were published by Harper & Bros, a very successful New York publishing house, known for its ambitious and uncompromising business practices. They paid £50 or £100 for each, which must have seemed remarkably little to Lytton as compared to the sums he received from the British publishers. Of course, the Harpers obtained only a brief head start in the race to publish, and not a legally defensible copyright. Worse still, the Harpers did not seem particularly grateful for the boon Lytton gave them, seeming to imply that he was in their debt with respect to his American reputation because of their expert handling of his works, grumbling that sheets arrived late or with insufficient notice, and complaining that his very popularity undermined the benefits which the bargain ought to have brought them. 'We send with this a copy of your last novel,' they remarked,

printed upon us within a few days after the appearance of our edition, in a different and inferior style, and sold at $37\frac{1}{2}$ cents per copy—about 1/6 sterling—the lowest price at which we could afford ours, so as to realise even the smallest profit, being more than double the sum. You are aware, of course, that having no copyright, we cannot prevent this interloping, and you can judge without any help from us, how materially it must injure us.[24]

Irritated at having to barter for each payment separately, Lytton proposed a contractual arrangement, whereby the Harpers would pay a fixed sum of £50 a volume for all his future works. The Harpers were exceedingly reluctant to be forced up to £150 for a novel, but evidently feared that other American publishers would be perfectly willing to pay this for a bestseller such as Lytton. To forestall this, they advised him 'candidly' that if he made arrangements with any other publishing house, they would reprint the works notwithstanding: 'from the magnitude of our disposable force, we could throw before the public one of your novels in twenty four hours after obtaining a copy—which no other house in the US could do—and even then sell it cheaper than others, getting it up in the same form.'[25] Predictably, Lytton was utterly enraged by these threats. The Harpers'

---

[24] Harper & Bros to Lytton, 15 Jan. 1835: D/EK/ C23/59/4.   [25] Ibid.

subsequent letters are more emollient and conciliatory, but do not back away from their central position; having embarked on a uniform edition of Lytton's works, they would complete it regardless of his wishes, if necessary. A contract was eventually signed that year, committing them to pay £50 a volume.[26]

In the spring of 1836 the Boston publishers Marsh, Capen & Lyon attempted to poach Lytton. He had no loyalty to the Harpers, given their high-handed approach to their dealings with him. Their coolness to Lytton contrasted sharply with Capen's respectful enthusiasm. A draft contract with the Boston firm was drawn up, under conditions of strict secrecy. But discussions were suspended in the autumn when it became clear that a bill proposing international copyright would be put before Congress. The issue had been highlighted by the activities of Lytton's London publishers, Saunders & Otley, who had opened a branch office in New York. The Harpers had reacted aggressively, reprinting their works, and disparaging the firm in the public press. Lytton therefore faced a delicate choice when issuing his new work, *Athens: Its Rise and Fall*. He prevaricated for a while, hoping vainly that agreement on international copyright would be reached quickly, but was forced to choose the standard pattern; simultaneous publication by Saunders & Otley in London, and Harper & Bros in New York. The Harpers refused point blank to pay for the advance sheets unless they in fact received the first copy to reach America, pointing out that Saunders & Otley had an obvious means of obtaining an early copy.[27]

Saunders & Otley continued to campaign for the bill, drafting a petition to Congress, signed by fifty-six British authors. Lytton was naturally one of those who signed. A Select Committee was appointed, chaired by Senator Henry Clay. It reported that justice required protection for foreign authors, and that America should enter into agreements with Britain and France. Clay submitted a bill, although the imminent end of the session meant that it was never likely to pass. Clay reintroduced the measure several times, but he was unsuccessful. Economic conditions were bad, which made the book trade's determined opposition more telling. Clay's final effort coincided with Dickens's famous lecture tour of America in 1842. Dickens's interest in copyright law was long standing, and he undoubtedly had a legitimate connection with the international question, given the massive popularity and extensive reprinting of his works in America. He pressed for international copyright in several speeches at dinners given in his honour, greatly provoking certain sectors of the American press. Dickens was defiant, writing to Forster: 'As the gauntlet is down, let us go on.' He asked Forster to arrange for a letter to be addressed to him, by the principal English authors who had signed Clay's petition, expressing their sense that Dickens had done his duty. It was Lytton who drafted the letter and also a memorial, thinking

---

[26] Harper & Bros to Lytton, 21 March 1835: D/EK C23/59/6; 7 April 1835: D/EK C23/59/7. Memorandum of agreement, 7 April 1835: D/EK C23/59/8.

[27] Harper & Bros to Lytton, 12 Sept. 1836: D/EK C23/59/16.

this might usefully be presented as a petition to Congress. Privately, Lytton seemed surprisingly unenthusiastic about the initiative: 'After all little is to be gained, I fancy, except by Dickens and Ainsworth, to whom we benevolently purvey—even if the Yankees yield.'[28] He was to take a different view later.

During this period the copyright status of foreign authors in Britain was often challenged, and conflicting decisions in different courts produced mounting confusion. In *Bentley* v. *Foster* (1839), Vice Chancellor Shadwell held that protection was given to a work first published in Britain, whether written by a foreigner or not.[29] The case concerned a novel by James Fenimore Cooper. This decision favoured Americans, holding that they could obtain British copyright by ensuring publication in Britain as little as one day before American publication.[30] However, in *Chappell* v. *Purday* (1845), Chief Baron Pollock in the Court of Exchequer undermined the prevailing understanding, finding that a foreigner could not have copyright if the work was published work abroad before publication in England. The see-sawing continued. Another Exchequer decision, *Boosey* v. *Purday* (1849) focused on the foreign author's place of residence when the work was first published. Publishers such as Murray and Bentley, who had paid substantial sums to American authors in the belief that first publication in Britain would secure copyright, were left vulnerable to reprinters, chief among whom were Bohn, and Routledge. Further legal action was begun. Then, in *Boosey* v. *Jefferys* (1850), the Court of Exchequer again held that a foreigner had no assignable copyright. The case was appealed, and on 20 May 1851 Lord Campbell held that wherever a foreigner was residing, first publication in the United Kingdom entitled him to British copyright.[31]

The matter was still not definitively settled, however, since the decision was soon taken to appeal *Boosey* v. *Jefferys* to the House of Lords. The case had considerable international significance, as was quickly recognized. There remained little incentive for any reluctant nation to conclude a copyright treaty with Britain, if privileges were already available to anyone who first published there. A public meeting was held at the Hanover Square rooms, to discuss the 'equitable adjustment of British and Foreign Copyright'. Lytton was Chairman of the meeting. In his speech he argued that Byron and Scott had called into existence a new reading public abroad, who 'receive their supplies of English works from foreign reprints, without contributing a single shilling to the maintenance of the

---

[28] Dickens to Forster, 24 Feb. 1842; Lytton to Forster, 24 March 1842: *The Letters of Charles Dickens: The Pilgrim Edition*, ed. Madeline House, Graham Storey, and Kathleen Tillotson, 12 vols (Oxford: Clarendon Press, 1965–2002), iii. 86 and 214 n. 3.

[29] *Bentley* v. *Foster* (1839) 10 Sim. 320.

[30] The reverse was not true. Even a year's residence in the United States did not entitle an English writer to American copyright unless he was intending to reside there permanently, as the English author Captain Marryat found to his cost. *Carey* v. *Collier* 5 F Cas. 58 (CCSDNY 1839).

[31] *Chappell* v. *Purday* (1845) SC 14 LJ Ex. 258. *Boosey* v. *Purday* (1849) 4 Exch. Rep. 145. *Boosey* v. *Jefferys* (1850) 20 Law J, Ch., 165. Appeal to the Court of Exchequer Chamber at 6 Exch. 580.

poets who charm or the scholars who instruct them'. He thought that a reciprocal copyright treaty was the fair solution. Lytton concluded with a staggering claim:

I need not say, Gentlemen, what an advantage it would be to us—to all literary men—to obtain a reciprocal Copyright in the United States of America. Had I been in possession of Copyright there when I first commenced writing, it would have made a difference to me now of about £60,000.[32]

Given that Lytton had received less than £2,500 from Harper & Bros in his entire writing career thus far, one can understand his motivation to alter the prevailing state of the law. He was soon to be involved in a highly secret attempt to secure Anglo-American copyright via Congress. The attempt almost succeeded—but not quite.

In 1849 Lytton's brother, Henry Bulwer, became British Minister to Washington. The following year, Edward's son Robert (then 18) was sent there also, to act as unpaid attaché in the British Legation. Lytton wrote to his son: 'Is there any chance, think you, of getting a Copyright for English Authors in America? Pray urge Henry to it. It might make me a rich man.' Robert's initial response was discouraging: it would be almost impossible to persuade a member of Congress to propose an international copyright bill, because it would be so unpopular with America's vast reading public, happily accustomed to cheap English reprints.[33] But later in the year he suggested a route which he admitted would sound pretty wild:

It *would* be hopeless to get a bill through Congress about international copyright unless, indeed, the authors of England were willing to subscribe among themselves for a certain amount—perhaps ten or twelve thousand pounds—for a sum to *buy the American Congress*, and then, *seriously*, and without joking—but in *sad and sober earnest*, I think the thing might be done. This, however, is confidential, and I fear the possibility can be turned to no practical use. I cannot very well explain my reasons for making this suggestion in a letter. But you would be amused, I think, by a peep behind the cowslips of politics here.[34]

Robert made further enquiries and grew more confident. He had learned of a lobbying group, known as 'The Organization', which would manage the passage of measures for a fee. Encouraged by his father, Robert made further enquiries. A figure of $60,000 was quoted; $20,000 in cash as an advance, the same on presentation of the Report and Bill, and the balance on its successful passage.

---

[32] *The Question of Unreciprocated Foreign Copyright in Great Britain: A Report of the Speeches and Proceedings at a Public meeting held at the Hanover Square Rooms, July 1, 1851*, With notes by Henry G. Bohn (London: Bohn, 1851), 9–11.

[33] Lytton to Robert Lytton, 21 Jan., 24 Feb. and 29 April 1851. The February and April letters are in D/EK C41 (1851). The January letter should be in the same folder but it is not, so I am reliant on James J. Barnes's transcription: *Authors, Publishers and Politicians: The Quest for an Anglo-American Copyright Agreement, 1815–1854* (London: Routledge & Kegan Paul, 1974), 177–8.

[34] Robert Lytton to Lytton, 8 Nov. 1851, also 13 Nov. and 7 Dec. 1851: D/EK C41 (1851).

John F. Crampton, the new British Minister in Washington, corresponded with Lytton on the matter. He also told the Foreign Office that he wished to negotiate a copyright treaty, having heard confidentially that Secretary of State Daniel Webster was willing to talk.

At this stage a major hitch occurred, when it was discovered that there had been a complete misunderstanding as to the amount required. Robert had inadvertently written home that hundreds of dollars were needed, not the thousands demanded. The Organization's representative was surprisingly understanding. Although willing to work for nothing themselves, £2,000 was already committed to printers whose influence was needed to carry the measure.[35] Money from England was urgently required in Washington. Lytton had little ready cash and could only offer £100. He wrote to Dickens, who, after discussing it with Forster, was extremely dubious about the scheme, but nevertheless agreed to hold a meeting in his house. The timing was particularly bad, being just at the height of the dispute over the Bookselling Regulations, which had increased tensions between authors and publishers. Although several of the principal publishers flatly refused to become involved, the necessary contributions were gradually secured. A draft treaty was finally agreed with Webster, but his unexpected death following a fall from a horse brought the appointment of a new Secretary of State, causing further delay. The Organization broke up, and opposition from the American publishers grew as details of the draft treaty were leaked to the press. Although the treaty was eventually signed, and discussions dragged on well into 1854, it was never ratified.[36]

Given the comparatively weak support offered by copyright law, Lytton had to rely on his own achievements and attitude to give him the advantage when negotiating with publishers. Always seeking to extract the best possible return from his works, he bargained fiercely. His first novels were published by the much derided Henry Colburn, known to his fellow publishers as 'the prince of puffers'. Colburn gave £500 for Lytton's first three-decker, *Pelham* (1828). Its success allowed Lytton to negotiate substantial advances for his next novels; £900 for *The Disowned* (1828) and £1,500 for *Devereux* (1829). The sensationally successful *Paul Clifford* (1830) was published by the new partnership of Colburn & Bentley, which lasted only two years. Lytton remained with Richard Bentley for a while after the split. Bentley became known for his Standard Novels—a single volume, issued monthly, attractive and elegant in a cloth binding, sold for a mere 6s. Several Lytton novels appeared in it, to the mutual benefit of author and publisher. Lytton's new novels continued to sell extremely well, particularly *The Last Days of Pompeii* (1834), for which he received £1,100. As a reliable best-seller, Lytton was a key part of Bentley's early success. But

---

[35] Crampton to Lytton, 19 April 1852: D/EK C11, p. 14; see also p. 12.
[36] Dickens to Bulwer Lytton 5 May 1852: *Dickens Letters*, vi, 662. Lytton to Dickens, 7 May 1852: D/EK C26/22. Barnes, *Authors*, 219–16.

the relationship did not continue unbroken. In 1834, Lytton offered Bentley a political pamphlet, *A Letter to a Late Cabinet Minister on the Present Crisis*. Lytton wanted £50 for one year's right to publish, but courteously assured Bentley that he would understand if the publisher was 'not in the pamphlet way' or if he disliked politics.[37] Bentley declined it. The pamphlet was extremely popular, and was thought to be influential in the general election, which the Whigs won. Worse still for Bentley, Lytton then offered his next novel, *Rienzi*, to Saunders & Otley, who had taken the pamphlet. They became his regular London publishers throughout the 1840s.

One vital matter therefore was to regain the rights to the Bentley works, so that they could be published in any future collected edition. But Bentley too could bargain well, and he did not give up his prizes easily. Lytton considered himself acutely aggrieved, because he knew that Bentley had made thousands from the deal. Forster was eventually entrusted with the legwork of negotiation, although their correspondence regarding 'Sharking Bentley' reveals Lytton's keen interest in details of both copyright law and the mechanics of publishing contracts. Lytton carried the rather contrived fishing metaphor through several letters to Forster:

This agreed, all points, are, I think, now settled by your angling and zeal most satisfactorily with Scylla Bentley. But now comes Charybdis Colburn. And I think it would be most desirable before we conclude with the first to deep plummet & sound the last.[38]

Lytton had to pay £750 to regain the rights he required to three novels, including *Pompeii*. His differences with Bentley were publicly known and discussed.[39] Presumably the parallel dispute between Bentley and Dickens, regarding the payments for the copyrights of several of his novels (including *Oliver Twist*), added to the acrimony.

Once the deal was done, Saunders & Otley could begin issuing their collective edition of Lytton (at 6s. per volume), completed in 1845. In 1847 Chapman & Hall announced a really cheap edition of Lytton's novels, patterned on their Dickens edition begun six months earlier. The double-column weekly parts were priced at only $1\frac{1}{2}$d., to tempt the most impecunious reader, because profit came only with massive sales. In the advertisements Lytton made much of the democracy of the format:

May these works, then, thus cheaply equipped for a wider and more popular mission than they have hitherto fulfilled, find favour in those hours when the shop is closed, when the

[37] Royal A. Gettmann, *A Victorian Publisher* (Cambridge: Cambridge University Press, 1960), 160.

[38] Lytton to Forster, 16 Sept. 1838. See also 10 Sept., 3 and 19 Oct. 1838. D/EK C27.

[39] Lytton himself commented bitterly in the preface to *Ernest Maltravers* (London: Saunders & Otley, 1840).

flocks are penned, and the loom has released its prisoners;—may they be read by those who, like myself, are workmen.[40]

Moneyed and leisured railway customers also wished to read Lytton's novels. It was a new and potentially highly lucrative market, although cover prices were driven down by the phenomenon.[41] Although early railway bookstalls sold a heterogeneous jumble of inferior and disreputable literature, the advance of W. H. Smith helped to raise standards significantly. One of the most successful exploiters of the new format was George Routledge & Co., with its 'Railway Library', inaugurated in 1848. Routledge was prepared to pay well for the rights to works which other publishers thought exhausted—and made a fortune doing so. In the 1853 Routledge offered Lytton £1,500 a year for five years, for the transfer of the Chapman & Hall cheap edition and the right to publish the works in the Railway Library. Lytton proposed £100 a year for each of twenty novels for *ten* years (to be paid in advance), and a division of profits on the library edition. Routledge accepted the amended proposition. Lytton handled the entire negotiation himself, specifying stringent particulars as to stock and plates, and insisting on complex requirements for the staging of payments.[42] The enterprise was a risky one. £20,000 was an enormous sum. Even Lytton thought that Routledge could not possibly make a profit on his works, and saw them as a loss leader: 'He strikes to establish a *prolonged series* of books—& pays high for a leading article to set up a periodical.'[43]

Lytton's sales in cheap editions were substantial and enduring. *Pelham* offers a useful illustration. Originally published in 1828, it was in and out of print until Routledge bought it in 1853. But 46,000 copies were sold in five years in the 1s. 6d. Railway Edition, followed by 35,750 copies in the 2s. Railway Library Edition of 1859. Yet although sales were lasting, they were not 'almost limitless',

---

[40] J. A. Sutherland, *Victorian Novelists and Publishers* (Chicago: University of Chicago Press, 1976), 33. Lytton had to overcome his distaste for the plebeian when publishing in cheap editions, and was (for similar reasons) highly resistant to issuing his works in parts. Salmon gives this advertisement as an example of the rhetorical strategy by which some mid-nineteenth-century novelists 'sought an affiliation with the common "necessity" of labor while simultaneous claiming to transcend it'. This tension between the materiality of modern print culture and the Romantic sanctification of authorship was one felt and explored by Victorian authors, but not resolved. Richard Salmon, '"Farewell Poetry and aerial flights": The Function of the Author and Victorian Fiction' in Francis O'Gorman (ed.), *A Concise Companion to the Victorian Novel* (Oxford: Blackwell, 2005), 144.

[41] Charles Wilson, *First with the News: The History of W. H. Smith, 1792–1972* (London: Cape, 1985), 101–9.

[42] George Routledge & Co. to Lytton, 27 Aug., 10, 24, 30 Sept. 1853; Lytton to George Routledge & Co., 30 Sept. 1853: D/EK C25/43. A draft Memorandum of Terms and draft Heads of Agreement exist in Lytton's hand.

[43] Lytton to John Blackwood, 15 Oct. 1853: M. O. Usrey, 'The Letters of Sir Edward Bulwer Lytton to the Editors of *Blackwood's Magazine*, 1840–1873, in the National Library of Scotland', Texas Technological College, PhD, 1963, p.133.

as the firm had hoped.[44] In 1861 Routledge offered terms of two-thirds profits for two further novels. Lytton, who preferred a guaranteed annuity, took this as an insult, driving Routledge to a defensive but transparently frank response:

I had not the slightest intention to undervalue the advantage and honour that would accrue to me from a continuance of our connection ... I am obviously enabled—as I am also willing—to bid as high for a renewal of the privilege of publishing the series of your admirable novels, as any other bookselling firm can be expected to do. I base my offer on the sale between July 1, 1860 to July 1, 1861 and they did not realize a profit on 31,000. Since that time trade is worse—and it is scarcely to be expected that the sale will be so large in seven years. ... I inclose the a/c of the sales of the double column edition for 12 months ending June 30 1861.[45]

When a further renewal was under discussion in 1868, Routledge claimed to be 'a very considerable loser' by their previous bargain. Lytton expressed hurt surprise, blamed Routledge for under-pricing the edition, and wondered whether he should take the copyrights back into his own hands, or dispose of them to someone else. Routledge gritted his teeth and offered either a five-year renewal at £600 a year, or a ten-year contract at £500. Lytton took two months to reply. For Routledge this would have been uncomfortably close to the expiry of their existing agreement, as Lytton was doubtless well aware. He preferred £600 a year for seven years, observing airily: 'That term is also more convenient for all my literary plans.'[46]

Lytton continued to go to every length to ensure that he extracted the maximum profit from his works. Always assertive and tenacious when engaged in these material questions, Lytton gave no sense that he thought his involvement in such matters at odds with his high calling. Rather, he saw the defence of rights as a proud necessity, which preserved the contemporary author's autonomy and integrity. In his publishing contracts Lytton had always been exceedingly careful to retain the right of selling foreign editions of his works. The opening volume in Tauchnitz's 'Collection of British Authors' was *Pelham* (1842), and in 1843 Lytton was one of the first authors to accept payment from Tauchnitz in return for the right to call the edition 'sanctioned'. His insistence on making his own arrangements sometimes entailed difficulties. In 1849 he sold *The Caxtons* for serialization in *Blackwood's Magazine*, and agreed to give the American rights to the Harpers. Unfortunately, *Blackwood's* was already the subject of a contract for reprinting in America—but with a different publisher. Lytton's agreement

---

[44] Q. D. Leavis, *Fiction and the Reading Public* (1932; London: Chatto & Windus, 1965), 306. In an advertisement announcing their agreement with Lytton, Routledge bragged that sale of such 'FIRST-CLASS WORKS' would increase the sale of the Railway Library 'to an almost limitless extent'. F. A. Mumby, *House of Routledge: With a History of Kegan Paul, Trench, Trübner and Other Associated Firms* (London: Routledge, 1934), 60.

[45] George Routledge & Co. to Lytton, 4 Nov. 1861. See also 16 Oct. and 28 Dec. 1861. D/EK 25/43.

[46] 46 George Routledge & Co. to Lytton, 10 March, 7 May, 6 and 10 July 1868. Lytton to George Routledge & Co., ?2 May, 2 and 8 July 1868: D/EK 25/43.

brought the two American enterprises into apparently irreconcilable conflict, much to John Blackwood's irritation.[47] Opportunities and infringers were both ruthlessly pursued, even overseas. Canadian territory, for historical reasons, had brought little practical reward for British authors. In 1871, when Canadian publishers began offering small but guaranteed royalties for the right to print cheap editions, Lytton was willing to deal directly with Hunter, Rose & Co. for his *King Arthur*, even though the sum involved was less than a hundred pounds. It must certainly have been the principle rather than the money which drove him to these lengths. The following year Blackwood offered £2,000 for a mere four-year right to *Kenelm Chillingly*, and the Harpers's London agents were delighted to give £750 for the American rights. It was to be Lytton's last novel. Although he supervised its publication, he did not live to see the extent of its success.

At Lytton's death in 1873, although Britain had signed bi-lateral copyright treaties with a few nations and the wider network was growing, the coverage within Europe was patchy. The Berne Convention, signed in 1886, created a 'Union for the protection of the rights of authors over their literary and artistic works.' Although a highly significant achievement, it did not include the major book producers of Holland and Russia. There was to be no protection in America either, until the Chace Act of 1891. Lytton worked tenaciously to secure the legal status of authors by giving them increased control of their work. But the full fruits of the efforts towards international copyright did not appear in his lifetime. Such rewards as Lytton enjoyed—which were remarkable for his time—stemmed from sheer market power and personal determination. If his career had begun at the end of the Victorian era, the picture would have been very different: authors with Lytton's status and popularity then entered the global market confident of significant international copyright protection, which could secure them considerable financial returns.

Yet in spite of all his striving for it, Lytton was well aware that money offered him somewhat hollow recompense. His last play, the comedy *Money*, represents greed as a social evil. Wicked characters readily trade fundamental values for fortune, whilst the hero Evelyn is tested, but eventually concludes that:

in the great comedy of life, it is our own fault if we do not find such natures, though rare and few, as redeem the rest, brightening the shadows that are flung from the form and body of the *time* with glimpses of the everlasting holiness of truth and love.[48]

The vice is shown to be not the money itself, but the way in which the sullied world chases after it. So, the message is that the virtuous *can* overcome all, live in the contemporary world, but remain unmired by it. However, just to be safe, Lytton leaves Evelyn with not just his Clara, but 'plenty of Money!'

---

[47] John Blackwood to Lytton, 17 July 1849: D/EK C15/33. John Jay to John Blackwood, 7 Aug. 1849: follows D/EK C15/34.
[48] *Money* (London: Saunders & Otley, 1840), Act V, sc. iii, ll. 319–22.

too. Lytton himself had only the fortune. Nor has posterity been willing to grant him the unchallenged immortality he desired. But, as far more than one of Camden's 'scribblers for bread', Lytton's exertions and achievements deserve present recognition and assessment. The question of Lytton's own artistic value was not resolved to his satisfaction during his lifetime. The idea that the market could function as a gauge of artistic worth both attracted and repelled him. Happy to embroil himself in the details of payment for his works, he was nevertheless squeamish about their production in cheap forms. Such tensions should not be dismissed as mere inconsistency, snobbishness, or hypocrisy on Lytton's part, but reveal the ambivalent relationship between author and market. Similar conflicts had been experienced by authors before. But the hugely expanded nineteenth-century literary marketplace, the efficiency of modern publishing, and the amounts of money involved in literary fame now helped make the exact shape of Lytton's problem a distinctively Victorian one.

4

'Vulgar needs': Elizabeth Barrett Browning, Profit, and Literary Value

Alison Chapman

Between March 1860 and November 1861, Elizabeth Barrett Browning published thirteen poems, all but two specifically on the Italian Question, on the front page of the New York *Independent* for $100 each.[1] This was double her fee from Thackeray's newly launched *Cornhill Magazine* where she published three poems in 1860 and 1861 for 10 guineas each; 'the American proposition', Barrett Browning writes to her sister Arabella, 'seems to myself extravagant'.[2] Her *Independent* contributions were also extraordinary, for, although she did publish in periodicals throughout her career, Barrett Browning often expressed anxiety about appearing in the popular press, especially after her marriage to Robert Browning, who was explicitly hostile to periodical publication.[3] Sending a poem to Henry Chorley of the *The Athenaeum* in 1849, for example, she complains that *Blackwood's Magazine* 'has behaved to me like a borderer and a thief […] so that I have learnt to be

The Berg Collection, the Harry Ransom Humanities Research Center, and the Armstrong Browning Library all gave valuable assistance during the research for this chapter. Thanks also to Francis O'Gorman for his insightful comments and editorial shrewdness.

[1] The poems are: 'A Court Lady' (29 March 1860), 'First News from Villafranca' (7 June 1860), 'King Victor Emmanuel Entering Florence' (16 Aug. 1860), 'The Sword of Castruccio Castracani' (30 Aug. 1860), 'Summing up in Italy' (27 Sept. 1860), 'Garibaldi' (11 Oct. 1860), 'De Profundis' (6 Dec. 1860), 'Parting Lovers' (21 March 1861), 'Mother and Poet' (2 May 1861), 'Only a Curl' (16 May 1861), 'The King's Gift' (18 July 1861), 'A View Across the Roman Campagna' (25 July 1861), and 'The North and the South' (7 Nov. 1861). $100 was worth just over £20, according to Barrett Browning's own calculations. See *The Letters of Elizabeth Barrett Browning to Her Sister Arabella*, ed. Scott Lewis, 2 vols. (Waco, Texas: Wedgestone, 2002), ii. 463, 478 (cited as Lewis hereafter and in text).

[2] See Lewis, ii. 478. The poems in the *Cornhill* are 'A Musical Instrument' (July 1860), 'A Forced Recruit at Solferino' (Oct. 1860), and 'Little Mattie' (June 1861).

[3] See, for example, Hewette Elwell Joyce, 'Mrs. Browning's Contributions to American Periodicals', *Modern Language Notes*, 35 (1920), 402–5. On Barrett Browning's abolitionist periodical publication, see Marjorie Stone, 'Elizabeth Barrett Browning and the Garrisonians: "The Runaway Slave at Pilgrim's Point", the Boston Female Anti-Slavery Society, and Abolitionist Discourse in the *Liberty Bell*', in Alison Chapman (ed.), *Victorian Women Poets* (Cambridge: Brewer, 2003), 33–55.

afraid of the whole race of periodicals.'[4] In 1859 the Brownings refused generous offers from the American *Atlantic Monthly* and British *Once a Week*, who had applied to them for poems 'at any price': 'We are told to ask what we please.' One unidentified and unsuccessful editorial suppliant from a periodical is informed by Barrett Browning in 1861 that 'My husband and I are averse generally to the periodical vehicle of publication'.[5] Barrett Browning's doubled and apparently contradictory attitude to periodical publication—both participation and rejection—is shared by other Victorian poets who also expressed a sense that poetic devaluation results from mass circulation.

This chapter reconsiders Barrett Browning's attitude to profit and periodical publication and argues that Barrett Browning's ambivalence is only half the story. In the late 1850s, her reconception of poetic value, and female public poetics in particular, led to a reconsideration of the worth of profitable periodical publication for political ends. Through her controversial commitment to the cause of Italian freedom, the *Risorgimento*, Barrett Browning reconfigures the vexed relationship between poetic value and financial gain into a profitable literary labour for foreign nationhood. Castigated for her commitment to Italy as the un-English 'poetess abroad' by the British periodical press in Britain,[6] Barrett Browning's 'extravagant' payments by *The Independent* and her venture into transatlantic popular print culture through this weekly are licensed by her politics.

LIVING BY VERSE

Barrett Browning was always keenly interested in her relationship to literary economics. In her letters she often discusses publishers' terms, sales figures and profits, reviews, and the public reception of her work. At the same time, she registers hostility to the literary marketplace and anxiety about the propriety of publication. The cost of publishing poetry may outweigh the benefits in hard economic or painful symbolic terms, in particular evinced through her concern with unauthorized circulation in the press that ranged from national and international copyright debates to anxieties over gossip, misrepresentation and mishandling by newspapers, magazines, and periodicals. In particular she discusses copyright issues, such as the debate around British copyright

---

[4] Elizabeth Barrett Browning to Henry Chorley, 9 Dec. 1849 (Armstrong Browning Library, Baylor University).

[5] See Lewis, ii. 444, 446 n., and Philip Kelley and Ronald Hudson, *The Brownings' Correspondence: A Checklist* (New York: Browning Institute, 1978), 110 (cited as Kelley and Hudson in text).

[6] See, for example, 'The Poetess Abroad', *Chambers's Journal of Popular Literature* (12 April 1860), 251–3, which laments of her *Poems before Congress* 'Alas, alas! why does a lady who can sing like this persist in writing leading articles?' (253).

law in 1842, as well as dissatisfaction with American exploitation of British authors.[7] There were many pirated editions in America of Barrett Browning's British volumes, due to the absence of legal copyright protection for foreign authors there. Even the many authorized American editions of *Aurora Leigh*, for which publisher Charles Stephen Francis gave her only $100, earned her no profit.

Barrett Browning's correspondence also discloses her distrust of publication in the periodicals as potentially a more risky form of circulation than volume publication. This suspicion was heightened after the reception of *Poems before Congress* (published as *Napoleon III in Italy* in America). The most stinging was Henry Chorley's review of *Poems before Congress* in the *The Athenaeum* (17 March 1860), which sharply criticized her 'Curse for a Nation' as a direct and unpatriotic attack against England for its policy to Italy, rather than against America for its slave trade as Barrett Browning intended. In a letter to Chorley, Barrett Browning explains that in publishing the poems she 'did not expect to help my reputation in England, but simply to deliver my soul', and she was not looking for 'compliments and caresses from the English press'.[8] Nevertheless, she sent no more poems to *The Athenaeum*, nor to any British periodical except *Cornhill*, a new magazine edited Thackeray who had solicited contributions from both the Brownings (Barrett probably agreed, when she had also at the same time turned down offers from *Once a Week* and the *Atlantic Monthly*, because of her friendship with Thackeray and his family (Lewis, ii. 444)). Reviews and publications in the periodicals were closely bound up together in circulating and advertising both poetry and poetic value. For the Brownings, as for other Victorian poets, however, publication in poetry editions and publication in periodicals was sharply differentiated by notions of literary value and monetary profit. While the two modes of publication were often mutually interdependent, as the example of *The Athenaeum* suggests and as I shall also argue in the case of *The Independent*, poets in this period frequently expressed hostility to periodical publication.[9] This hostility was especially acute for women, for the association between feminized poetry of sensibility and the annuals of the 1840s and 1850s aligned periodical poetry with the ephemeral. With the collapse of the British poetry market in the 1830s, as periodicals and gift books dramatically undercut sales of poetry volumes, poets as Lee Erickson has

---

[7] Barrett Browning's correspondence is especially engaged with Thomas Hood's 'Copyright and Copywrong' articles in the *Athenaeum*. For a discussion about the link between copyright, coverture and *Aurora Leigh*, see Cheri Larsen Hoeckley, 'Anomalous Ownership: Copyright, Coverture, and *Aurora Leigh*', *Victorian Poetry*, 36 (1998), 135–61. For more on the 1842 Copyright Act, see Catherine Seville, 'Edward Bulwer Lytton Dreams of Copyright: "It might make me a rich man" ', above, 55–72.

[8] *The Letters of Elizabeth Barrett Browning*, ed. Frederic G. Kenyon, 2 vols (London: Smith, Elder, 1897), ii. 379; hereafter cited as Kenyon.

[9] See, for example, Katherine Ledbetter, 'Protesting Success: Tennyson's "Indecent Exposure" in the Periodicals', *Victorian Poetry*, 43 (2005), 53–73.

demonstrated faced a painful dilemma: 'vulgar popularity' versus 'insubstantial isolation'.[10]

Barrett Browning's *Aurora Leigh* dramatizes such a conflict. Aurora's poetry volume that finally wins her acclaim and financial success is the result of hard literary labour in London, where for three years she lived in a garret and funded her poetry by writing prose for the periodicals because 'there came some vulgar needs':

> I had to live, that therefore I might work,
> And, being but poor, I was constrained, for life
> To work with one hand for the booksellers,
> While working with the other for myself
> And art.

> (3: 301–5)

The 'vulgar needs' of Aurora that drive her to write prose for mass circulation in the popular press suppresses, through re-inscribing the apparent separation between literary value and economic profit, the interdependent relationship between periodicals and poetry. 'In England, no one lives by verse that lives' (3: 307) declares Aurora, wryly expressing a popular view that poetry, as pure art, is unsullied by the market: the hand that writes for popular print culture is separate from the hand that writes poetry. The vulgarities of literary business occasioned by the collapsed poetry market, nevertheless, drive poets into the arms of the periodicals which circulate their name as a commodity to readers through publisher's advertisements, judge their literary value in the reviews, and provide lucrative payments through poetry contributions. While Aurora does not write poetry for the critics in the press (see, for example, 7: 738–44), her success is measured by Vincent Carrington in terms of positive reviews from three or four 'common critics' (7: 553). The narrative is, however, coyly silent about details of the book and its success: we do not know its title, how much Aurora makes from it, nor the extent of its readership. The silence is telling in its problematic celebration and elevation of the book's claims to truth over its commercial success. Aurora ironically argues that, as a woman who dares to publish, she is freed from concerns of the literary marketplace: responding to Carrington's quip 'We think here you have written a great book, | And you, a woman!' (7: 563–4), she retorts 'least care have we for the crowns and goals | And compliments on writing our good books' (7: 742–4). This refusal by a woman poet to base a poem's worth on its market value springs partly from the legacy of de Staël's *Corinne* (1807), in which love and fame for a woman poet were seen to be incommensurable, something reiterated in poems by Barrett Browning's precursors such as Felicia Hemans in 'Woman and Fame' (1829).

At the start of Book 2 of *Aurora Leigh*, the poet-heroine's private attempt to crown herself in the style of Corinne's public coronation at the Capitol

---

[10] Lee Erickson, *The Economy of Literary Form: English Literature and the Industrialization of Publishing, 1800–1850* (Baltimore: Johns Hopkins, 1996), 25.

is interrupted by an amused cousin Romney who makes a marriage proposal. *Aurora Leigh* displaces the heroine's relationship to the market, attempting to hold literary value separate from monetary exchange. Part of the ideological project of *Aurora Leigh* to dismantle the poetess as an object of consumption, and to challenge the dependence of woman's poetry on a discourse of sensibility circulated by annuals, is contingent on separating literary value from profit, a separation that emerges as a failed repression in the narrative. This is because the success of Aurora's book betrays its dependence on the periodical market for its origin and its public acclamation and circulation, just as *Aurora Leigh* itself was to circulate as a successful commodity in the marketplace which advertises, evaluates, and consumes it. While writing for periodicals was seen on the one hand to be a form of cultural devaluation, on the other it was a marketing vehicle for disseminating poetic status and celebrity. Monetary profit and literary value were two sides of the same coin.[11]

This co-dependence between notions of symbolic and monetary return for poetry was both productive and problematic for Barrett Browning. Linda Shires suggests that the poet negotiates the complexities of the periodical market, the commodification of her poet-persona in the popular press, and the interests of her own politicized poetics through plural yet incommensurate identities, or 'cross-dwelling' as a social critic of traditional domesticity, a respectable wife and mother in a domestic household, and someone who can also enter into the world of periodical editors and their practices.[12] This multiple personal and professional identity may authorize Barrett Browning's social critiques, but, in the controversy during this period over her un-English poems about Italy, it is clear that 'cross-dwelling' also involves an uncomfortable slippage in the periodicals between private and public personae that has a cost, as well as a profit.

ITALIAN INVESTMENTS, AMERICAN PROFITS

Part of the reason that Barrett Browning was willing to enter the periodical market for profit at all after her marriage was down to the hard fact of her finances, just as Aurora Leigh was compelled to write with one hand for the booksellers. After their marriage, the Brownings received a modest £200–£300 per annum, and managed to live within their means through the cheapness of Florence (Lewis, i. 174, 270). Their income largely came from dividends from Barrett Browning's £4,000 legacy from her paternal grandmother, her shares from a West Indies packet ship *David Lyon*, together with profits from poetry volumes. After their

[11] Compare Jonathan Rose, 'Was Capitalism Good for Victorian Literature?', *Victorian Studies*, 46 (2004), 489–501.

[12] Linda Shires, 'Elizabeth Barrett Browning: Cross-dwelling and the Reworking of Female Poetic Authority', *Victorian Literature and Culture*, 30 (2002), 327–43.

son's birth, John Kenyon sent them £100 a year as a gift, although sometimes he forgot, and the ship money was often disappointing, especially as their trips to England depended on that income. Before Kenyon's generous legacy, Barrett Browning often lamented her poverty to her sisters, on one occasion attesting that their resources were so low that her husband has to forgo a haircut and she new shoes (Lewis, i. 270). When Moxon sends the Brownings £75 profit in 1847, payable after the expenses of publication have been met, Barrett Browning declares to Arabella 'I assure you we shall make our way by poetry yet' (Lewis, i. 59). Sometimes, however, profits fail to materialize, as with the 'impertinence' of Chapman and Hall in 1854 who neglected to send their account despite Browning's two letters (Lewis, ii. 88). Browning's 1858 account book for Casa Guidi, now in the British Library, details all their household costs, itemizing everything from a skeleton (as an aid to Robert Browning's anatomical drawings) to numerous postage stamps, suggesting how very careful the Brownings were about expenditure.[13]

Despite their modest and sometimes precarious income, they invested in Italy in material as well as symbolic means. With poetry profits from Moxon of £50 sent in 1848 they bought Italian furniture and paintings for their new apartment in Palazzo Guidi, for 'as a mere investment for money, nothing could be wiser' (Lewis, i. 174); with part of Kenyon's legacy they invested in Tuscan funds, which in June 1857 realized £550 a year but, with war in Italy two years later, go 'down to the floor' (Lewis, ii. 403 n., 405); in 1859 they subscribed all they can afford, 10 scudi (just over 10 guineas) per month, to support the war of independence (Lewis, ii. 411).[14] In May 1861, their Tuscan funds were down again, and Robert Browning wanted to buy more: his rashness—caught, Barrett Browning declared, from her—worried their Italian friends, but they were 'alarmed by neither sinking funds nor rising loans. We have strong faith in Italy—*Italia fatta*'.[15] For Barrett Browning, monetary investment in Italy was a point of honour; despite the collapse of the Tuscan funds, she figures the money as gathering both moral and monetary interest. To Arabella Barrett she writes in March 1859, on the verge of war, 'I wish pecuniary loss were all the evil to be feared. Still … be easy for us even there—we shall *not* sell out in a hurry—we shall hold on—& funds like peoples, will rise again' (Lewis, ii. 400). Two months later she writes to Anna Jameson making clear how extensive is their investment

[13] Robert Browning's account book for expenses at Casa Guidi 1858, British Library (Ashley 5715). See also the accounts listed in the back of their address book, which give some figures for income and expenses for 1851 and 1852 (Harry Ransom Humanities Research Center, University of Texas at Austin).

[14] According to Edward McAleer, 47 pauls was equivalent to one pound sterling; see *Dearest Isa: Robert Browning's Letters to Isabella Blagden* (Austin: University of Texas Press, 1951), 390 (cited in text as McAleer, *Dearest Isa*).

[15] Kenyon, ii. 441. The phrase *Italia fatta* seems to mean here both the literal sense of Italy made, and also the connotation of Italy grown up, as if the nation will mature into wholeness from its current infancy of political fragmentation.

in Tuscany, as well as how severe the risk: 'There's comfort in having nearly all one's money in the Tuscan funds, so as to have the honour of risking something when so many noble human beings risk all.'[16] With the deposition of the Grand Duke of Tuscany, and the formation of a provisional government in Florence, there was more economic uncertainty, but Barrett Browning again assures her sister: 'there's no danger we think of the funds, though they are of course down to the floor—Tuscany wont [*sic*] sink, nor Italy Arabel—And really I have a sort of pleasure in sharing the risk a little' (Lewis, ii. 405). Just over a month later, on 3 June 1859, she writes of their decision not to leave Italy for England despite great political and military volatility: 'nearly all our property is in this country, & the most vulgar motives should keep us on the spot. To withdraw our funded monies at this time of excessive depreciation would be ruin of course—& indeed we have too much faith in ultimate events to be tempted to do any such thing [...] our interests are here ... just as our hearts are in this case' (Lewis, ii. 409). Barrett Browning's belief in the 'rising again' of funds and peoples, implied in the very term *risorgimento* (connoting both resurgence and resurrection), allows her to identify not only her public poetic persona with the Italian struggle for resurgence, but also her family private finances. A domestic politics also ripples here under the surface, for Barrett Browning invests in a politics with which her husband might not have entirely agreed. They may have 'vulgar motives', as their property is at stake, but also they also have made figurative and indeed prophetic investments for the future of Italy too, implied in that suggestive word 'interests'. Hearts and money are both given to the cause: investment in Italy is financial, political, moral, and spiritual.

It is exactly this set of dynamics that licenses Barrett Browning's extraordinary relationship with the New York *Independent*, which so far has only attracted notice in terms of Robert Browning's apparent inconsistency in supporting the venture.[17] After the hostile reception in the periodicals to *Poems before Congress*, published in Britain on 12 March 1860, Barrett Browning was approached by the editor of the New York *Independent*, Theodore Tilton, with an offer to publish in his newspaper for a large fee. By this time, arrangements had been made for an American edition of the volume with Francis, re-titled *Napoleon in Italy and Other Poems*, and Barrett Browning's first appearance in *The Independent* was from that volume. 'A Court Lady', published on 29 March 1860, was possibly placed by Francis as an advertisement to the American edition (and as a common act of American piracy) (Gladish, 47–8); indeed, an advertisement for the volume appears in the same newspaper (3). The poem's appearance on

---

[16] Elizabeth Barrett Browning to Anna Jameson, 10–14 May 1859 (Armstrong Browning Library, Baylor University). For more on risk and Victorian financial culture, see Jane Moody, 'The Drama of Capital: Risk, Belief, and Liability on the Victorian Stage', below, 91–109 and Francis O'Gorman, 'Speculative Fictions and the Fortunes of H. Rider Haggard', below, 157–72.
[17] See Robert W. Gladish, 'Mrs Browning's Contributions to the New York Independent', *Bulletin of the New York Public Library*, 71 (1967), 47–54 (cited as Gladish in text).

the front page was introduced by Tilton as coming 'fresh from the pen of one of the most gifted women of the age' (1)—the freshness not quite true, as it happens—and the poem was highlighted on the left of the page with the heading 'Our Special Contributors'.

For Barrett Browning, *The Independent* was a channel through which she could quickly publish poems for profit *en route* to her American publisher Francis, where they would be collected for the second edition of *Napoleon III in Italy*. Writing to Fanny Haworth, she links this outlet to the controversy over *Poems before Congress* in Britain, implying that she has found a more sympathetic as well as more lucrative audience:

> being turned out of the old world, I fall on my feet in the new world, where people have been generous, and even publishers turned liberal. Think of my having an offer (on the ground of that book) from a periodical in New York for a 100 dollars for every single poem, though as short as a sonnet—that is, for its merely passing through their pages on the road to the publishers proper.[18]

To her sister Arabella she tells of the 'literary propositions' from America, which have earned her £45 'for their merely passing through a periodical into my next edition', and that 'sympathy and pay come double' from America (Lewis, ii. 463, 500). For Barrett Browning, the fact that these poems are seen to be 'merely passing through' *The Independent* on the way to her publisher Francis apparently dissolves anxieties about the 'race of periodicals' and their monetary transactions. Indeed, although she admits to Arabel that 'anti-English as I am said to be, I prefer an English audience very much' (Lewis, ii. 500), she also writes to an unknown correspondent on 22 April 1861 that whatever she publishes in periodicals now 'is absorbed by an American engagement, which besides paying extravagantly, leaves my poems as good as manuscript for the English public' (Kelley and Hudson, 110). Thus, after the reviewers' condemnation of anti-English sentiment in *Poems before Congress*, bypassing English periodical readership protects the market for her English poetry volumes, but also protects Barrett Browning from the sting of the British periodicals.

TRANSATLANTIC CIRCULATIONS

The attraction of writing for *The Independent* was various. Like the front-page journalism of her friend Margaret Fuller, who was foreign correspondent in Europe for the American *Tribune*, Barrett Browning's contributions on the front page secured her prestige among an American public who warmed to her pro-Italian ideology. The readership was sympathetic because of the politics of the

---

[18] Kenyon, ii. 387.

newspaper, which was founded in 1848 to campaign for abolition. Its pages were committed to reporting domestic and foreign news and, in particular, the Italian Question, which was seen as analogous to the slavery issue. Indeed, the correspondence between Barrett Browning and Tilton suggests that the association between the *Risorgimento* and abolitionism validated her contributions to the newspaper on Italian politics, and were part of her symbolic and monetary investments in Italian nationhood. Unease about popular print and mass circulation was also shifted because of her commitment to a more vigorous public poetics for the cause of Italy; while her politics had isolated her in Britain because of the periodicals' hostility, it would make her campaign for Italy across the Atlantic.

Barrett Browning's first surviving letter to Tilton invokes the familiar reluctance of publishing in the popular press: 'We do not often write for periodicals whether at home or abroad.'[19] She makes an explicit link between Italy and America, praising his country's generous sympathy for the cause of 'rescued nations', eliding the lucrative payments to her with the cause of Italy itself. Furthermore, she picks up on the sense of the poems circulating directly between Italy and America, bypassing England (and the hostile periodical press): 'The poems go straight to you from the brain, & not round by England. When you have done with them, have the goodness to pass them to Mr Francis for the next edition—of "Napoleon III in Italy." ' The implication is that the poems are written 'fresh from the pen' with the newspaper and her second American edition in mind; furthermore, she refers to the controversial reviews of *Poems before Congress* in the British press, implying that *The Independent* readership is more sympathetic than a home audience: 'My book has had a very angry reception in my native country as you probably observe, but I shall be forgiven one day, and meanwhile, forgiven or unforgiven, it is satisfactory to one's own soul to have spoken the truth as one apprehends the truth.' This insistence on publishing for truth and not critical acclamation repeats the terms of her letters to Chorley over his misreading of 'A Curse for a Nation', as well as the distinction reiterated through *Aurora Leigh* about poetry's truths kept unsullied from the marketplace. Nevertheless, the spectre of lucrative publication hovers over this letter: she now seeks a favourable reception and a substantial payment, for both will be profitable for Italy. In addition, the repeated mention of angry British reception suggests that, as with the critics' misreading of 'A Curse for a Nation', there is a certain slippage between nations in the transatlantic circulation between Britain, America, and Italy.

Another letter from Barrett Browning to Tilton, dated 20 July 1860, continues their dialogue on Italian politics while expressing ambivalence about publishing

---

[19] Elizabeth Barrett Browning to Theodore Tilton, 6 May 1860 (Harry Ransom Humanities Research Center, University of Texas at Austin). This letter is misdated 20 Oct. 1860 in the *The Brownings' Correspondence: A Checklist* (449): a postscript on the back of the letter gives the date as 6 May.

for payment. Implying that her considerable profit is not anything directly to dowith her, she writes that she sends him 'two new poems on Italian affairs with a certain reasonable shyness' at his generous payment: 'If these mss. destined for a future edition of my Italian volume, should suit you, they are at your service; if not let them pass simply into Mr. Francis's hands for the book.'[20] Tilton's reply, dated 1 September 1860, tries to tempt her to contribute more to his pages with several extremely profitable offers, and, crucially, links the issue of gain to the Italian Question. Invoking Harriet Beecher Stowe's contribution to abolition with *Uncle Tom's Cabin* (1852), Tilton asks Barrett Browning to do the same, in prose and in his newspaper, for Italian oppression:

Why will you not do for the oppressed in Italy what she has done for the oppressed in the United States? I propose that you write a story, to be printed chapter by chapter in The Independent, giving to the American People an insight into Italian life, manners, traditions, sufferings, and struggles for Freedom? Such a work, written out of the heart, and constructed of scenes of which your own eyes have been the witnesses, would win the whole world's thanks.[21]

Tilton here suggests that international politics makes news, something that was part of the nineteenth-century's invention of the news as a sellable item and inextricable from the developing media culture, but also that poetry has an intrinsic part to play in journalism. Tilton concludes his transatlantic analogy with a rhetorical question that suggests Barrett Browning has a moral debt to her adopted homeland that would be discharged by publishing for profit: 'Do you not owe it to Italy?' His attempt to entice Barrett Browning on to his pages mixes political obligation with a reformulated feminine sensibility: she must write from the heart to win a transatlantic sympathy for Italy, and such is her duty for freedom.

This combination of public politics with private affect is a prelude to Tilton's financial offers in his letter, and despite his confident tone it suggests the necessity of smoothing the way to a lucrative offer with an appeal to both her place in the public sphere and her feminine empathy, recalling Shires' notion of 'cross-dwelling'. Tilton makes several financial offers: the publication of the story in his newspaper along these lines, addressed to the American people, at a rate of $100 a week for six to eight months, after which Francis will bring out the columns in a book 'for your benefit'; regular weekly contribution to his newspaper for a year of whatever 'scrap' she desires, for an annual payment of $2,600 (or $50 per week); and if both offers are declined, he reminds her of his previous offer for irregular contributions of poetry at $100 per poem. He adds that all offers are open to both Brownings, although Barrett Browning relayed to him in her previous letter that her husband has a 'disinclination

---

[20] *Descriptive Catalogue of the Gluck Collection of Manuscripts and Autographs in the Buffalo Public Library* (Buffalo, 1899), 11 (cited in text and hereafter as Gluck).
[21] Armstrong Browning Library, Baylor University.

to the periodical channel'.[22] The prose story he suggests, more lucrative than regular poetry contributions, is valuable for the communication to his American readership of the Italian struggle for freedom: 'My object in proposing such a task is to excite in this country a more tender & sympathetic interest in the struggle of Italy for her political & moral elevation.' Tilton's vision for *The Independent* is clearly invested in the transatlantic circulation of writing and politics, mapping the newspaper's founding principle in abolitionism with Italy's freedom from foreign oppression, which in turn reaffirms the newspaper's interventions in American national identity in the prelude to the Civil War. His correspondence with Barrett Browning attempts to market and appropriate her celebrity status as a transnational woman writer, a controversial and newly radicalized figure after the hostile British periodical reception to *Poems before Congress*, in order to reaffirm the literary and political value of his newspaper. His manipulations of her over-determined identity in the print media are based on Barrett Browning's transatlantic circulation, and on what she can offer his attempt to fashion his newspaper's alignment with high culture; his apparently sentimental sympathy for Italy, in other words, is mediated through his ambitions for the place of *The Independent* in the competitive world of politicized news media. Indeed, Tilton concludes his letter with a reassurance about the literary value and political aim of his paper, both in his view closely linked:

I may mention that the object for which The Independent was started ten years ago, was to aid in the overthrow of American Slavery. To this end, it wishes to build up, if possible, the highest literary reputation, and the greatest moral influence, among the periodical pen of the United States. [...] I believe that in welcoming you to its columns, I am welcoming you to a circle of goodly men & women.

By writing for his paper, Barrett Browning will advance the cause of Italy, publish for a mass circulation of sympathetic readers and supporters in America, and be part of a 'circle' of esteemed contributors. By agreeing to his offer to contribute and join this network, literary reputation, moral influence and lucrative payment all represent investments in the Italian cause.

Barrett Browning continues to emphasize in her letters that she has not sought profit in her newspaper publications. In a letter sent early in 1861, she writes 'Now I send you something—or nothing as you may decide—(3 poems)—I don't insist on its being something—remember *that*' (Gluck, 12). Nevertheless, the symbolic and material circulation of politics and poetry between Italy and America is underlined by the fact that Tilton has been sending her complimentary copies of *The Independent* as well as news of American politics in his letters (Gluck, 12). Such an exchange between Italy and America is given a prominent metaphor in Barrett Browning's last surviving letter to her American editor. In April 1861 she sends 'Mother and Poet' and 'Only a Curl' to Tilton,

---

[22] Barrett Browning to Theodore Tilton, 20 July 1860 (Gluck, 12).

together with fresh news from Italy. After analysing Prince Napoleon's speech from the Italian pro-*Risorgimento* newspaper *Il Monitore*, and criticizing *The Independent*'s own Italian correspondent for his ignorance, she expresses her support of abolition and comments on recent American politics:

Our Italian cause sweeps on its way triumphantly. [...] A thrill of life and liberation is running through Europe. Let us not forget to praise the great Czar for the freeing of the serfs. Never can America admit a compromise on slavery, in the face of that action. Never can a 'President' named by the northern states, submit to carry a 'fugitive slave law' in face of that action. It is not possible.[23]

The 'thrill of life and liberation' connecting European nations is also reaching America and the cause of abolition. This sense of an interrelationship between Europe and America fashions Barrett Browning into the transnational women poet, whose pro-Risorgimento poems not only witness to the cause of Italy's freedom from foreign oppression, but also link that struggle with other European nations and with American abolitionism. Furthermore, the word 'thrill' suggests not only an active and politicized application of the poetics of affect inherited from Landon and others, but also implies that Italy and America are connected by a symbolic nerve that communicates and has a mediating influence, as well as a figurative and material economy, of its own.

The means of communication of that 'thrill' is the periodical press, especially the news media. Barrett Browning often expresses the affect of reading newspapers on Italian politics in acute bodily terms; for example, to Anna Jameson in May 1859 she writes of experiencing 'really physical *palpitations* in reading the newspapers'.[24] What the historian Clara Lovett terms the 'national democratic network'[25] in Italy after the unsuccessful revolutions of 1848 were partly sustained by regional and local newspapers. The Brownings were avid readers and subscribers to many of the most prominent Tuscan publications, even to the extent of asking diplomat Odo Russell to smuggle extra copies of *Il Monitore* and *La Nazione* into his diplomatic bag when they wintered in Rome in 1859–60; eventually the police seized an extra copy of *La Nazione*, banned in Rome because of its anti-papal policy (Lewis ii. 430; McAleer, *Dearest Isa*, 67). In 1859, Barrett Browning reports that she reads through three newspapers a day (Lewis, ii. 430), including not only Tuscan pro-*Risorgimento* papers but also *Galignani's Messenger* and British newspapers.

As Virginia Jackson notes, however, the metaphor of a vibrating chord over the Atlantic is specifically associated in the nineteenth century with transatlantic

[23] Elizabeth Barrett Browning to Theodore Tilton, April 1861 (Berg Collection, New York Public Library).

[24] Barrett Browning to Anna Jameson, 10–14 May 1859 (Armstrong Browning Library, Baylor University). Italic original.

[25] See Clara M. Lovett, *The Democratic Movement in Italy, 1830–1876* (Cambridge, MA: Harvard University Press, 1982).

literature. Referring to a speech by William Bryant in 1868, she argues that transatlanticism was typified by the metaphors of telegraphy, electric currents, and vibrating chords that unite nations with an active influence on the welfare of people: such figures were influenced by initiatives from 1858 to establish a transatlantic telegraphic cable. This is a fantasy of literature as communication, as an affective thrill that posits living presence, what Jackson terms 'the transatlantic imaginary'.[26] Bryant's speech celebrates poetry, rather than periodical literature, but the palpitations received by Barrett Browning on reading the newspapers are part of the affective discourse of transnationalism that he describes, the 'thrill of life and liberty' that vibrates across the Atlantic. Furthermore, Barrett Browning's contributions to *The Independent* repeat this rhetoric of affective communication and influence, as they also explore issues of value and investment. Indeed, for Barrett Browning there may also be here a connection between the thrill of transatlantic circulations of liberty and newsprint, and new uncanny technologies of affective communication offered by spiritualism. Networks of communication for Barrett Browning, in a distinctly proto-Modernist way, resonate through thrilling material and ethereal channels.[27]

VIRTUE AND VALUE

Several of Barrett Browning's poems in *The Independent* are written as a type of reportage. Not only do they communicate recent political and military events, they also borrow and satirize the discourse of newspapers, especially the British *Times* which she often condemned in correspondence as pro-Austrian and anti-Napoleon. The poems Barrett Browning almost certainly first sends to Tilton herself are 'First News from Villafranca' and 'King Victor Emmanuel Entering Florence'. The former, written in response to the unexpected and (to Barrett Browning and many other Italian patriots) deeply disappointing peace agreed on 11 July 1859. Unlike 'A Tale of Villafranca', published in *The Athenaeum* on 24 September 1859, this poem represents the patriots' angry first reaction to the armistice: it both responds to the 'first news' from the site of the peace, and transmits an interpretation of events for a transatlantic audience. The angry refrain 'Peace, peace, peace, do you say?' refutes the news while also transmitting

[26] Virginia Jackson, 'American Victorian Poetry: The Transatlantic Poetic', *Victorian Poetry*, 43 (2005), 157–64, 157.

[27] For the connection between telegraphy and transatlantic spiritualism, see Bridget Bennett 'Crossing Over: Spiritualism and the Atlantic Divide', in Janet Beer and Bridget Bennett (eds), *Special Relationships: Anglo-American Affinities and Antagonisms, 1854–1936* (Manchester: Manchester University Press, 2002), 89–109. For an account of Barrett Browning's political and poetical investments in spiritualism, see Alison Chapman, 'Risorgimenti: Spiritualism, Politics, and Elizabeth Barrett Browning', in Alison Chapman and Jane Stabler (eds.), *Unfolding the South: Nineteenth-century British Women Writers and Artists in Italy* (Manchester: Manchester University Press, 2003), 70–89.

it to the reader: 'What!—with the enemy's guns in our ears? | With the country's wrong not rendered back?' (stanza 1). In particular, the poem struggles to understand the actions of Napoleon III in brokering the peace, and ends by sending news fresh from the scene that simply denies that there will be any peace at all: 'Peace, peace, is still your word? | *We* say you lie then!—that is plain. | There *is* no peace, and shall be none' (stanza 5). The oral transmission of the first news of the peace, straight from the scene itself, is thus oddly both reported in the poem and refuted. By the concluding stanza, the news is seen merely to be a pause in the continued violent struggle for Italy's freedom: 'such a peace as the ear can achieve | 'Twixt the rifle's click and the rush of the ball.' Furthermore, the sense of poetry as both the mediation of news, and also of more value than journalistic reportage, is heightened by the poem's first publication just under a year after the first news itself, when subsequent events in Italy prove the poem's message to be proleptically true. Barrett Browning sends this poem, apparently now about old news, to Tilton on 7 May 1860, just after Tuscany peacefully ejects its Austrian Duke but also in the expectation of further war, especially in the south. Indeed, the other poem sent at this time both reports and celebrates its new King entering Florence after the plebiscite in Tuscany approves union with Piedmont. This poem, written after a description of the Florentine festivities was sent to the Brownings in Rome from Isa Blagden (*Dearest Isa*, 60), reports on events as a both an expatriate's eye-witness account and also as a participant in the action. The speaker merges the voice of the Italian patriot with that of the commentator and reporter, repeatedly exclaiming 'King of us all, we cried to thee, cried to thee', as it describes the scene, while also asking the King's minister Cavour to 'witness' to events and to know that there is more to be done for Italy, for 'Deeds unfinished will weigh on the doer' (stanza 8). The strangeness of this poem rests in its shifting of tone and register, as it mimics the cries of patriots, enters a dialogue with Cavour, and addresses the news for a foreign readership. Both these two poems sent to Tilton mimic and transform the accounts of newspaper journalism, so that the poetry fuses eye-witness reportage, the voice of the Italian patriot, and political prophecy.

Other poems sent to Tilton have a similar hybrid voice based on reportage, suggesting an important and dynamic new alliance between verse and the new media. For example, 'The Sword of Castruccio Castracani' is based on Victor Emanuel's visit to Lucca and celebrates him as the hero of liberated Italy, 'Garibaldi' on the pivotal point in the campaign in Sicily with the 'Thousand', and 'The King's Gift' on Garibaldi's daughter's acceptance of a token from Victor Emanuel signalling renewed friendship between the patriots. 'Summing up in Italy', subtitled 'Inscribed to the Intelligent Publics Out of It', is clearly written for foreign periodical readers, but it also satirizes the reports in British newspapers that refuse to acknowledge the heroism of Napoleon, Cavour, and King Victor Emmanuel for Italy, concluding ironically in the voice of 'thoughtful reviewers' (stanza 9). While the *Independent* poems play on the discourse of the periodicals, however, they also thematize obligations and gifts, turning the sense of investing in Italy into a moral and material exchange that transcends 'vulgar' monetary value. For example, they refer to Tuscany who 'gave all things away' in gratitude to their new King, the King's gift of jewels to Teresa Garibaldi, and the Tuscans who give their loved ones to the cause (as in 'Parting Lovers' and 'Mother and Poet'). Indeed, in all the *Independent* poems about Italy that call for and celebrate the gift of freedom and nationhood, freedom depends on obligation to the patriots and leaders, as well as an exchange with other nations.[28] Such gift exchanges are perhaps most clearly seen in the last poem written by Barrett Browning, 'The North and the South', which is based on a dialogue between north Europe and Italy, in which both ask to be given the best of the other. Finally, the South calls for a 'seer' and 'poet' who will bring 'baptismal flame', in a passage reminiscent of the call in *Casa Guidi Windows* (1851) for 'Some poet's hand' to bring the patriotic ideal into reality (1: 1092). While the poem concludes by honouring Hans Christian Anderson, the implication is also that this very poem, and in turn Barrett Browning herself, has such ability. Poetry is not only reportage, and not only for American newspapers at a lucrative price, it is also discharging a patriotic debt to Italy, and is both prophetic and performative. Robert Browning's countermanding of this poem from the *Cornhill* to *The Independent* seems to acknowledge the poem's reverberations for American politics, while also suggesting that his hostility to the 'periodical channel' was not perhaps simply one of rejection (there are other complications: his publication, for instance, of *The Ring and the Book* in parts a few years later (1868–9), mimicked the reading experience of serial publication). Browning sent the poem to Tilton with a letter that supports the 'Great Cause' of American republicanism (Gluck, 16) and the poem in *The Independent* is immediately followed by Horace Greeley's essay 'The North and the South', which urges that it may now be necessary to crush the rebellion and save the Republic. Greeley argues that 'The Nation must put forth its full strength in support of its authority and integrity' in order to save the north and the south from a greater calamity (1). Read in the context of the American Civil War, Barrett Browning's poem is endowed with an even greater (if poignant) transnational urgency and posthumous agency.

In letters to home to Britain, especially after the hostile reviews of *Poems before Congress*, Barrett Browning had defended Italian politics as an appropriate subject for poetry, articulating explicitly her new form of public poetics. In letters to Anna Jameson early in 1860, for example, she asks whether Italy is 'unfit for poetry' even if people disagree with her politics, and defends her political poems

---

[28] Even the non-political poem, 'Only a Curl', written for an American correspondent who had lost a child, is based on the notion of gift economy: the parents are comforted by the notion that God has not taken back the gift that is their child, but rather added to it. For more on the theory of the gift economy, see Judith Still, *Feminine Economies: Thinking Against the Market in the Enlightenment and the Late Twentieth Century* (Manchester: Manchester University Press, 1997).

as written by somebody 'who meant it, thought it, throbbed it out with heart and brain'.[29] To Chorley, in the aftermath of his *Athenaeum* review of *Poems before Congress*, she writes: I don't dream and make a poem of it. Art is not either all beauty or all use, it is essential truth which makes its way through beauty into use'.[30] Although she modestly adds 'Not that I say this for myself', recognizing the possibility of artistic failure, this statement suggests that she conceived poetry to have a use or affect, a dynamism that unites value and virtue, two concepts closely identified in the gift exchanges of her Italian poems.

Barrett Browning conceived the performativity of poetry in terms of affect, as if the thrill of life and liberty that she campaigns for and witnesses in Italy can be communicated and enacted through reading itself. Newspapers might convey the palpitation of affect, as she comments to Anna Jameson, and poems for *The Independent* also trope news as a bodily and electric impulse. The galvanic, emotional affect of first news of Villafranca is conveyed by the stuttering staccato rhythms of that poem, which also rather horrifyingly mimic the gunfire predicted imminently to continue. The rush of the patriotic crowd's warmth to King Victor entering Florence is conveyed by repeated exclamations and non-sequential narrative, transmitting the chaotic energy of the festivities into the poem's form. In other poems, military news is relayed by telegraph, suggesting an analogy with the poetry itself as another technology of communication. 'Garibaldi' ends abruptly with news of military success in Sicily, and the triumph of Garibaldi's Thousand, delivered by a telegram: '*Palermo's taken, we believe*'.[31] Laura Savio, in 'Mother and Poet', learns tragic news that her son has been killed in battle through the telegraph: 'without pause, up the telegraph-line | Swept smoothly the next news from Gaeta:—*Shot*' (stanza 12). The brevity and speed of telegraphic news, seen in 'Mother and Poet' as inhumanely abrupt and relentless, like the bullet itself, is a modernity humanized by Barrett Browning's political poetics into a communication of presence, of bodily empathy, pulse, and thrill.

By the late 1850s, after the reviewers' condemnation of the un-English sentiments of *Poems before Congress*, the 'periodical channel' of transatlantic newspaper for lucrative payment attracted Barrett Browning for a number of reasons. According with her reconception of politicized public poetry as an affective performance, publishing in *The Independent* brought her a sympathetic transatlantic network that was profitable to advancing Italy's cause. The poems for Tilton explore the concept of the gift and obligation, the link between monetary and moral value, and the relationship between value and virtue, but they also explore the cost of circulating the private in the public sphere. In particular, 'Mother and Poet', based on the Italian 'poetess and patriot' Laura

---

[29] Kenyon, ii. 364, 362.   [30] Kenyon, ii. 383.
[31] For an account of Garibaldi's victory, see George Macaulay Trevelyan, *Garibaldi and the Thousand (May 1860)* (London: Nelson (1920)), ch. 17.

Savio who lost two sons to the wars of independence, is a dramatic monologue that painfully exposes the human price of war and, as Angela Leighton argues, a refusal to write poetry as a woman (as with 'Only a Curl', that explicitly denies the sentimental platitudes expected of a woman's elegy for a child).[32] Despite Savio's refusal in the poem to write 'a great song for your Italy free' as a poetess, the poem nevertheless mixes private and public discourses through the metaphor of nation building as childbearing: 'the birth-pangs of nations will wring us at length | Into wail such as this' (stanza 19). And, although Savio refuses to write as the patriotic poetess she was 'only last year' (stanza 2) before her sons' deaths, Barrett Browning's text fashions her as a bereaved woman poet, re-configuring gender and nation-building into an acknowledgement and witness of the cost of freedom.

Such realignment of private and public are also seen in the pages of the *Independent* themselves where Tilton quotes from Barrett Browning's private letters to him, evidently not meant for publication. After her refusal to write a prose story based on Italy's sufferings, Tilton may be taking what prose he could out of the eminent transatlantic poet, for the price offered shows that, for a newspaper editor interested in copy, prose is valued more highly than poetry. His editorial comment introducing 'First News from Villafranca' on 7 June 1860 appropriates Barrett Browning's letter to him, in which she explains that the poems come to him 'direct from the brain, without going round by England', turning her words into an advertisement for the exclusiveness of her contribution: 'The accompanying poem', Tilton wrote, 'came to us direct from Italy, without going round by England' (1). *The Independent* quotes her letters at length as a preface to her poems on 16 August 1861, 21 March 1861 and, on 2 May 1861, 'A Note from Mrs. Browning', extracts her correspondence about Napoleon (1). When publishing 'Mother and Poet', Tilton's preface spells out the links with America:

The following magnificent poem [...] will find an echo in a hundred thousand mothers' hearts to-day, whose sons are now on the battle-field of their country, fighting for liberty in America as Mrs. Browning's heroes are fighting for liberty in Italy. God bless the woman who moves two nations with one song! (2 May 1861, 1).

Finally, when news of her death reaches New York during publication of 'A View Across the Roman Campagna' on 25 July 1861, Tilton prints an extravagant eulogy, a hagiographical account of her 'life of suffering': 'Not a finer genius ever came into the world, or went out of it; not a nobler heart ever beat in a human bosom; not a more Christian life was ever lived; not a more beautiful memory ever gathered round the name of man or woman' (1). This homage is wrapped around what he erroneously terms her last poem, 'A View Across the Roman Campagna', recommending Francis's three volume edition of her poems 'clad in

---

[32] Angela Leighton, *Victorian Women Poets: Writing Against the Heart* (Hemel Hempstead: Harvester Wheatsheaf, 1992), 109–10.

blue and gold—fit apparel for a poet!', and reminding his readers of her special relationship with *The Independent.* Barrett Browning's debt to Italy, symbolically discharged by printing her poems in this American newspaper, is converted into editorial prose and publishers' profit. Although her sense of the vulgarity of profits from periodicals, and the literary devaluation of mass print circulation, were overcome by her investments in Italy, in the end the newspaper commodifies the poet as a celebrated object of consumption. In Tilton's eulogy, the thrill of Italian life and liberty, channelled through the American press, markets Barrett Browning's body as a sign of heroic liberal transnationalism, marrying when 'Night was on the nation' in Italy, and dying on the dawn of Italian unification: 'the poetess was a prophetess. In her new home, she sat and watched for the day dawn through Casa Guidi windows. It waited long, but dawned at last, and she saw it—and died!' (1). Nevertheless, the analogy of the *Risorgimento* with abolitionism might still validate newspaper transactions, certainly in the eyes of Robert Browning, who continued to offer poems and proofs sheets to Tilton and Francis.33 At the start of America's own bloody conflict, and at the end of Italy's successful bid for national unity, such poignant analogies were profitable indeed.

33 See, for example, Robert Browning to Theodore Tilton, 11 Sept. 1861 (Gluck, 15–16).

5

The Drama of Capital: Risk, Belief, and Liability on the Victorian Stage

Jane Moody

To cross the threshold of a theatre entails the implicit recognition of a contract which is both financial and aesthetic. The entertainment promised by the ticket is predicated on the spectator's willingness to give credit—however provisional and contingent—to stage illusion. In a variety of periods, the interweaving of aesthetic and economic value systems at the heart of performance has created productive confusions between pleasure and profit. This chapter investigates the theatrical terms and generic conventions through which the stage represented the protagonists and paraphernalia of Victorian capital. My argument suggests that these depictions of fraudulent joint-stock companies, deceitful promoters, and collapsing banks cleverly exploited the uncertain economy of the theatre's own mimetic conditions.

At the close of a comedy by Tom Taylor whose financial plot pivots on the presence and power of a receipt, the speculator addresses the spectators directly, suggesting that notes of hand—a term which evokes financial credit, promises of love as well as their own applause—are 'payable on demand'.[1] In this ironic inversion, the credit conventionally granted by the audience to performance is brought into comic opposition with the debts due to the financier; suddenly, the spectators find themselves caught between credit and debit, suspended between the licence of theatrical illusion and the remorseless, unbending demands of capital. At first glance, such an address recalls the self-conscious theatricality of prologues and epilogues written for the Georgian stage. On closer inspection, however, Reuben's rhetoric markedly departs from such elaborately fawning

For suggestions about plays exploring the themes discussed here, I am grateful to Helen Day Mayer, Sos Eltis, Heidi Holder, David Mayer, and Kate Newey. I would like to thank Miles Taylor for useful references and Lawrence Rainey for several fruitful conversations about capital and melodrama which helped to define the shape of this argument.

[1] Tom Taylor, *Payable on Demand*, performed at the Olympic Theatre in 1859 (London: T. H. Lacy, no date), Act II, 53. Throughout this essay, references are to Act and page no.; the place of performance is London unless otherwise specified.

compliments. Rather, like so much Victorian drama, *Payable on Demand* plays on the fears of a society newly alert to the anxieties and embarrassments of a capitalist system. Indeed, the articulation and imaginative transformation of capital in a public space was to a large extent an achievement of the theatre.

The growth and collapse of capital markets proved a dramatic subject with strong appeal at the Victorian box-office. This phenomenon, however, is all but invisible in scholarly work on the subject where the novel's position as the definitive genre of capital remains undisputed.[2] My argument, written against the grain of these assumptions, investigates the way in which a cultural form built on appearances, characterized by insoluble contradiction, and defined by extreme forms of distortion, acquired a special kind of explanatory power in the age of high capital.

The instability of the relationship between the actual and the imaginary lies at the heart of theatrical illusion. That uncertainty is mediated by genre (the inflated, fantastical world of burlesque; the dream-world solutions provided by melodrama; comedy's celebration of incongruous improbability) but it also possesses material dimensions (the rise of the proscenium arch; the dimming of the house lights) which are historically specific, though sometimes conflicting in their stage effects. In a variety of ways, theatrical representations of capital brilliantly exploited the peculiar position of dramatic mimesis as a site of mediation between symbolic and other worlds. As the natural province of disorder, for example, the stage delighted in exhibiting the forms of fantasy, trickery, and transgression which capital produced. In particular, the emergence and institutional construction of financial risk created uncertainties which the Victorian stage seemed both to celebrate and repudiate. Indeed, the theatre's fascination with risk can perhaps be explained by its own equivocal position on the boundaries between the real and the unreal.

GAMES

A magnificent carriage, covered in dust, arrives at the house of Affable Hawk. From it descends a man, enveloped in a fur pelisse, carrying a box under his arm. The creditors are jubilant: finally Mr Sparrow has returned from Calcutta with what is presumed to be 'an incalculable fortune' to repay them. Hawk, too, breathes a sigh of relief, but for a different reason. He knows the man descending

---

[2] An exception which proves the rule is Linda V. Troost's persuasive essay, 'Economic Discourse in the Savoy Operas of W. S. Gilbert', in *Theorizing Satire: Essays in Literary Criticism*, ed. Brian A. Connery and Kirk Combe (London: Macmillan, 1995), 193–207. See also Jennifer A. Wagner-Lawlor, ' "Who Acts John Bull?": Speculating on English National Character and Modern Morality', *Victorian Review*, 23 (2003), 64–96. Historians are starting to pay attention to drama's crucial role in the mediation of Victorian finance. See James Taylor, *The Joint Stock Company in Law, Politics and Culture in Nineteenth-century Britain* (London: Royal Historical Society, 2005).

from the postchaise to be none other than his friend Sir Harry Lester who has agreed to impersonate his absconded business partner. Such an appearance, he hopes, will buy sufficient time to drive up the price of shares in the Great Indian Emerald company and, having profited to the tune of £20,000, to repay all his creditors. In a characteristic confusion of metaphors, Hawk laughs to himself, relishing the prospect of triumph: 'All the steam is on, and away we go. The moment Mahomet had three followers who believed in him, he had won his empire. I have moved the mountain.' The provision of credit, Hawk is all too aware, depends on a kind of belief akin to religious faith.[3]

The man in the fur pelisse, reports Mrs Hawk, cannot bear to meet his former partner until he has wiped out the past. Hawk is impressed by his wife's participation in the performance: 'Bravo, my dear! You do it capitally!' (Act III, 95). Such remorse also delights the creditors, and any remaining scepticism about this capitalist *deus ex machina* disappears when the man proceeds to pay off Hawk's debts in bills and cash. When he sees the cheque for £10,000, now in the possession of Frederick Noble, even the suspicious Mr Prospectus is convinced. Hawk, however, becomes increasingly perplexed by the success of his own Stock Exchange hoax: 'Damn it, they're all paid! I see fire—the room spins round! This is fairy land—enchantment—devilry!'(Act III, 101). Moments later, these intimations of madness are forgotten when Sir Harry Lester appears and Hawk realizes that the elusive man in the parlour is indeed Sparrow himself. Delighted by his new identity as a creditor, Hawk declares his intention to abandon the game of speculation, while advising spectators to imitate his energy and perseverance in playing this game until they, too, reap the rewards of financial success.

In this denouement of George Henry Lewes's comedy, *The Game of Speculation* (Lyceum, 1851) can be glimpsed the self-conscious convergence and playful collusion of capitalism and performance on the Victorian stage. From one perspective, Sparrow's serendipitous arrival is a predictable event which merely recapitulates a stock device familiar to British audiences from countless sentimental comedies: in particular, his appearance as a rich nabob echoes that of Sir Oliver Surface in Sheridan's *The School for Scandal* (1777). The moral status of these two colonial characters, however, is very different, for Sparrow's decision to abandon his business partner and vanish with the cash has reduced Hawk and his family to beggary. The play emphasizes the legitimacy of Hawk's game of speculation by explaining its origins in turning 'my very ruin into an amusement' (Act I, 55). But Lewes's appropriation of the game as his play's defining metaphor also highlights the parallels between mimesis and capital. Like the stage, the vertiginous world of speculation requires the simultaneous participation of many individuals; the limits and rules of the game take its players

---

[3] George Henry Lewes, *The Game of Speculation* (Lyceum, 1851), reprinted in *The Lights O' London and Other Victorian Plays*, ed. Michael R. Booth (Oxford: Oxford World's Classics, 1995), Act III. Subsequent references will be given within the text.

into unfamiliar, sometimes disturbing territory. Yet the self-consciously ludic quality of Hawk's game perhaps offers the audience some playful consolation for the frightening risks entailed by a speculative society.

The scene's rhetoric and dramatic construction highlight that credit—belief, confidence, faith, trust—on which capitalism and theatre alike depend. As Hawk reminds himself in his incongruous allusion to Mahomet, the creditors' belief is all that is necessary for his plot to succeed. Yet Sparrow's arrival proves even more plausible—to everyone except Hawk—than Lester's intended performance. Despite some initial scepticism (Mr Prospectus 'does not quite believe in the return of Mr Sparrow' (Act III, 98), the receipt of their money in Bank of England notes provides the creditors with what they regard as definitive evidence of Sparrow's identity. What makes Sparrow credible is not a telling scar or other physical mark (so often the proof of identity in melodrama) but the kind and amount of money which he produces. Significantly, however, Sparrow never appears on stage: like Hawk, the audience is invited to put its trust in the confidence of the creditors.

Lewes's source for *The Game of Speculation* was Balzac's *Mercadet, ou le Faiseur* (1848). The identity of Godeau, the name of the speculator's business partner in the French drama, has engendered not a little discussion about his influence on the still more mysterious Godot in Samuel Beckett's play. Though Beckett refuted the connection, the possibility that the twentieth century's most celebrated drama of existential crisis may have drawn on a play about the uncertainties of capital remains intriguing. Admittedly, Lewes's main interest in Balzac's play was the creation of a suitable 'vehicle' for his friend and employer, Charles James Mathews: he famously completed the adaptation in less than thirteen hours. But despite this haste, *The Game of Speculation* enjoyed a success 'unexampled in the annals of modern drama'.[4]

Only a few years earlier, hisses had greeted the first performance of Boucicault's speculative satire, *The School for Scheming* (Haymarket, 1847). Though the play went on to have a respectable run, such disapprobation attests to the tensions produced by the theatrical business of calling speculation to moral account in the Victorian period. In Lewes' play, however, speculation moved into the field of light comedy. Moreover, the star of the piece was an elegant and charismatic performer famous for his skill in embodying the idiosyncrasies of English gentlemen.[5] Mathews went on to make this ingenious swindler one of his most famous roles, taking the character of Affable Hawk abroad on tours to Australia and America and choosing it for his farewell performance at Paris in 1877. As these migrations attest, the game of speculation effortlessly crossed the boundaries of nation and culture.

[4] Letter from Lewes, 1852, cited by Rosemary Ashton, *G. H. Lewes: A Life* (Oxford: Clarendon Press, 1991), 36.

[5] James Robinson Planché in *The Life of Charles James Mathews, Chiefly Autobiographical*, ed. Charles Dickens, 2 vols (London: Macmillan, 1879), ii. 278.

Though delighted with the play's popularity, Lewes was disconcerted by the moral implications of Mathew's brilliance. Such was his 'artistic merit', declared Lewes, with a mixture of admiration and half-disapproval, that 'it almost became an offence against morality, by investing a swindler with irresistible charms, and making the very audacity of deceit a source of pleasurable sympathy'.[6] The problem involved in dramatizing speculation, recognized Lewes, is the difficulty of patrolling the rules and moral limits of the game.

The Game of Speculation explores the uncertainties—thrilling and danger-ous—when the old calculations of wealth based on land have been transformed into the liquidity of capital. In Lewes's play, Affable Hawk (Mercadet, the Napoleon of Finance, in the French play) has turned to speculation in order to pay off his tradesmen and to provide a grand dinner, plus a dowry of £20,000, in order to persuade Sir Harry Lester (a man whom he believes to own land which is ripe for speculation) to marry his daughter Julia. As so often in Victorian culture, the questionable morality of speculation is offset through the provision of an explicitly sentimental rationale.[7]

Hawk is a speculator of considerable virtuosity. During the first act alone, he cunningly extracts money from Earthworm, persuades Hardcore to lend him £300 as well as to sell his shares in the Emerald Mine Company, and secures the loan of some plate from Prospectus for his dinner. Though impressed by Sir Harry's catalogue of his estates (especially the possession of a salt marsh 'which might be worked by a company, and give enormous dividends' (Act II, 79)), Hawk advises him on the superiority of hard cash, precisely because it is always 'at hand'. (Balzac's De La Brive had seen these advantages through the lens of political upheaval: the advantage of capital was that, in the event of revolution, it could be easily transported elsewhere.)[8] But having discovered that Sir Harry's credit is as shady as his own, Hawk persuades him to impersonate Sparrow in order to rescue his own position.

In a variety of ways, Lewes's play helps explain what was at stake in per-formances of capital on the Victorian stage. For Victorian actor–managers, especially those intent on seeking patronage from middle-class audiences, capital was a profitable dramatic subject. Many of these plays proudly exhibited the furniture of the Victorian office: the material illusions involved in scenes

---

[6] *On Actors and the Art of Acting* (London: Smith, Elder, 1875), 65. Cf. the review published in *The Leader* (4 Oct. 1851), 949: 'The adventurer is almost, but not quite, a heartless schemer: he has still in him enough stuff o' the conscience for you to sympathize with him, and you relish his successes.' For a complaint about the cultural transposition of Balzac's tragic speculator into the exuberant playfulness of Mathews's Affable Hawk, see the remarks on Mathews (published anonymously but written by the dramatic critic Percy Fitzgerald) in the series 'Players of our Day' published in the *Gentleman's Magazine* in 1872. Mathews's reply is reprinted in *Life of Mathews*, ii. 264–70.

[7] This tendency confirms the broader arguments made in G. R. Searle, *Morality and the Market in Victorian Britain* (Oxford: Clarendon Press, 1998).

[8] Honoré de Balzac, *Mercadet*, trans. Robert Cornthwaite (Lyme: Smith and Kraus, 1994), 43.

featuring a 'Stockbroker's Office, with view of Capel Court and Entrance of the Stock Exchange' provided an intrinsic part of their appeal.[9] By 1863, business settings had become so ubiquitous (and conventional) that a dramatic character can marvel at the sight of a bill broking office precisely because, though she has often seen such rooms on stage, 'they ain't a bit like the real thing.'[10] Props, in particular, were used to evoke the conflicts over property and technology which dominated contemporary clashes between labour and capital. In the printed text of Henry Arthur Jones's *The Middleman* (Shaftesbury, 1889), a play whose conflict arises from the disputed ownership of a new glaze, the props required included 'several pieces of Biscuit Ware ... to be obtained from a pottery works'.[11] The sheer intangibility of capital seemed to demand a form of stage realism which compensated for the invisibility of its subject by exhibiting capital's material production.

The meaning of these plays was shaped, too, by the theatre's position in a highly competitive cultural market increasingly in search of national and even international profit. By the late nineteenth century, theatre management had become a site for speculation in its own right. Indeed, the success of Walter Watts, a clerk who embezzled £70,000 and invested the proceeds in the luxurious management of the Marylebone and Olympic theatres, exemplified the audacity of 'high art crime'.[12] The capital invested in and generated by London theatres was peculiarly visible and, in the case of individuals such as Dion Boucicault, contentious.[13] In April 1851, just six months before his appearance in *The Game of Speculation*, Mathews petitioned the Bankruptcy Court for protection against arrest under the Debtor and Creditor Private Arrangements Act: the account he gave in court of hairbreadth escapes from his creditors would go down in financial history.[14] The case reveals the precarious dependence of actor–managers on the vagaries of private credit but it also alerts us to the public knowledge which audiences brought to their interpretations of Mathews's characters. As the actor later remembered, 'every allusion I had to make to duns and bailiffs was hailed by the audience as the emanation of a light heart, and the most unctuous

[9] Scene directions in Tom Taylor, *Settling Day*, performed at the Olympic in 1865 (London: T. H. Lacy (1865)).

[10] Emily in Tom Taylor, *The Ticket-of-Leave Man* (Olympic, 1863), reprinted in *Plays by Tom Taylor*, ed. Martin Banham (Cambridge: Cambridge University Press, 1985), Act III, 194.

[11] Henry Arthur Jones, *The Middleman* (French's Acting edn, London: n.d.). The play is reprinted (though these directions are omitted) in Booth's collection, *The Lights O' London*.

[12] David Morier Evans, *Facts, Failures, and Frauds: Revelations Financial, Mercantile, Criminal* (London, 1859; repr. Newton Abbot: David and Charles, 1968), 74.

[13] Boucicault famously became rich on the back of his own profit-sharing theatrical revolution. See further, John R. Stephens, *The Profession of the Playwright: British Theatre, 1800–1900* (Cambridge: Cambridge University Press, 1992), ch. 3.

[14] David Morier Evans, *Speculative Notes and Notes on Speculation*, first published 1864 (New York: Augustus M. Kelley, 1969), 187.

enjoyment.'[15] Hawk's gesture of pulling the strings of an imaginary puppet draws attention to the skills of entrepreneurial manipulation shared by actor and character.[16]

The anxieties associated with capital made it an ideal subject for various forms of laughter. Different genres, however, mediated capital in distinctive ways. This diversity, not to mention the instabilities produced by the profusion of hybrid forms in this period, has not been properly recognized.[17] Michael Booth has emphasized the usurpation in mid-century melodrama of the traditional evil aristocrat by deceitful men of capital, notably the proprietors of banks which later collapse.[18] But melodrama was by no means the only genre preoccupied by the moral problems of capital. Burlesque's self-conscious disavowal of rationality and reality, as we shall see, became a powerful instrument for displaying the corrosions of romantic intimacy and political accountability which capitalism produced. Comedy, too, was gripped by capitalist fever. By nature an acquisitive form driven by the desire to own the material world, comedy delighted in the conflicts between the thrills and the spills of capital.[19] In these Victorian dramas, the stock impostor metamorphoses into the ebullient, deceitful, and predatory company promoter, intent on flogging the latest joint-stock company: plays from Taylor's highly successful *Still Waters Run Deep* (Olympic, 1855) to Jones's *The Rogue's Comedy* (Garrick, 1898) rehearse and expose the attractions of this delusive modern prophet.[20] Whereas stock market crashes taught investors painfully real lessons about the folly of investing in 'ludicrous' schemes, the theatre identified the boundary between legitimate and illegitimate risk as a rich arena for ludic exploration.[21]

[15] Dickens, *Life of Mathews*, ii. 96.

[16] Cf. Jones, *The Middleman*, Act IV, where Batty Todd uses a similar gesture to illustrate his manipulation of both labour and capital

[17] Though largely concerned with early cinema, Ben Singer's recent work extends the important arguments made by Peter Brooks about melodrama's constitutive relationship to the making of capitalist modernity. But Singer's worryingly broad and indistinct definition of melodrama seriously over-simplifies the generic terrain. See Ben Singer, *Melodrama and Modernity: Early Sensational Cinema and its Contexts* (New York: Columbia University Press, 2001). On the interdependence of comedy and melodrama, see Michael R. Booth's excellent introduction to *English Plays of the Nineteenth Century*, 5 vols (Oxford: Clarendon Press, 1969–75), iii.

[18] As pointed out by Michael R. Booth in *Theatre in the Victorian Age* (Cambridge: Cambridge University Press, 1991), 164–7.

[19] Eric Bentley, *The Life of the Drama* (London: Methuen, 1966), 304.

[20] This stage figure becomes prominent following the rise and fall of the notorious railway impresario, George Hudson. See especially, Edward Stirling, *The Railway King*, performed at the Olympic in 1845, in *Duncombe's British Theatre* (1828–52), vol. liv.

[21] Significantly, the language of ridicule and the ludicrous is invoked in Evans's discussion of the companies 'for the pretended sale of milk, bread, fish etc.' which came into existence in the bull market immediately preceding the panic of 1825–6. See D. Morier Evans, *The History of the Commercial Crisis, 1857–1858 and the Stock Exchange Panic of 1859* (1859, Newton Abbot: David and Charles Reprints [1970], 1.

RISK AND SEX

Like Affable Hawk, the hero of Tom Taylor's *Still Waters* congratulates himself on playing what he calls a desperate game: 'but I've won it, and the stake was worthy of the risk' (Act III, sc. i, p. 54). The image of life as a game, I have suggested, was an important tool for exploring and conceptualizing the problem of risk. But risk in these plays is rarely a purely financial question. On the contrary, its rewards and costs become inseparable from sex.

Recent discussions on the nature of agency and social structure in post-industrial modernity have focused in fruitful ways on the nature of risk. The analysis of our contemporary world, where risk is no longer chosen but ubiquitous and unavoidable (a 'self-endangering civilization', in the terms of Ulrich Beck), throws light in unexpected ways on languages of risk in the Victorian period.[22] Sociologists define risk as '[a] situation or event in which something of human value ... has been put at stake and when the outcome is uncertain.'[23] Risks involve hazards to property, to profit, and to the legitimacy of people or organizations; they are characterized by the stake which an individual or a group takes in the possibility of commercial or other advantage in the future. High capitalism, of course, is unthinkable without risk,[24] and the nineteenth century marked its democratization and institutional construction in Britain. During this period, thousands of people became exposed to risk through their participation in the purchase of shares; the introduction of limited liability in 1855 attempted to contain the risk of investing in joint-stock companies;[25] changes to the status of married women's property altered the conditions of risk by granting women control over their own fortunes and, as a consequence, the freedom to invest and lose money.[26] To a large extent, the growth of the British economy and the empire depended on the acceptance of risk and uncertainty as the price of growth and expansion.[27]

Such a transformation helped to produce new financial plots for Victorian playwrights and performers. Characters invest and lose money in foreign companies; fortunes collapse in the wake of international panics; clashes take place

---

[22] See especially Anthony Giddens, *Modernity and Self-Identity: Self and Society in the Late Modern Age* (Cambridge: Polity, 1991) and Ulrich Beck, *Risk Society: Towards a New Modernity* trans. by Mark Ritter (London: Sage, 1992).

[23] Carlo C. Jaeger et al., *Risk, Uncertainty, and Rational Action* (London: Earthscan, 2001), 17.

[24] See Anthony Giddens, *Runaway World: How Globalization is Reshaping our Lives* (1999; London: Profile, 2002), ch. 2.

[25] For more on practices of representation in relation to risk in the period, see Francis O'Gorman, 'Speculative Fiction and the Fortunes of H. Rider Haggard', below, 157–72.

[26] See also Nancy Henry, '"Ladies do it?" Women Investors in Fact and Fiction', below, 111–31.

[27] See further, Elaine Freedgood, *Victorian Writing about Risk: Imagining a Safe England in a Dangerous World*, Cambridge Studies in Nineteenth-century Literature and Culture, 28 (Cambridge: Cambridge University Press, 2000), 95.

between labour and capital and between the exigencies of provincial capitalism and the luxury enjoyed by indolent metropolitan consumers.[28] The emergence of women as financial agents made possible a variety of comic scenarios in which women heal a crisis of capital.[29] The communal nature of performance allowed audiences both vicarious release and the bond of imaginary partnership (a vicarious version of the precarious joint stock company) in such events. What many of these plays about capital share is a fascination with the representation of risk.[30]

Risk, as Anthony Giddens points out, is closely linked to innovation; it is a discourse inseparable from ideas of probability and uncertainty.[31] As an institution which trades on the simultaneous truthfulness and deceitfulness of its own representations, the theatre had a particular interest in the rhetoric of risk. Ulrich Beck observes that '[b]y contrast to the tangible clarity of wealth, risks have something *unreal* about them. In a fundamental sense they are both *real* and *unreal*'.[32] The shock effects of capitalism produced experiences of belief and disbelief which mirrored the theatrical border between reality and illusion. 'Is this real or sham?' demands Pennythorne when he learns that Alice's father has speculated and lost his daughter's fortune in the comedy, *One Thousand Pounds* (Prince of Wales, 1866), 'It's not put up to try me, is it?' 'It is too real', replies Alice, 'We have lost every shilling.'[33] Pennythorne's last-ditch hope that the news might be no more than a cruel hoax unwittingly draws the spectators' attention to the realization that, at another level, this loss is indeed only a sham.

---

[28] A large number of manuscript plays, submitted for licensing to the Examiner of Plays, and now held in the Lord Chamberlain's collections (hereafter LC) at the British Library, inform the argument made here. These include *King Capital*, performed Oldham, 1866, LC MS 53064V; Edward Howard, *True Forgiveness* 'illustrating the commercial crisis of 1866' (London: Lacy, 1870); [Alfred Wigan], *Business is Business; or, A Satisfactory Settlement* (Brighton, 1874), LC MS 53159E, featuring a comic clash between a Liverpool capitalist and his leisurely metropolitan son-in-law; [Augustus Harris and Henry Pettitt], *Pluck: A Story of £50 000*, performed Drury Lane, 1882, LC MS 53275B which includes a scene in which a mob storm a bank; [Sydney Grundy], *Mammon* (Strand, 1877), LC MS 53184E; Sir Charles Young, *Jim the Penman*, performed Haymarket, 1886 (London: Samuel French, n.d.), one of a large number of forgery plays in the period; [Augustus Harris and Paul Merritt], *The World*, performed Drury Lane, 1880, LC MS 53234N; Henry Arthur Jones, *Wealth*, performed Haymarket, 1889 (London: Lacy, n.d.) which depicts a stock market panic and features a Sheffield millionaire; [Augustus Harris and Henry Pettitt], *A Million of Money*, performed Drury Lane, 1890, LC MS 53457H; [W. J. Patmore and A. B. Moss], *Capital and Labour*, performed Victoria Opera House, Burnley, 1890, LC MS 53584B; [Edward Righton], *Insurance Money; or, The Story of a Coffin Ship*, performed Lyric, Hammersmith, 1894, LC MS 53549L; C. T. Dazey, *The War of Wealth*, performed Bolton, 1895, LC MS 53567H.

[29] See Taylor's *Settling Day* in which two women combining financial savvy and sentimental self-sacrifice lend their capital in order to rescue a bank.

[30] Plays from the pre-Victorian period tend to explore questions of capital from rather different perspectives. See, for example, George Colman (the Elder), *The Man of Business*, performed Covent Garden, 1775 (London: T. Becket, 1775); Frederic Reynolds, *Speculation*, performed Covent Garden, 1795 (London: Longman, 1795).

[31] Giddens, *Runaway World*, 25.   [32] Beck, *Risk Society*, 33.

[33] Henry J. Byron, *One Thousand Pounds* (New York: Robert De Witt, n.d.), Act III.

The disclosure of these boundaries, both explicit and implicit, seems to offer a form of communal reassurance necessarily absent from the world beyond the playhouse.

The laws of the stage, and those which define Victorian society, come into comic opposition in these dramas about risk. When Hawk explains his plans to buy time from his creditors by 'resuscitating' someone, Sir Harry demurs. Such 'melodramatic situations', he explains to the arch plotter, are 'no longer taken in good part' in 'real life' (Act III, 89); what is tolerated on stage triggers the intervention of the police outside it. The final confrontation between hero and villain in Taylor's *Still Waters* takes the form of a debate about risk which similarly pivots on the boundary between actual and symbolic worlds. In this scene, the suave villain Captain Hawksley, proprietor of a dubious company dealing in Galvanic Navigation, arrives at John Mildmay's villa intent on killing the man who has discovered his criminal past. Having been challenged to a duel, the apparently dull and phlegmatic hero proceeds to outwit the villain (and avoid his own assassination) by proceeding to analyse the risks involved:

You have often boasted you can hit the pip of an ace at twenty paces. I never fired a pistol at anything more formidable than a sparrow. I am willing to risk my life against yours on equal terms; but if we stand up opposite to each other at twelve paces, each with a loaded pistol—skill against no skill—what becomes of the equality of risk? (*crosses back*) Your friend has loaded one of these pistols—let us leave the other unloaded—put both under the cloth—each draw one, and fire together across the table; now, close your eyes and choose. You hesitate! (Act III, sc. i, p. 56).

Mildmay's rational calculation of risk makes a mockery of the duel as a form of honourable arbitration. All the dumbfounded villain can do is to dismiss the challenge by declaring it beyond the province of credibility: '[s]uch a way of fighting was never known but in a novel. I decline this unheard-of proceeding' (Act III, sc. i, p. 56). Again, Taylor invokes mimesis as an analogy for the operations of a society based on risk. Ironically, the character who is most alert to this resemblance is a master in the arts of duplicitous speculation.

In many of these plays about capital, the risks involved in speculation become inseparable from the threat posed by illicit love; women, in other words, come to embody the seductiveness and thereby the cost of capital. In *Still Waters*,[34] a play uneasily poised between comedy and melodrama, it is Captain Hawksley's seduction which makes the household vulnerable to financial risk. Before the play begins, Mildmay's father-in-law, Mr Potter, has invested one thousand pounds in Hawksley's Galvanic Navigation Company. In the opening scene, Potter's sister, Mrs Sternhold has urged her brother to buy some more shares. But since

---

[34] Taylor's play is based on a French novel entitled *Le Gendre* by Charles Bernard. The drama became a stock comedy and was later turned into a silent film.

Potter is overdue on a payment of £8,000 to the trustees under his daughter's marriage settlement, he encourages Mildmay to invest this money in Galvanics, a speculation alleged to guarantee a return of 8 per cent. Initially Mildmay accepts this proposal with laconic good-humour and even considers making a further investment from his own funds.

Mildmay then overhears Mrs Sternhold accusing Hawksley of transferring his illicit attentions from her to the naive Mrs Mildmay; he also discovers that Hawksley forged a bill presented at his own counting house. Having concluded that his laissez-aller principles have endangered the household's moral and financial safety, Mildmay decides to take action. In a masterful display of sangfroid, he compels Hawksley to buy back the shares and to return Mrs Sternhold's love letters as the price of his silence about the forged bill.[35] The pathetically grateful Mrs Sternhold and his repentant wife are now all too eager to acknowledge Mildmay's patriarchal authority.

In order to triumph as a comic hero, Mildmay has to confront the various risks facing the Brompton household. As we have seen, the capitalist discourse of risk permeates the comedic plot. At one level, the problems Mildmay faces are familiar ones, with their roots deep in theatrical tradition: sexual conquest is a favourite activity of the comic trickster.[36] Hawksley, however, occupies a new position between the private and public spheres: now, the dangers of illicit love explicitly figure the risks of capital. Drama, a cultural form intensely preoccupied by the erotic, revels in the evocation of these sexual threats. What such plays rehearse is the dilemma that the very risks necessary for the exploitation of capital are potentially fatal to the security of a middle-class household.

Anthony Hope Hawkins's drama, *The Price of Empire* (St James', 1896) deploys the analogy between the risks of capital and the dangers of the flesh to even more disturbing ends.[37] When the action begins, members of a syndicate have just received a telegraph from Ruston, the mysterious director of the company established to exploit the resources of Omofaga (a territory whose geographical identity is never disclosed) requesting an additional investment of £70,000 in order to buy out the rights of a German baron. The investors' lack of knowledge about Omofaga, not to mention the shadowy character of Ruston himself, increases the sense of contingency and foreboding. Throughout the play, characters oscillate between acceptance and repudiation of the risks involved in empire.

[35] As Allardyce Nicoll shrewdly points out, the play is among the first in the period to acknowledge illicit love as 'a fact of life'. See *A History of English Drama, 1660–1900*, 6 vols (Cambridge: Cambridge University Press, 1952–9), v: *Late Nineteenth-century Drama, 1850–1900*, 101.

[36] See Harry Levin, *Playboys and Killjoys: An Essay on the Theory and Practice of Comedy* (New York: Oxford University Press, 1987), 41.

[37] Anthony Hope Hawkins was a well-known barrister and liberal politician who wrote novels (including *The Prisoner of Zenda* which was a runaway success) under the pseudonym of Anthony Hope. *The Price of Empire* was never published, but a typewritten script is extant in LC MS 53594R. Subsequent references are given within the text.

Ruston attempts to counter the investors' doubt by declaring the success of Omofaga a certainty. This statement prompts a series of exchanges which reveal the assumptions on which risk is constructed:

ADELA   A certainty for who[m]?

SEMINGTON   What the public think a certainty is a certainty—for the public. That's philosophy, eh, Ruston?

RUSTON   Is it? I never read any and your extract doesn't raise my opinion of its value.

SEMINGTON   And what the public thinks a certainty is a certainty—for the Promoters. That's finance.

MRS DENISON   (*smiling*) This is an age of finance, isn't it?

ADELA   Some people call it by another name.

RUSTON   Call it—or me—what you choose. In ten years Omofaga will be a British province. (Act II, 11–12)

Adela is the sceptical investor of the play, a rich, witty woman stubbornly reluctant to accede to the faith on which the venture depends. Throughout, Hawkins presents Ruston's enterprise as one whose success depends on a secular form of religious belief. As Ruston tells the syndicate, 'You give me faith, and I'll give you a kingdom' (Act II, 12). Such rhetoric, however, raises the spectre of fanaticism as when the car of Juggernaut (a frequent point of reference in the play) crushes its devotees under a huge machine. But what preoccupies the investors is the cost of this enterprise: 'A few millions—a few lives—a few tears?' (Act II, 13). Just as Lady Semington mistakes the red crosses on the map denoting the Company forts for tombstones (Act II, 9), so her fellow investors wonder whether their hopes, their money, or even their own bodies will end up being buried in Omafaga. The boundaries between empire, religion, and performance in *The Price of Empire* are polemically uncertain, each precariously dependent on kinds of faith offered by individuals who are no longer sure if they are speculators, worshippers, or merely spectators. Indeed, the play's language subtly exploits the antipathy as well as the intense rivalry between the church and the stage as purveyors of belief.

Like Hawksley, the risk embodied by Ruston is figured in terms of sexual charisma: capital, as we have seen, brings the sexes into forms of dangerous proximity. Ruston is a particularly ambiguous character. Though the play follows Victorian conventions by portraying the ultimate failure of his sexual designs, the moral uncertainty of the ending implicitly acknowledges the territorial ambition of the imperial capitalist. Notably, the burgeoning illicit relationship between Ruston and Maggie Denison is presented as an open secret or rather a 'forbidden subject' which intrudes into almost every conversation. At a villa in Dieppe, during a night shrouded in mist, Ruston and Mrs Denison dream of running away together to Omofaga: beyond the villa lies a casino, another telling image of the losses and extraordinary winnings which depend on the operation of chance. But when news arrives that the Prime Minister has refused to recommend the

Omofaga railway to the Cabinet, Ruston returns to London and the threat of an elopement recedes.

By the end of the play, Harry Denison has decided to leave the Board: his wife is seeing a doctor and seems to be suffering from some kind of breakdown. But the business of the syndicate, still riven by conflict and uncertainty, continues: in the eyes of the investors, the seductive profits of empire still outweigh its manifest risks. So whereas Hawk and Mildmay take advantage of the capital markets only to repudiate the game of speculation in the final act, the Omofaga investors remain on the imperial stage, paralysed by hope and fear.

LIABILITY

In the world of international capital, where the collapse of a bank in one nation could produce ruin thousands of miles away, the concept of liability (a word which first emerges in 1794 to refer to the condition of being answerable by law or equity) began to permeate everyday life. By the 1840s, the term 'liabilities' connoted the financial obligations which characterize a capitalist society. Whereas the language of risk emphasizes the chances involved in taking a stake in the future, the emerging discourse of liability reveals the haunting of the present by financial obligations made in the past. The consequences of such liabilities—and the psychological confusion they produce—are a recurring theme in Victorian theatre.

Burlesque, a genre in which fantastical events are made out of all too predictable conventions, shrewdly exploited the social instabilities produced by capitalist markets; melodrama, by contrast, came to embody the experience of financial catastrophe. In this part of the essay, I focus on one of the period's defining moments of theatrical capitalism, a moment which witnessed the dramatic conversion of fateful contingency into capitalist sensation.

W. S. Gilbert, a man who made spectacular profits from the dynamic theatrical market at the end of the century, was fascinated and disturbed by the crises of individual and social identity which liability brought into being. *Engaged*, his bitterly absurd and disconcerting burlesque, turns on the status of a marriage contracted between two strangers for the sole purpose of protecting the woman from an unwanted suitor. Having declared themselves man and wife in the garden of a house on the border between England and Scotland, the two individuals part. Each is now entailed to a partner whose identity is unknown to them; the legal status of the marriage is only compounded by its geographical uncertainty.

At the heart of Gilbert's play is a comic situation taken to absurd extremes. The objects of our laughter are two characters attempting to cope with an extraordinary level of contingency. For Belinda, the situation is one of doubt and confusion: 'Can I marry? Have I married? May I marry? Who am I? Where am I? What am I? What is my condition in life?'[38] In Belinda's case, a liability incurred in the past engenders a sense of psychological paralysis; by contrast, the quixotic Cheviot attempts to erase the past and to avoid the fixity entailed by commitment (marriage, as he points out, is 'a very risky thing') by engaging himself successively to Belinda, Maggie, and Minnie. To each, he insists, he is passionately devoted; each he declares, using an almost identical phrase, is 'the tree upon which the fruit of my heart is growing; my Past, my Present, and my Future' (Act I, 156). Adding insult to injury, Cheviot attempts to defend his action by invoking the language of probability: both Belinda and Minnie, he points out 'has an even chance of becoming my wife' (Act III, 182).

The uncertain status of Cheviot and Belinda's marriage rehearses the liabilities which a capitalist society brings into being. The moment when Minnie discovers that Cheviot is liable for all his capital in the Royal Indestructible Bank is a good example. Belvawney has tried to secure Minnie's love for himself by starting the erroneous rumour that the bank has collapsed. Minnie reacts accordingly, repudiating Cheviot as a romantic prospect precisely because his position is not fully 'assured'. Reviewers were horrified that characters could harbour such mercenary values beneath the silvery rhetoric of theatrical love: *Figaro* called the play 'nauseous and repulsive' and complained about laughter being 'extorted' from the audience in spite of their 'sense of honour or of decency'; *The Hornet* thought the play's 'cold-blooded, brutal cynicism' had never been equalled, while Clement Scott complained that Gilbert 'takes a delight in vivisecting the human heart.'[39] Critics have tried to explain this reaction by suggesting that audiences somehow failed to understand the play's critique of melodramatic conventions. Such an interpretation, however, misses the point about Gilbert's wholesale mockery of capital. In *Engaged*, the contingencies of modern capital have come to define the construction of identity. Indeed, the difficulties experienced by these characters in coming to terms of 'settlement' (a word precariously moored in the play's language between financial payment, marriage, and psychological certainty) are at once patently absurd and surprisingly serious. What the critical dissent about the play reveals is an anxiety about the legitimacy of its symbolic world, a reluctance to grant stage licence to the calculating identities Gilbert regarded as the social and psychological products of capitalism.[40]

If *Engaged* offers a ludicrous perspective on the identity crises engendered by a capitalist society, *Utopia, Limited* (Savoy, 1893) explores their political and constitutional consequences. From one point of view, Gilbert's comic opera, set on a dreamy island in the South Pacific, represents the triumphant exhibition

---

[38] *Engaged*, reprinted in *London Assurance and Other Victorian Comedies* ed. Klaus Stierstorfer (Oxford: Oxford University Press, 2001), Act II, 167.

[39] Quotations from reviews are cited from Jane W. Steadman, *W. S. Gilbert: A Classic Victorian and his Theatre* (Oxford: Oxford University Press, 1996), 151.

[40] See further, Gunter Gebauer and Christoph Wulf, *Mimesis: Culture–Art–Society*, trans. Don Reneau (Berkeley: University of California Press, 1992), 3.

of theatrical capital. Indeed, the enormous production costs of this lavish show, featuring the burlesque reconstruction of an English court (using hundreds of electric light bulbs and a specially constructed parquet floor), ate into the still substantial profits made in a run of almost 250 performances. But from another perspective, *Utopia, Limited* sets out to expose one of the most crucial and controversial innovations of Victorian capital: the introduction of limited liability.

The position of limited liability on Utopia as an imperial export creates rich opportunities in the play for spectacular exoticism and densely ironic mimicry.[41] So coruscating, indeed, was Gilbert's script that many satirical lines were deleted in rehearsal or, in response to affronted spectators, after the first performance.[42] Among the 'flowers of progress' which Princess Zara brings to the island on returning from her fashionable education at Girton College is Mr Goldbury, a company promoter who advocates '[s]tupendous loans to foreign thrones', speculates in ginger-pops and peppermint-drops and regards no scheme too great or too small '[f]or Companification'.[43] The immediate conversion of Utopia into a limited company has various unintended consequences: the King's new status as a Corporation, for example, utterly destroys political opposition. And as the evil courtiers discover, the plea of limited liability also ruins once profitable businesses: customers simply avoid their bills by applying to be dealt with under the Winding-up Act. As in *Engaged*, *Utopia* takes advantage of the arbitrary, self-consciously incredible world of burlesque. Such a theatrical universe entertains an audience with absurd improbabilities but at the same time engenders scepticism and even heresy. For *Utopia* presents limited liability as a form of secular religion which has corroded the nation's political fabric, disenfranchising its own citizens in the name of 'dull Prosperity' (Act II, 646). Burlesque provides the generic framework for the creation of anti-worlds which disclose disturbing insights into the nature of the self and modern society.

Burlesque deals in laughter and the anxieties which laughter releases. But the emergence of capitalism also created a need for plots which testified to and somehow mastered the attendant terrors of this world. The depiction of capital as a place of shock and shocking reversal became the special domain of melodrama and the play which most notably marks this act of territorial possession is Boucicault's *The Poor of New York* (Wallack's, New York, 1857). To thousands of playgoers on both sides of the Atlantic, this drama exhibited the inescapable character of liability in the modern world. What is more, in a

---

[41] See Carolyn Williams's persuasive argument in '*Utopia, Limited*: nationalism, empire and parody in the comic operas of Gilbert and Sullivan', in *Cultural Politics at the Fin de Siècle*, ed. Sally Ledger and Scott McCracken (Cambridge: Cambridge University Press, 1995), 221–47.

[42] John Wolfson includes a facsimile rehearsal libretto in *Final Curtain: The Last Gilbert and Sullivan Operas* (London: Chappell, 1976).

[43] *Utopia, Limited* in *The Complete Plays of Gilbert and Sullivan* (New York: Cerf and Klopper, n.d.), Act I, 618. Subsequent references are cited within the text.

remarkable convergence of the financial and aesthetic contracts between stage and auditorium, *The Poor of New York* elevated that most tangible proof of liability—the receipt—into an instrument of moral retribution.

'Never did wickedness and commerce seem so intimately allied as during the great panic of 1857,' remarked David Morier Evans.[44] The trigger for the international commercial panic of that year—following almost a decade of breathtaking expansion—was the collapse of the Ohio Life Insurance Company with liabilities of $7m.[45] Banks and other institutions swiftly followed, creating financial disarray, mass unemployment, hunger, and destitution both in America and in Europe. The actor and playwright Dion Boucicault witnessed the crisis at first hand in New York, and shrewdly anticipated the market for a play which captured the citizens' experience of confusion, perplexity, and despair. Given that Boucicault had spent four years living and working in Paris, France was an obvious source of dramatic raw material; money and materialism, too, dominated the plays in the contemporary Parisian repertoire.[46] Having identified a seven-act drama by Edouard Brisebarre and Eugène Nus entitled *Les Pauvres de Paris* (Ambigu-Comique, Paris, 1856), he and his collaborators set to work converting the play into *The Poor of New York*.[47] The drama would receive almost three thousand performances at Wallack's Theatre; local adaptations on both sides of the Atlantic brought the total to many hundreds more. The chaos of the world's first financial emergency became the stuff of melodrama.

Boucicault's play marks the metamorphosis of melodrama into a form—and a commercial vehicle—of international capital capable of generating extraordinary receipts. Such a phenomenon disgusted Charles Dickens who pronounced one of the London adaptations of the play 'the most depressing instance, without exception, of an utterly degrading and debased theatrical taste that has ever come under my writhing notice.'[48] In the character of the munitions manufacturer, Andrew Undershaft, George Bernard Shaw would create his own trenchant refutation of Gideon Bloodgood, Boucicault's evil banker. Such distinguished indictments have ensured the position of *The Poor of New York* as an almost demonic anti-script in Victorian theatrical history.[49] But rather than accepting these judgements at face value, we need to be alert to the clues they provide

[44] Evans, *History of the Commercial Crisis*, 11.

[45] On the financial boom of the 1850s marking the emergence of the first global industrial economy, see Eric Hobsbawm, *The Age of Capital, 1848–1875* (London: Weidenfeld & Nicolson, 1975), ch. 2.

[46] See further, Neil Cole Arvin, *Eugène Scribe and the French Theatre, 1815–1860* (Cambridge Mass: Harvard University Press, 1924).

[47] The play was advertised as having been written 'by the *** Club': Boucicault's collaborators were three New York journalists.

[48] Dickens, letter to John Forster [?8 Oct. 1864] in *The Letters of Charles Dickens*, 12 vols (Oxford: Clarendon Press, 1965–2002), x. 433–4, 434.

[49] As Robert Hogan complains, the play contains 'every stale staple of popular theatre ... virtue in distress, the scrap of paper that makes everything come right, feast, wedding and dual action on a divided stage'. See *Dion Boucicault* (New York: Twayne, 1969), 67.

about a fundamental transformation taking place in the 1850s in the relationship between capitalism and mimesis.

Boucicault's source dramatizes the fortunes of a Bordeaux banker who becomes rich on the profits of a dead man's cheque while his penniless debtors struggle to survive. Many years later, however, Planterose, the banker's canny clerk, manages to produce the receipt (see Act VII, scene ix, when Planterose enters '*un papier à la main*'), enabling the banker to be apprehended and the embezzled fortune to be restored to the family.[50] At the heart of this highly sentimental play, then, is a symbolic token which proves the moral and financial liability of the fraudulent capitalist. The ideological ambivalence of Boucicault's play arises from the blending of sentimental rhetoric with what is arguably a celebration of the jeopardy and contingency at the heart of a capitalist society.

In Brisebarre and Nus's drama, Boucicault discovered a plot which could model the changing relationship in capitalist modernity between social structures and individual agency. Eschewing the melodramatic cosmologies of providence and fate[51] whose operation traditionally underpins the final triumph of good over evil, the new and spectacular climax of *The Poor of New York* dramatizes the moral retribution which an extraordinary risk makes possible.[52] In this scene, immediately recognized as a technological tour de force (and using fireproof scenery invented by Boucicault himself), Badger fights his way into the burning house and emerges clutching the receipt just as the building collapses around him. The elemental force of fire provides a new kind of theatrical language for the amoral and uncontrollable forces of capitalism as well as offering audiences a thrilling environment for a compensatory fantasy of human agency. Indeed, Boucicault's conversion of capital's terrifying power into a source of spectatorial sublimity establishes the theatrical terms for what we might call the capitalist aesthetics of Victorian sensation culture.[53]

Boucicault later explained the success of *The Poor of New York* by declaring that in the minds of his spectators 'the actual, the contemporaneous, the *photographic* had replaced the works of imagination'.[54] The play's geographical transposition to the streets of New York (famous scenes included Union Square on a snowy night, the desperate poverty of tenement lodgings and the opulent furnishings

---

[50] Edouard Brisebarre and Eugène Nus, *Les Pauvres de Paris* (Paris: Michel Levy frères, n.d.).

[51] On the idea that fate and destiny have no part to play in a modern society, see Giddens, *Modernity and Self-Identity*, ch. 4.

[52] Significantly, the resolution of *The Poor of New York* tempers the moral clarity of *Les Pauvres*: the handcuffed banker is released rather than being imprisoned on the grounds of his redeeming love for his daughter. British reviewers were perplexed by what they saw as a comedic resolution to a melodramatic plot. See *The Times* review of *The Streets of London* (3 Aug. 1864).

[53] On the 1860s as the 'age of sensation', see Jenny Bourne Taylor, *In the Secret Theatre of Home: Wilkie Collins, Sensation Narrative, and Nineteenth-century Psychology* (London: Routledge, 1988). Singer rightly emphasizes the crucial relationship between sensation and technology in late nineteenth-century melodrama. See Singer, *Melodrama and Modernity*.

[54] 'Leaves from a Dramatist's Diary', *North American Review*, 149 (1889), 228–36, 230.

of Bloodgood's house in Madison Square) and its temporal alignment with the contemporary financial panic of 1857 are designed to dissolve the boundaries of space and time between off-stage and on-stage capital. Boucicault also jettisons the religious and sociological language of the French source, choosing instead to present capital as a secular and economic phenomenon (see Badger's allusions to 'a want of confidence ... [which] pervades the community') which recognizes boundaries of neither class nor geography.[55] Significantly, rich New York playgoers seem to have regarded this panoramic approach as a distasteful innovation. In their critiques of Badger, the wily clerk, as 'too fierce, gruff and melodramatic', it is as if reviewers were attempting to defend the integrity of theatrical mimesis from the uncomfortable vulgar truths of capital.[56] The problem with a 'photographic' approach to the representation of financial crisis on stage was that it left nothing to the imagination.

The geographical rootlessness of modern capitalism provided Boucicault with both a dramatic subject and an international market. He went on to create 'localized' versions of *The Poor of New York*, written on the urban fabric of burgeoning world cities—both in North America (Boston and Philadelphia) and the British Isles (London, Leeds, Manchester, Liverpool, and Dublin). Only perfunctory textual changes were necessary: a manuscript prepared for production at Liverpool refers to characters 'carrying bag to the—Hotel' and scenes set in 'An open place near—' as if the names of the city's streets, coffee houses, and hotels would be supplied when rehearsals began.[57] But these dramas of urban capital drew enormous audiences: *The Streets of London* (Princess's Theatre, 1864), featuring a spectacular recreation of Trafalgar Square, a druggist's shop 'brilliant with red bottles', and 'the best burnt house ever destroyed upon any stage' brought in profits of £32,000.[58] In an ironic reversal of the modern restructuring of local relations across indefinite spans of time and space,[59] capitalism transformed stage geography by creating a demand for local plays about the international economy.

Boucicault recognized melodrama's savage power to embody the frightening contingencies and shocking reversals which define a capitalist society. The success of *The Poor of New York* in its various versions disturbed critics because it challenged cherished beliefs about the boundaries between theatrical mimesis and the money-grubbing world of capital. In these critiques, then, a crisis of capital is reconfigured as a crisis of taste. The vantage point of theatrical history

[55] Cf. Evans, *Speculative Notes*, 36–7, who points out that commercial panics enter both 'the palace of the millionaire and the hovel of the peasant'.

[56] *The Herald* (10 Dec. 1857), cited *Annals of the New York Stage*, ed. G. C. D. Odell, 15 vols (New York: Columbia University Press, 1927–49), vi. 22–3.

[57] Manuscript entitled 'The Poor of —' submitted to the Examiner of Plays by the Theatre Royal, Liverpool, LC MS 530290.

[58] *The Times* review (3 Aug. 1864); John Hollingshead, evidence given to the *Select Committee on Dramatic Literature* (1866), 193, cited Tracy C. Davis, *The Economics of the British Stage, 1800–1914* (Cambridge: Cambridge University Press, 2000), 213.

[59] See further Anthony Giddens, *The Consequences of Modernity* (Cambridge: Polity, 1990).

also enables us to see that *The Poor of New York* produced the technological foundation for a modern culture of sensation which would further corrode these fragile illusions. Faced by Badger's receipt, Dickens protested despairingly about the financial and 'photographic' contract on which the play was based whilst Shaw would respond with *Major Barbara*, a brilliantly pugnacious drama about the ethical conflicts raised by the operation of high finance. In this way, *The Poor of New York* left an indelible trace on the scripts we now call theatrical modernism. As my argument has sought to demonstrate, however, Boucicault's play also demands attention precisely because it marks the spectacular collapse of theatrical mimesis into capital.

6

'Ladies do it?': Victorian Women Investors in Fact and Fiction

Nancy Henry

Like buying a home or executing a will, investing capital—whether in joint-stock companies or government securities—is simultaneously a public and a private act. It may involve consultations with trusted advisers or attendance at open shareholder meetings, and it may also make the investor a contributor to the extension of national markets or the expansion of empires. In Victorian Britain, women could not vote in political elections, but they could buy shares and, as shareholders, vote for company directors. Charlotte Brontë, Elizabeth Gaskell, and George Eliot were among the growing number of women who supplemented their income by investing in companies that funded railways, canals, and public utilities. *Shirley* (1849), *Cranford* (1851–3), and *The Mill on the Floss* (1860) are among the many Victorian novels in which female characters use inherited money to make loans (Shirley), purchase bank shares (Deborah Jenkins), or speculate in trade (Aunt Glegg). Many of the authors who created these characters were themselves active in the stock market. This chapter examines the ways in which Victorian novelists both participated in economic transformations and contributed to the discourse about those transformations through the financial plots of their novels and specifically through the figure of the investing woman.

In the eighteenth century, both cautious investing and speculation became available to middle-class Britons who were not involved directly in trade. By the Victorian period, with excess capital abundant, investing had affected social and cultural as well as economic habits and attitudes. Mary Poovey has defined this new 'culture of investment' as 'the various ways that financial relationships organize individuals' experience of modern society, not to mention their personal lives; and the complex system of financial arrangements that informs so many Victorian novels and poems'.[1] As Poovey emphasizes, financial relationships

I would like to thank Graham Handley and Francis O'Gorman for comments on this essay. For ongoing support for this project I thank Mary Poovey and Maura O'Connor.

[1] Mary Poovey (ed.), *The Financial System in Nineteenth-Century Britain* (New York; Oxford: Oxford University Press, 2003), p. ix.

structured personal lives, and the representations of those lives in literature was part of the larger cultural context in which people were thinking and writing about the psychological, ethical, and practical implications of their new financial instruments and institutions. Novels have explored the way financial relationships structure women's lives at least since Defoe's *Moll Flanders* (1722). But increasingly throughout the nineteenth century, literature reflected the active role taken by women as investors in publicly held companies or lenders to private businesses, and registered the degree of social tolerance for such independent activity.

It would be difficult to consider women and investment in the nineteenth century without invoking the model of 'separate spheres', by which many historians and literary critics have understood and interpreted Victorian culture. The simultaneously public and private nature of financial acts seems to obviate the distinction between a public/male sphere and a private/female sphere. And yet, the activities of investing women, especially their presence in 'the City,' frequently called up the rhetoric of separate spheres in the Victorian press. For example, in 'Scenes from the Life of an Unprotected Female' (1850), *Punch* satirized Miss Martha Struggles's journey to collect her dividends from the Bank of England as she is bounced from counter to counter repeating: 'If you please, I've come for my dividends—'.[2] The image of women negotiating the male world of the City remained comical throughout the century. In 1893, *All the Year Round* published an account of 'Dividend Day' that recalled that 'not long ago a handsome carriage and pair might, on dividend days, be seen waiting in Gresham Street while its mistress, with the greatest precautions to avoid being seen, made her way to the Bank to draw a quarter's annuity'.[3] And yet, the notion that women were too incompetent to collect their dividends (or that successfully collecting them was indiscreet) is only humorous because women *were* going to the City to collect dividends, freely crossing the imagined line between private and public spheres.

In her critique of the separate spheres metaphor in historical studies, Amanda Vickery argues that, rather than a descriptive account of restrictions on women, 'the broadcasting of the language of separate spheres looks like a conservative response to an unprecedented *expansion* in the opportunities, ambitions and experiences of late Georgian and Victorian women'.[4] In concluding that the conceptual device of separate spheres is inadequate and misleading, she also points out that, in fact, 'there is little unanimity among historians as to what public and private should be held to mean in this context'.[5] Women's involvement

---

[2] 'The Bank', 'Scenes from the Life of an Unprotected Female' (Scene 11), *Punch, or the London Charivari*, 18 (Jan. 1850), 22–3, 22.

[3] 'Dividend Day,' *All the Year Round* (11 Nov. 1893), 462–4, 462.

[4] Amanda Vickery, 'Golden Age to Separate Spheres? A Review of the Categories and Chronology of English Women's History', *Historical Journal*, 36 (1993), 383–414, 400.

[5] Ibid. 412. The usefulness of the concept of separate spheres, so dominant as a model to explain both the position of women and the constitution of bourgeois society under capitalism,

in financial markets as a routine fact of their daily lives, influencing where they went (into the City), what they read (financial journalism), and how much they earned, should cause us to question further the value of insisting on the model of separate spheres.

Just as the position of women investors defies simple dichotomies between public and private, the position of investing authors exposes another less metaphoric but equally ambiguous opposition in Victorian culture between the monetary values of the business class and the 'prestige' values of the aristocratic and 'rentier' classes.[6] In *Literature, Money and the Market* (2002), Paul Delany argues that in the nineteenth century, 'a prestige order and a monetary order co-existed in an uneasy mixture of rivalry and mutual dependence'.[7] Although most Victorian authors needed to work for a living, they upheld the values of the *rentier* and many sought to separate themselves from those who cared about money. As Colin Nicholson has argued about financial transformations in the eighteenth century, the canonical writers—or 'most remembered voices'—'set themselves determinedly at variance with what was happening while privately seeking to profit from it'.[8] The moral outrage against modern greed and corruption in many Victorian novels suggests that similarly conflicted attitudes toward the market continued into the Victorian period.

Many Victorian authors spiced up their novels with frauds, swindles, and bubbles. Critics of Victorian literature have tended to focus on these spectacular facets of the financial plot and to find in them evidence of the novelists' moral objections to capitalism.[9] Yet many of the same Victorian authors embraced

---

has come into question in both historical and literary studies. Worked out initially by scholars such as Martha Vicinus, Mary Poovey, and Catherine Hall, it has been subject to revision by these scholars themselves, as well as by historians of Victorian British history such as Antoinette Burton, Maura O'Connor, and others. For overviews of the development and discrediting of the separate spheres model, see Vickery, 'Golden Age to Separate Spheres?' and Richard Price, *British Society, 1680–1880* (Cambridge: Cambridge University Press, 1999), ch. 6.

[6] By '*rentier*', I mean those capitalists who were successful enough to retreat from the business world and live off their invested capital. As David Kynaston explains: 'British overseas investment, some £200 m in the mid-1850s, increased about fivefold over the next twenty years and, in conjunction with the permanent effects of the railway boom, a fully fledged *rentier* class was born.' See *The City of London*, i (London: Chatto & Windus, 1994), 167.

[7] Paul Delany, *Literature, Money and the Market from Trollope to Amis* (Basingstoke: Palgrave, 2002), 9. Delany provides a fascinating and convincing account of the *rentier*'s influence. See especially 'English Literature and Rentier Culture' (ch. 8).

[8] Colin Nicholson, *Writing and the Rise of Finance: Capital Satires of the Early Eighteenth Century* (Cambridge: Cambridge University Press, 1994), 18.

[9] Several important works on literature and finance were published in the mid-1980s. See John Reed, 'A Friend to Mammon: Speculation in Victorian Literature,' *Victorian Studies*, 27 (1984), 179–202; John Vernon, *Money and Fiction: Literary Realism in the Nineteenth and Early Twentieth Centuries* (Ithaca: Cornell University Press, 1984); Barbara Weiss, *The Hell of the English: Bankruptcy and the Victorian Novel* (Lewisburg: Bucknell University Press, 1986); Norman Russell, *The Novelist and Mammon: Literary Responses to the World of Commerce in the Nineteenth Century* (Oxford: Clarendon Press, 1986). For a challenge to arguments about the representations of the financial swindle, see Tara McGann, 'Literary Realism in the Wake of Business Cycle Theory: *The Way We*

capitalism in their daily lives, and whether we find their involvement inevitable or hypocritical, it is a fact that complicates our understanding of the culture's attitudes toward the economic system that so influenced their lives.

In the 1990s, following the 'fall' of communism, the expansion of global markets, the popularity of tax-free investments (401(k)s, IRAs, ISAs), the international media obsession with fluctuating markets, and the dot-com bubble, an inclination on the part of Victorianists to condemn capitalist practices from either a Marxist or a genteel perspective seems to have diminished. While it would be impossible to determine a simple cause for this apparent lack of interest in rehearsing the flaws and injustices of the capitalist system, there is no doubt that a new body of scholarship has emerged that is devoted to understanding Victorian capitalism and the ways in which financial arrangements conditioned individual lives.[10]

This new work has caused some astonishment. In a review essay entitled 'Was Capitalism Good for Victorian Literature?', Jonathan Rose writes: 'We are now witnessing the emergence of something quite unprecedented—a capitalist criticism'.[11] After asking: 'Is such a thing possible? And who on earth is doing it?', he advances the intentionally provocative thesis that literary criticism concerned with aspects of capitalism and not explicitly anti-capitalist must be implicitly pro-capitalist.[12] Yet this conclusion derives more from an assumption that literary studies are inherently anti-capitalist than from evidence in the works he discusses, which 'treat capitalism like sex: as a fact of life.'[13] To the extent that we can define a new movement within literary and historical studies that has disregarded expectations that investigations of past capitalist practices will be political (i.e. anti-capitalist), it would be misleading to call it 'capitalist criticism'. Rather, much of this new work is looking to uncover neglected aspects of Victorian culture. Just as Vickery argues that 'our preoccupation with the ideology of separate spheres may have blinded us to the other languages in play in the Victorian period',[14] so I would like to suggest that 'our' preoccupation with criticizing capitalism may

---

Live Now (1875)', below, 133–56 and Francis O'Gorman, 'Speculative Fictions and the Fortunes of H. Rider Haggard', below 157–72.

[10] Examples from historical and literary studies include: George Robb, *White Collar Crime in Modern England: Financial Fraud and Business Morality, 1845–1929* (Cambridge: Cambridge University Press, 1992); *The Culture of the Market: Historical Essays*, ed. Thomas L. Haskell and Richard F. Teichgraber III (Cambridge: Cambridge University Press, 1993); P. J. Cain and A. G. Hopkins, *British Imperialism: Innovation and Expansion* (London: Longman, 1993); Timothy Alborn, *Conceiving Companies: Joint-Stock Politics in Victorian England* (London: Routledge, 1998); *The New Economic Criticism*, ed. Mark Osteen and Martha Woodmansee (London: Routledge, 1999); *Victorian Studies*, 45 (2002), Special Issue on Victorian Investments, ed. Cannon Schmitt, Nancy Henry, and Anjali Arondekar; Gordon Bigelow, *Fiction, Famine, and the Rise of Economics in Victorian Britain and England* (Cambridge: Cambridge University Press, 2003); Margot Finn, *The Character of Credit: Personal Debt in English Culture, 1740–1914* (Cambridge: Cambridge University Press, 2003).

[11] Jonathan Rose, 'Was Capitalism Good for Victorian Literature?' *Victorian Studies*, 46 (2004), 489–501, 489.

[12] Ibid. 490.   [13] Ibid. 500.   [14] Vickery, 'Golden Age', 401.

have blinded us to some important dimensions of the Victorians' interactions in the financial world, particularly, for example, the ways in which investing women benefited from and contributed to the Victorian culture of investment.

Since the end of the seventeenth century, investing has been an acceptable way for British women to make money. In the early eighteenth century, women comprised a significant minority of shareholders in the Bank of England, the South Sea Company, and the East India Company. Aristocratic and middle-class women were part of a new and diverse class of investors that included professional authors. In 1710, for example, Jonathan Swift urged Stella to buy Bank of England stock, 'which is fallen near thirty *per cent*' and 'will certainly soon rise'.[15] In 1720, Alexander Pope gave Lady Mary Wortley Montagu the unfortunate advice 'to Buy the South Sea-Stock at the present price, which will certainly rise'.[16] Catherine Ingrassia describes the infectious appeal of investing for women who 'because of class or gender, previously lacked any opportunity for meaningful financial improvement or autonomy'.[17] The 'financial revolution' began to uncouple social status from economic power. Anyone with capital to invest could contribute to the expansion of markets or help fund the national debt while generating more capital for herself. Even to defenders of the landed interest like Swift and Pope, the game was irresistible. As Pope remarked when asking his broker about a new African stock: ''tis Ignominious (in this Age of Hope and Golden Mountains) not to Venture'.[18]

Even the South Sea Bubble—the manic speculation in South Sea Company stock that ruined many British investors in 1720—did not deter women from investing. Three years after the bubble burst, women still made up 20 per cent of shareholders in the South Sea Company.[19] In 1756, women made up a third of all

---

[15] *Journal to Stella*, ed. Harold Williams (Oxford: Clarendon Press, 1948), i. 74. At the same time Swift announced his own plan to buy into the Bank of England.

[16] The price soon plummeted. See *The Correspondence of Alexander Pope*, ed. George Sherburn, 5 vols (Oxford: Clarendon Press, 1956), ii. 52. Pope later ranted against corruption, greed, and specula-tion, especially in relation to the South Sea Bubble in the 'Epistle to Bathurst' ('Of the Use of Riches,' 1733). Swift satirized the unsinkable directors of the South Sea Company and their gullible followers in 'The Bubble' (1720). For details about the investments of Pope, Swift, and Gay, see Nicholson.

[17] Catherine Ingrassia, *Authorship, Commerce, and Gender in Early Eighteenth-century England* (Cambridge: Cambridge University Press, 1998), 17. Following J. G. A. Pocock's observation that 'economic man' (as opposed to propertied man) was perceived as feminine—ruled by passions, fantasies and appetites—Ingrassia shows that speculative investment was associated with 'hysteria, disorder, and unregulated passions, with the same "feminizing" forces that motivated the economic man' (19). She also argues that in the eighteenth century 'women's participation in speculative investment obscures the binary categories of public and private, or financial and domestic, as women insert themselves into a public financial space' (20).

[18] Pope, *Correspondence*, ii. 33.

[19] The primary source for statistics on female investors in the eighteenth century is P. G. M. Dickson's *The Financial Revolution in England* (1967; Aldershot: Ashgate, 1993). Dickson gives figures for 1707–9, 1719–24, and 1744–53 for 14% annuities, 5% annuities, South Sea stock, Bank stock, and East India stock. Between 1719–24, for example, women made up about 20 per cent of the investors though the amount they owned was less, about 11% in both the South Sea Company and East India Company (282). His figures are based on samples, and historian Amy

investors in the East India Company.[20] And at the end of the eighteenth century, as Leonore Davidoff and Catherine Hall have shown, women still contributed 20 per cent of loan capital: 'Female capital supported the joint stock companies behind municipal utilities and railways. Widows and spinsters were the core of those investors requiring a steady income without administrative worries'.[21] Davidoff and Hall have done much to uncover the 'hidden investment' of women in the nineteenth-century British economy, yet few historians of the Victorian period have asked what we might learn from the actions of actual female investors or from the representations of female investors in Victorian fiction.[22]

The inclusion of women was part of the democratic nature of joint-stock companies and the stock market generally. Some observers applauded the diversity. In his paean to global commerce, Addison's *Spectator* sees the stock exchange as 'a great Council, in which all considerable Nations have their Representations'.[23] In contrast, Thomas Gordon, in 'A Learned Dissertation on Old Women, Male and Female' (1720), complained that Englishmen were being 'enchanted by a Stupid *Kennel of Stock Jobbers* who cheat us out of our Money and our Sex'.[24] This derogatory characterization of the market's openness continued into the nineteenth century. William Alexander observed in 1807 that the General Court of the East India Company was a 'popular senate, no distinction as to citizenship—the Englishman, the Frenchman, the American; no difference as to religion—the Jew, the Turk, the Pagan; no impediment as to sex—the old women of both sexes'.[25] Throughout the nineteenth century, financial writers and social commentators like D. Morier Evans and Samuel Smiles expressed

Froide has revised his numbers upwards in 'The Silent Partners of Britain's Financial Revolution: Singlewomen and their Public Investments' (unpublished paper).

[20] This number declined in the second half of the century because investing in the company became more speculative and less safe, losing its appeal to cautious British and Dutch widows and spinsters. See H. V. Bowen, 'Investment and Empire in the Later Eighteenth Century: East India Stockholding, 1756–1791', *The Economic History Review*, NS 42 (1989), 202.

[21] Leonore Davidoff and Catherine Hall, *Family Fortunes: Men and Women of the English Middle Class, 1780–1850* (Chicago: University of Chicago Press, 1987), 211. See also their comments on women's involvement in early nineteenth-century joint-stock companies such as the Birmingham Botanical and Horticultural Society (422–3).

[22] While little has been published, several historians are engaged in research that promises to transform this area of study. Work-in-progress includes George Robb's ' "Ladies of the Ticker": Women, Investment, and Fraud in England and America, 1850–1930' (unpublished paper); Maura O'Connor's 'Sensationalizing Speculation: English Women's "Tales of the Stock Exchange" ' (unpublished paper); and Janette Rutterford and Josephine Maltby's ' "The Widow, the Clergyman and the Reckless": Women Investors in England, 1830–1914', *Feminist Economics*, 12 (2006), 111–38.

[23] Saturday, 19 May 1711. *The Spectator*, ed. Donald F. Bond, i (Oxford: Clarendon Press, 1965), 293.

[24] Thomas Gordon, 'A Learned Dissertation on Old Women, Male and Female' (London, 1720), 8.

[25] Quoted in C. H. Philips, *The East India Company, 1784–1834* (Manchester: Manchester University Press, 1961), 2. Anyone who bought shares in the company's stock became a Proprietor. Until 1773, one needed only £500 to vote. After the Regulating Act of 1773, £1,000 was required

mixed views about the phenomenon of female investors. In 1875 Alexander Innes Shand wrote that 'it is no secret that the fair sex, and ladies of the highest station too, are in the habit of throwing themselves into the national game with characteristic feminine impetuosity'.[26]

Despite detractors and sceptics, women enjoyed the right to vote in joint-stock companies. In 1720, most of the female shareholders in the South Sea Company owned enough stock to vote and were theoretically eligible to hold a governing position.[27] In 1798, Colonel Sweny Toone ran for the East India Company's Court of Directors and complained: 'Mrs. Morgan, Mrs. Metcalfe, Mrs. Floyer and all the beauty of Portland Place are canvassing against me. Hard upon a man who loves the sex so well!'[28]

In 1852, John Stuart Mill testified before the Select Committee of the House of Lords inquiring into the Acts for the 'Better Government of Her Majesty's Indian Territory'. He was asked about the qualifications of the East India Company's Court of Proprietors to elect the Court of Directors, specifically whether the '899 ladies who have votes',—that is, roughly half of the 1,765 voters—'exercise a sound discretion in the selection of the individuals, knowing their qualifications and claims?' Mill replied: 'I do not believe any portion of the Court of Proprietors exercise much discretion of that kind'.[29] Whether exercised with discretion or not, women's votes counted. In her 1854 pamphlet outlining and protesting restrictions on women, Barbara Bodichon included investing as one of the few forms of power available to women. That power was financial and indirectly political because East India shareholders could vote and therefore 'a woman can take part in the government of a great empire by buying East India Stock'.[30]

While it may come as a surprise to some that women were such active investors in eighteenth- and nineteenth-century markets, readers of nineteenth-century literature will be familiar with the investing widows, spinsters, and wives who populate the novels of the period. The type of the old female investor can be traced to Jane Austen. Her last, unfinished novel, *Sanditon* (1817), includes an old woman who promised to become as tyrannical and insufferable as *Pride and Prejudice*'s (1813) Lady Catherine de Bourgh, but with the difference that Lady

for one vote and additional votes were given: two votes for £3,000, three votes for £6,000 and four for £10,000 (Bowen, 198).

[26] Alexander Innes Shand, 'Speculative Investments' [1876], in Poovey, *Financial System*, 195. On other nineteenth-century financial writers' opinions about women, see G. R. Searle, *Morality and the Market in Victorian Britain* (Oxford: Clarendon Press, 1998), 164

[27] Froide, 'Silent Partners'.   [28] Quoted in Philips, *East India Company*, 6.

[29] John Stuart Mill, *Writings on British India*, ed. John M. Robson, Martin Moir, and Zawahir Moir from *The Collected Works of John Stuart Mill* (Toronto: University of Toronto Press, 1990), xxx. 46. Mill was also asked: 'Do you think the English and foreign Jews, who hold a large amount of stock, exercise a sound discretion in the election of Directors, with reference to the good government of India?' (46). As when asked about women, he refused to concede that Jews were less qualified than any other group of shareholders.

[30] Barbara Leigh Smith Bodichon, *A Brief Summary, in Plain Language of the Most Important Laws Concerning Women; Together with a Few Observations Thereon* (London: n.p., 1854), 4.

Denham was risking her money by becoming a partner in a speculative venture. Mr Parker, the developer of the seaside resort at Sanditon, tells the heroine Charlotte that Lady Denham was his 'Colleague in Speculation'. She was a 'very rich old Lady, who had buried two Husbands, who knew the value of Money'.[31] Women who inherited money might entrust it to the safe and reliably profitable financial programme that funded government debt. Beginning in 1749, 'the consols,' or 'the funds', paid a fixed rate of 3 per cent annual interest (and thus were also known as 'the three per cents'). More adventurous heiresses could put their capital 'out' into speculative ventures. Either way, women with money to invest were courted by members of their own family looking for a legacy and by men looking for investment capital.

Thackeray's mid-century novels, representing an earlier generation, attest to women's financial and political power as investors in the Funds, the East India Company, and in colonial banks. In *Vanity Fair* (1847–8), Sir Pitt Crawley's unmarried half-sister has 'a balance at her banker's which would have made her beloved anywhere' and is described by Becky Sharp as 'the great rich Miss Crawley, with seventy thousand pounds in the five per cents'.[32] Becky's early hope for her marriage to Rawdon depends on his inheriting Miss Crawley's money. When this scheme fails, Becky continues her social ascension, but still thinks wistfully that she could 'be a good woman if I had five thousand a year' and wishes, at least for a moment, that she could 'exchange my position in society, and all my relations for a snug sum in the Three per Cent. Consols'.[33]

Thackeray also reflected ironically on the gender and racial equality of the East India Company's Court of Proprietors in the early part of the century. The much sought-after mulatto heiress from St Kitts, Miss Rhoda Swartz, in addition to her West Indian plantations, was said to have 'a deal of money in the funds; and three stars to her name in the East India stockholders' list', indicating that she owned at least £6,000 worth of stock and was entitled to three votes.[34] Miss Swartz is such a silly character that the image of her voting at a shareholders' meeting implicitly mocks the system, as does the suggestion of female board members in *The Newcomes*. When Rosey Newcome comes into her fortune, 'Poor Clive, by right of his wife, was now rich Clive'.[35] Rosey 'possessed not only B.B.C. [Bundelcund Bank Company] shares, but moneys in bank and shares in East India Stock, so that Clive in the right of his wife had a seat in the assembly of the East India shareholders, and a voice in the election of directors of that

---

[31] *Sanditon, in Works of Jane Austen*, ed. R. W. Chapman, *Minor Works* (Oxford: Clarendon Press, 1988), iv. 375.

[32] William Makepeace Thackeray, *Vanity Fair*, eds. Geoffrey and Kathleen Tillotson (1847–8; London: Methuen, 1963), 87, 98.

[33] Ibid. 409, 410.   [34] Ibid. 193.

[35] William Makepeace Thackeray, *The Newcomes* Biographical Edition, viii (1853–5; London: Smith, Elder, 1898), 673.

famous Company'.[36] The banking Barnes brothers are represented thanks to the matriarchal line, since 'the old lady, who founded or consolidated that family, had had three stars before her own venerable name, which had descended upon her son Sir Brian, and her grandson Sir Barnes'.[37]

In *The Newcomes*, the multinational Bundelcund Bank prides itself on its diversity: 'the greatest capitalist in India as well as the youngest ensign in the service might invest at the largest and safest premium, and borrow at the smallest interest, becoming, according to his means, a shareholder in the B.B.'[38] Furthermore, the bank boasts of what we would call transparency, for 'the books of the bank were open to every shareholder': 'the ensign or the young civil servant was at liberty at any time to inspect his own private account as well as the common ledger.'[39] Subscribers in London include Miss Cann, 'who took a little fifty-pound-note share', 'dear old Miss Honeyman', and Mrs. Mackenzie, who has Clive buy £1,500 worth of shares for 'her and her darling girls'.[40] The women follow the lead of poor Colonel Newcome, and like him, lose their money when the bank fails at the novel's climax.

While both *Vanity Fair* and *The Newcomes* look back to the early decades of the nineteenth century, they were written at mid-century when novels became increasingly preoccupied with matters of finance as they affected wider ranges of society. By placing dramatic crises at the centre of plots such as these, many novelists seemed to express hostility toward the capitalist system in which they participated through the public marketing of their books and the private management of their wealth. In *The Cash Nexus* (2002), Niall Ferguson observes that 'As an occupational group, professional writers have always been conspicuously ungrateful for the benefits conferred by economic progress.'[41] And Jonathan Rose seems to express the obvious when he remarks: 'Surely every important Victorian author deeply distrusted speculative capitalism.'[42] Carlyle's outcry against the 'cash-payment' nexus in *Chartism* (1840) and *Past and Present* (1843) and Arnold's denunciation of 'philistinism' in *Culture and Anarchy* (1869) are among the best-known attempts to define a moral divide between culture and capital, intellectual and businessman. Yet it was precisely because that division had become so blurred that their insistence on it became so zealous.

The production of literature depended on the capitalist marketplace, and many authors were good businessmen. When they invested the profits of their writing in the stock market they moved out of the specialized market of literature and gained an interest in larger capitalist ventures. The stock market provided a meeting ground for prestige culture, with its moral objections to capitalism, and business culture, with its scepticism about the higher values

---

[36] Ibid. 675.   [37] Ibid. 674.   [38] Ibid. 516.   [39] Ibid. 516.
[40] Ibid. 517.
[41] Niall Ferguson, *The Cash Nexus: Money and Power in the Modern World, 1700–2000* (New York: Lane, 2002), 5.
[42] Rose, 'Was Capitalism Good for Victorian Literature?', 491.

upheld within that moral critique. The stock market and the institutions that served it brought together *rentiers*, artists, businessmen, and financiers and taught them to speak a common language in pursuit of a common interest—making money.

Few critics of the market were willing to address their own dependence on it. Arnold's correspondence, for example, reveals just how interested he was in money and how it may have affected his literary judgement.[43] Ferguson mentions Dickens, Zola, Maupassant, and Karl Marx as authors who looked to the stock market to help fund the publication of works that exposed the injustices of capitalism. In 1864, after inheriting money, Marx wrote to his uncle that he had been 'speculating—partly in American funds, but more especially in English stocks': 'It's a type of operation that makes small demands on one's time, and it's worth while running some risk in order to relieve the enemy of his money.'[44] Marx claimed to have speculated, buying low and selling high, dipping in and out of the market for a fast profit. His British contemporaries were more inclined to invest conservatively, looking for sustained growth over time.

The distinction between investing and speculating was a technical one given a moral overlay by the Victorians. Either to invest or to speculate is to expect to get money without working for it, and it is a questionable moral logic that insists on distinctions about the amount of time we choose to leave the money in the market. Both practices involve risk; both run contrary to the Protestant work ethic. Marx was untroubled by the moral distinction, revealing in his exploitation of the stock exchange to further his anti-capitalist writings. In contrast, many Victorian novelists worked diligently to uphold the moral difference between investing and speculating. Their novels played an important part in turning speculators into villains and investors into respectable citizens who were prey to these unscrupulous gamblers. Ferguson is right in pointing to a contradiction in the 'ungratefulness' of Victorian authors to what he calls 'economic progress', given that they were susceptible to collective social 'manias' like the railway bubble of the 1840s, as well as eager to take advantage of safer investment opportunities. While novels like *Little Dorrit* (1855–7), *The Newcomes* (1853–5), and *The Way We Live Now* (1874–5) wove complicated financial plots, making the credit economy and speculation into targets of moral outrage, the novelists themselves took care of their investments: Dickens preferred Russian bonds; Thackeray American securities, and Trollope colonial investments.[45]

[43] See Bill Bell, 'From Parnassus to Grub Street: Matthew Arnold and the House of Macmillan', *Macmillan: A Publishing Tradition*, ed. Elizabeth James (Basingstoke: Palgrave, 2002).

[44] Francis Wheen, *Karl Marx* (London: Fourth Estate, 1999), 268.

[45] In *The Age of Atonement* (Oxford: Clarendon Press, 1988), Boyd Hilton observes: 'Risk being inseparable from profit, the line between fair trade and foul is impossible to draw' (122). In *Wall Street in the American Novel* (New York: New York University Press, 1980), Wayne W. Westbrook identifies 'The Puritan prejudice against gambling and speculation' as the source of 'an innate and lasting prejudice of the American novelist against high finance as well as success on Wall Street' (8). See also Searle, *Morality*.

Significantly, Ferguson does not mention any female authors among those who simultaneously criticized and benefited from the capitalist marketplace. We do not count a major female author among the great critics of capitalism, in the company of Marx, Dickens, Thackeray, Trollope, Maupaussant, and Zola despite the fact that authors Catherine Gore, Margaret Oliphant, Elizabeth Gaskell, the Brontës, Mary Elizabeth Braddon, and George Eliot incorporated bank failures and bankruptcies into their plots, and many of them were as committed financially and emotionally to the stock market as their male contemporaries.[46] Investing was available to women in ways that other forms of social advancement were not. Perhaps for this reason, those like the Brontës, Gaskell, and George Eliot—all of whom earned their own incomes from writing—were more tempered in their critiques of capitalism per se.

In Charlotte Brontë's *Shirley*, both Caroline and Shirley contemplate the implications of a woman entering business. Caroline wishes that she might be an apprentice to Robert Moore and keep the books for his mill.[47] The novel in general is preoccupied with the secrets and mysteries of business as they appear to the women. Speaking of Moore, the narrator observes: 'The secrets of business—complicated and often dismal mysteries—were buried in his breast.'[48] Shirley owns the property on which the mill stands and helps Moore by lending him money. She therefore includes herself when thinking about the character of business: ' "I cannot get out of my head a certain idea that we manufacturers and persons of business are sometimes a little—a very little selfish and short-sighted in our views." '[49] The novel exhibits an ambivalence about capitalist pursuits, reflecting Brontë's own mixed feelings about her investment activities.

In 1842, Charlotte and her sisters had invested inherited money in the York and North Midland Railway. Her first advisor was her former teacher, Margaret Wooler, to whom she wrote in 1845:

We have never hitherto consulted any one but you on our affairs—nor have we told any one else of the degree of success our small capital has met with, because, after all, there is nothing so uncertain as rail-roads; the price of shares varies continually—and any day a small share-holder may find his funds shrunk to their original dimensions—Emily has made herself mistress of the necessary degree of knowledge for conducting the matter, by

---

[46] Edward Copeland has considered representations of consumer culture in women's fiction from the late eighteenth and early nineteenth centuries in *Women Writing about Money* (Cambridge: Cambridge University Press, 1995). In discussing the expansion of Victorian commerce and the credit economy into genteel society in Trollope's *The Last Chronicle of Barset* and Margaret Oliphant's *Phoebe Junior*, Elsie B. Michie argues that Oliphant 'confuses groups that late Victorians sought desperately to keep separate, gentlemen and those who openly express commercial desires. It was this collapsing of the distinction between the two factions of the middle class that made Oliphant seem vulgar to contemporary reviewers.' See 'Buying Brains: Trollope, Oliphant, and Vulgar Victorian Commerce', *Victorian Studies*, 44 (2001), 77–97, 90.

[47] Charlotte Brontë, *Shirley*, ed. Andrew and Judith Hook (1849; Harmondsworth: Penguin, 1974), 99, 104.

[48] Ibid. 146.   [49] Ibid. 322.

dint of carefully reading every paragraph & every advertisement in the news-papers that related to rail-roads and as we have abstained from all gambling, all 'mere' speculative buying-in & selling-out—we have got on very decently.[50]

Charlotte's emphasis on the moral distinction between gambling/speculation and cautious investing is typical of her discussions about finance. She frequently concludes detailed exchanges about her investments with a moral reminder of more important things that recalls the ambivalence found in *Shirley*.[51]

And yet the Brontës were caught up in the railway mania of 1845–6, and when the financial crisis came, their shares had lost much of their value. Charlotte subsequently asked her publisher, George Smith, to advise her on how to dispose of the railway shares, in which she had also invested earnings from *Jane Eyre* (1847). She explained her past investments in the York and North Midland, revealing the close attention she paid to her finances: 'The original price of Shares in this Railway was £50. At one time they rose to 120; and for some years gave a dividend of 10 per cent; they are now down to 20, and it is doubtful whether any dividend will be declared this half-year.'[52] Smith advised her to place her money in the Funds, to which she agreed. As her London contact, he took on the responsibility of collecting and sending her dividends.

In 1850, after investing the income from *Shirley* in the Funds, she wrote to Smith that 'the dividend business had better be deferred till I come to London; I shall then have an opportunity of emulating "Mrs. Martha Struggles" by going to the Bank for myself'.[53] The ironic reference to *Punch*'s 'Scenes from the Life of an Unprotected Female' shows Charlotte's familiarity with the popular press's satirical representations of independent women like her who, as investors, were required to enter the City and collect their dividends. Charlotte, however, was far from an inept investor. She wrote to Smith in 1850:

Rest assured I regard these matters from a less unpractical point of view than you perhaps imagine. Though women are not taught the minutiae and the mysteries of business, yet in the course of observation they manage to gather up some general idea of the leading principles on which it is conducted.[54]

By referring to the 'mysteries of business', she echoes the language of *Shirley* in which Caroline 'mused over the mystery of "business," tried to comprehend more about it than had ever been told her—to understand its perplexities, liabilities, duties, exactions'.[55] Perhaps the mystery accounts for the hint of pleasure revealed by Lucy Snowe in *Villette* (1853) on her first visit to the City: 'At the West-end you may be amused, but in the city you are deeply excited'.[56]

---

[50] *The Letters of Charlotte Brontë*, ed. Margaret Smith, 3 vols (Oxford: Oxford University Press, 1995–2004), i. 390.
[51] Ibid. ii. 264, 267.   [52] Ibid. ii. 264.   [53] Ibid. ii. 386–7.   [54] Ibid. ii. 436.
[55] Brontë, *Shirley*, 188.
[56] *Villette*, ed. Mark Lilly (1853; Harmondsworth: Penguin, 1979), 109.

Throughout Victorian literature, women were excited by the prospect of speculation. Both the incompetent and the shrewd female investor were developed as types. Dickens's *Nicholas Nickleby* (1838–9) begins with the story of Nicholas's father's financial ruin. Old Nicholas wonders how to maximize the small capital he possesses:

> 'Speculate with it', said Mrs. Nickleby.
> 'Spec—u—late, my dear?' said Mr. Nickleby, as though in doubt.
> 'Why not?' asked Mrs. Nickleby.
> 'Because, my dear, if we *should* lose it ... if we should lose it, we shall no longer be able to live, my dear'.
> 'Fiddle', said Mrs. Nickleby.[57]

The consequences are disastrous as: 'A mania prevailed, a bubble burst, four stockbrokers took villa residences at Florence, four hundred nobodies were ruined, and among them Mr. Nickleby.'[58]

In *David Copperfield* (1849–50), the indomitable Miss Betsey Trotwood, under the misimpression that her financial adviser Mr Wickfield is responsible for her ruin, assumes the blame in a strange, disassociative narrative in which she speaks of herself in the third person. 'Betsey', she says

> thought she was wiser, now, than her man of business ... and she took it into her head to lay it out for herself. ... First, she lost in the mining way, and then she lost in the diving way ... and then she lost in the mining way again, and last of all, to set the thing entirely to rights, she lost in the banking way.[59]

After the revelation that she had not in fact made bad investments, but rather that Uriah Heep had defrauded her, Miss Betsey recoups her five thousand pounds in the Consols and is redeemed as a wise and responsible manager of her own money.

In Gaskell's *Cranford*, Miss Deborah Jenkins, guardian of gentility and Johnsonian high culture, is also an independent investor. She made her own decision, against the recommendation of her adviser (the narrator Mary Smith's father), to purchase shares in the Town and Country Bank. She is invited to attend shareholder meetings and vote for a director. So is Miss Matty, who inherits the shares and becomes the victim of the bank's collapse. Miss Matty tells Mary that Deborah ' "was quite the woman of business, and always judged for herself; and here, you see, they have paid eight per cent, all these years".'[60] While poor Miss Matty's ruin is one of the central dramatic episodes of the novel,

[57] Charles Dickens, *Nicholas Nickleby* ed. Paul Schlicke ([1838–9], Oxford: Oxford University Press, 1990), 4–5.

[58] Ibid. 5.

[59] Charles Dickens, *David Copperfield*, ed. Jeremy Tambling (1850; Harmondsworth: Penguin, 1996), 473.

[60] Elizabeth Gaskell, *Cranford*, ed. Graham Handley (London, 1995), 173.

Deborah's 8 per cent on her investment over the years provides the context for the unmarried sisters' independence.

In 1849, shortly before writing *Cranford*, and building on the success of *Mary Barton*, Gaskell invested £1,500 in St Katherine's Docks, the working docks next to the Tower Bridge and Tower of London constructed by the St Katherine's Docks Company earlier in the century. She wanted the money to be put into the 'general fund at its present value; and in the division to form part of the moiety which is to be invested for me'.[61] In 1862, we find that she held shares in the Sheffield and Lincolnshire Railway and that she managed the business affairs when her husband was away. She wrote to her cousin and financial advisor Edward Holland that she had 'a great "spite" at the Catherine [*sic*] Dock shares, which is not diminished by their diminishing dividend, but I quite agree with you that this is not the time for selling out'.[62]

George Eliot too, was an investor in St Katherine's Docks. Her career as a shareholder began with the profits from *The Mill on the Floss*, £2,000 of which she invested in the Great Indian Peninsular railway. Over the next two decades, her diversified portfolio was comprised of stocks and bonds in colonial and domestic securities.[63] In *The Mill on the Floss*, Tom Tulliver, in need of capital, turns to his Aunt Glegg. Upon learning she may receive 'Ten or twelve per cent', the profit-minded Aunt Glegg reproaches her husband: ' "Haven't you allays told me as there was no getting more nor five per cent".' To which Mr. Glegg replies, ' "You couldn't go into trade, could you? You can't get more than five per cent with interest".'[64] Lured by the promise of speculation, she becomes a primary investor in Tom's scheme to dig his father out of debt.

But perhaps even more interesting than Aunt Glegg's financial inclinations are the novel's passing references to other lady speculators. Aunt Pullet refers to Mrs Sutton as 'an old lady as had doubled her money over and over again, and kept it all in her own management to the last', and Bob Jakin mentions a lady named Bucks, 'wi' a cork leg' who 'let out thirty pounds' to a draper who sent out his goods to be traded and got her ' "eight per zent fust go off—an' now you can't hold her but she must be sendin' out carguies wi' every ship, till she's gettin' as rich as a Jew".'[65] The independence suggested by these background characters contrasts to the helplessness of Mrs Tulliver and Aunt Moss, two women crippled by their husbands' financial failures.

The title character of Trollope's *Miss Mackenzie* (1865) is a spinster heiress with money to invest. In *An Autobiography* (1883), the author calls her 'a very

[61] *The Letters of Mrs Gaskell*, ed. J. A. V. Chapple and Arthur Pollard (1966; Manchester: Mandolin, 1997), 827.

[62] Ibid. 690.

[63] On Eliot's colonial investments, see Nancy Henry, *George Eliot and the British Empire* (Cambridge: Cambridge University Press, 2002).

[64] George Eliot, *The Mill on the Floss*, ed. Nancy Henry (1860; Boston: Houghton Mifflin, 2004), 279.

[65] Ibid. 69, 301.

unattractive old maid, who was over-whelmed by money troubles'.[66] His narrator generalizes: 'Like all other single ladies, she was very nervous about her money. She was quite alive to the beauty of a high rate of interest, but did not quite understand that high interest and impaired security should go hand in hand together.'[67] Miss Mackenzie, although 35 years old and never considered attractive, is not too old to be courted when she inherits money from a brother. While she is tempted to place the money in the 'Three per Cents', 'she had gone to work with the figures, and having ascertained that by doing so twenty-five pounds a year would be docked off her computed income', she prefers to look out for a higher paying investment.[68] Such an opportunity comes when her surviving brother, the partner in an oil-cloth business, asks her to lend him the money to buy some property at a promised but not guaranteed rate of 5 per cent. Four men with ideas about how she should invest her money try to woo her, and her power to make her own decisions about what to do with her money drives the plot of the novel. Until she finds that there has been a mistake; the fortune is not hers but her cousin John Ball's. Already one of her suitors, he graciously (and genuinely) offers to marry her.

One year later, in *The Last Chronicle of Barset* (1866–7), Trollope created another wealthy woman preoccupied with money matters. Mrs Van Siever is 'a weird old woman, so small, so ghastly, and so ugly!'[69] She is a silent partner in a shady City firm that engages in speculation and money lending. When she comes to the City to collect her interest on her loans and investments, her partner, Dobbs Broughton, complains: ' "Likes her money! By George she does; her own and anybody else's that she can get hold of. For a downright leech, recommend me always to a woman. When a woman does go in for it, she is much more thorough than any man" '.[70] Dobbs, a fraudulent social climber throwing West End dinners and foreshadowing *The Way We Live Now*'s Melmotte (without the Jewish taint), represents Mrs Van Siever in much the same way Bob Jakin represents Mrs Bucks. The suspicion is that women, rather than naturally equipped to provide a haven from the cutthroat business world, are, when given the chance, just as ruthless and successful as men at making money. This suspicion, often invoked humorously, challenged assumptions at the heart of separate spheres ideology and caused authors such as Trollope to hint at the unnaturalness of businesswomen.

Trollope's narrator, for example, in addition to emphasizing the ugliness of Mrs Van Siever, is compelled to make a distinction between the private woman

[66] Anthony Trollope, *An Autobiography*, ed. David Skilton (1883; Harmondsworth: Penguin, 1996), 123.

[67] Anthony Trollope, *Miss Mackenzie*, ed. A. O. J. Cockshut (1865; Oxford: Oxford University Press, 1992), 36.

[68] Ibid. 37.

[69] Anthony Trollope, *The Last Chronicle of Barset*, ed. Sophie Gilmartin (1866–7; Harmondsworth: Penguin, 2002), 371.

[70] Ibid. 367–8.

and her public persona. By night she is a society lady, but when she enters the City in her 'work-a-day business dress, as we may call it, she looked to be very old'.[71] Crossing from the West End into the City and wearing her business dress, the ugly woman looks even older and more repulsive to her cohorts in speculation, a physical manifestation of her leech-like behaviour. The unforgiving Mrs Van Siever, who in fact only wants what is due to her from her corrupt partners, presses Dobbs for her money and thus contributes to his financial ruin and bloody suicide.[72]

Financial ruin also leads to suicide in *The Prime Minister* (1875–6), in which a wealthy female investor is Ferdinand Lopez's last hope. Having failed to extract an expected inheritance from his wife's father, he approaches the wealthy Lizzie Eustace to invest in a mysterious Central African product called 'Bios'. Lopez 'fired her imagination with stories of the grand things to be done in trade'.[73] When she asks: '"Ladies do it?"', he responds, '"Yes; why not women as well as men? Anyone might do it who had money in his pocket and experience to tell him, or to tell her, what to buy and what to sell. And the experience, luckily, might be vicarious"'.[74] He proposes that she invest jointly with him, asking: '"Would you object to hold it with me?"' The narrator observes that 'Lopez, as he asked the question, looked at her as though he were offering her half his heart.'[75] Lizzie refuses both the offer of shares and his proposal that she run away with him to Guatemala. It is this final rejection that drives him to suicide.

Whether old and masculine like Deborah Jenkins, Aunt Glegg, and Mrs Van Siever, or younger and sexually available like Miss Swartz, Miss Mackenzie, and Lizzie Eustace, investing women in Victorian fiction constitute a counter tradition to the image of the helpless female ruined either by an irresponsible husband or by an unscrupulous swindler. The interpretations of their independence in a variety of texts are a measure of what society would tolerate and how far the democratizing influence of capitalism—and the openness of the market to 'the old women of both sexes'—might extend. As women entered business, and business entered literature, some authors and reviewers responded by contending that both moves were inappropriate and threatening to the purity of women and of literature.

---

[71] Anthony Trollope, *The Last Chronicle of Barset*, 371.

[72] Elsie Michie argues that *The Last Chronicle of Barset* conforms to Bourdieu's observation that 'the urge to calculate, repressed in men, finds more overt expression in women, who are structurally predisposed to be less concerned with the symbolic profits accruing from political unity' (quoted in Michie, 81). It is not economic man that is feminine but females who are economic. Men like Trollope in his representations of men like Mr Crawley might escape or transcend the 'vulgarity' of commercial transactions by associating women with economics and men with asceticism, honor, as well as intellectual and spiritual pursuits (Michie, 86). Interestingly, in her discussion of the Crawley plot as a response to economic transformations, she does not mention the Dobbs Broughton/Mrs Van Siever plot line.

[73] Anthony Trollope, *The Prime Minister*, ed. Jennifer Uglow (1876; Oxford: Oxford University Press, 1983), ii. 73.

[74] Ibid. ii. 73.   [75] Ibid. ii. 135.

The discomfort with female knowledge about finance, as well as with business as a subject for fiction, is registered in responses to the Irish-born Charlotte Cowan Riddell (1832–1906), known in her time as 'the novelist of the City'. A typical review observed of her novel, *A Life's Assize* (1871), that 'it is very far from being a lady's novel—is, in fact, peculiarly not a lady's novel' and is 'singularly masculine'.[76] At this time, Riddell published under her own name. The comments about the book's masculinity were directed at her as a female author, and though grudgingly complimentary, they add the less flattering 'peculiar' and 'singular'.

Riddell's first successful novel, *George Geith of Fen Court* (1864), was published under the pseudonym F. G. Trafford. It too unapologetically displays knowledge of the City and of finance, and offers a self-conscious social and aesthetic statement about the importance of representing the financial world in fiction:

The trials of sensitive men who cannot make sixpence a year, have been repeated till even young ladies are weary of making heroes of them. Gold-diggers, emigrants, hunters, explorers, all find words with which to interest the public ear. It is only trade, only that which is the back-bone of England, only that which furnishes heiresses for younger sons; only that which sends forth fleets of merchantmen, and brings home the products of all countries; only that which feeds the poor, and educates the middle classes, and keeps the nobility of the land from sinking to the same low level as the nobility of all other lands has done; it is only this, I say, which can find no writer worthy of it, no one who does not jeer at business and treat with contempt that which is holy in God's sight, because it is useful, and proves beneficial to millions and millions of his creatures.[77]

Riddell's narrator complains about authors who jeer at business, and within the novel this general prejudice becomes not merely a fact but a theme. George Geith, the aristocratic son turned City accountant, declares:

I am not going to follow the example of the citizens, and despise that which has kept me off the parish. Business is a capital invention, and the City is a place where any man with courage and industry may push his way. The City is the proper land for younger sons to emigrate to, if younger sons could but be induced to think so.[78]

Geith points out that the opportunity to start anew—what the colonies represented to many younger sons—might be found within England in the land of business, so mysterious to, or effaced by, the genteel classes. Geith's love interest, Beryl Molozane, daughter of a well-meaning but inept aristocrat who has lost his money speculating in Welsh mines, explains that the burden is on the men of business to counteract the prejudice against them: 'The outer world can know nothing of business, except what it hears from the initiated.'[79] Riddell established herself as an initiate to City life, an emissary from this foreign territory. Her mid-Victorian

[76] Review of *A Life's Assize* in *Harper's Magazine*, 43 (June 1871), 139.
[77] Charlotte Riddell, *George Geith of Fen Court* (1864; London: Warne, n.d.), 98.
[78] Ibid. 181.   [79] Ibid. 182.

novels introduced middle-class readers of realist fiction to the ordinary business-men of the City, much as George Eliot introduced them to rural Midlanders, Trollope to the provincial clergy, and Gaskell to the northern working classes.

Furthermore, in arguing that business 'keeps the nobility of the land from sinking to the same low level as the nobility of all other lands', Riddell confronts the reality of class slippage—of impoverished noblemen who have immigrated to the City and learned to work for a living. In contrast to many of her contemporaries, she is more interested in downward than upward mobility. *George Geith* registers every possible kind of class prejudice relating to this 'fall'. Geith's aristocratic cousins disdain his work as an accountant, while he only reluctantly overcomes his distaste for the vulgarity of other City people. He is a conspicuously new kind of hero, held up as a model of hard work and a convert to City values. As he tells Mr Molozone, who is indignant at being asked to wait in line: 'We businessmen cannot afford to be other than democrats and the peer and the peasant stand on an equality in a City office.'[80]

In Riddell's novel, fiscally irresponsible aristocrats and gentry refuse to see that their land owning does not support their habits. Living for the present, they run up debts and drive their families to ruin. In contrast, the accountant Geith is neither a pleasure seeking nor a sensitive man. He gave up his 'living' as a clergyman on his family's estate because 'he liked business better than preaching, or praying, or visiting the fatherless and widows in their afflictions.'[81] Like Robert Moore in *Shirley* and John Thornton in Gaskell's *North and South* (1854–5), he has come down in the world and must work his way back up. The difference is that Geith is a City businessman rather than a Northern industrialist.[82] Having learned to toil in the present for future rewards, he realizes that he cannot re-cross that 'broad line of demarcation' that separates the life of 'independence and business' from that of 'dependence and pleasure'.[83]

Not only did Riddell represent the two-way traffic between the world of dependence and pleasure and the world of independence and business; she exposed herself to criticism by displaying her financial knowledge. Despite the backhanded compliment 'masculine', which might be considered an accomplish-ment for a female author, critics insinuated that no matter how realistically

---

[80] Ibid. 21. In *The Decline and Fall of the British Aristocracy* (New Haven: Yale University Press, 2000), David Canadine discusses the phenomenon of the 'working patrician', which he calls a 'contradiction in terms' (405). He argues that from the 1880s, 'going into the City was a new means of life support eagerly embraced' by the aristocracy, and this move constituted a 'major upheaval' (406). It is interesting that Riddell identifies this trend as early as 1865.

[81] Riddell, *George Geith*, 17.

[82] For discussions of the different kinds of businessmen in Victorian fiction, see Herman Jansonius, *Some Aspects of Business Life in Early Victorian Fiction* (Purmerend: Muusses, 1926); Ivan Melada, *The Captain of Industry in English Fiction* (Albuquerque: University of New Mexico Press, 1970); James Raven, *Judging New Wealth: Popular Publishing and Responses to Commerce in England, 1750–1800* (Oxford: Clarendon Press, 1992); *The Representation of Business in Literature*, introd. and ed. Arthur Pollard (London: Institute of Economic Affairs, 2000).

[83] Riddell, *George Geith*, 106.

treated, business and trade were not subjects suited to fiction. A reviewer of her novel *The Senior Partner* (1882) observes that 'we scarcely know whether, as a general rule, her novels should be reviewed in the columns that are set apart for literature, or whether they would not more fitly receive a notice side by side with the works on foreign exchanges or the currency'.[84] Critics as prominent as G. H. Lewes and Anne Thackeray Ritchie praised Riddell for her realism, but the knowledge about finance that made her fiction realistic was also suspicious to the guardians of literary taste.[85]

Riddell's novels invited the application of binary, gendered terms by critics even as she defied those categories through her 'masculine' knowledge and representation of the financial world. Her work also called up genteel, literary prejudice against fictionalizing business and City life. The neglect of her work today may owe something to our continued prejudice against a female novelist who defended capitalism and capitalists with less moral ambiguity than Brontë or Gaskell.

Women's involvement in the market continued to have transgressive connotations for late Victorian authors who exploited the dramatic effect of such transgression. Riddell's Irish compatriot Oscar Wilde made good use of the dangerous investing woman in *An Ideal Husband* (1895). Mrs. Cheveley announces: ' "I am not in the mood tonight for silver twilights, or rose-pink dawns. I want to talk business" '.[86] Wilde reversed the stereotype of the male swindler and female victim with Mrs Cheveley's determination to blackmail Sir Robert Chiltern into investing in the Argentine Canal Company, a Stock Exchange swindle. Toward the end of the nineteenth century, the woman with knowledge of finance began to be represented not merely as unwomanly, but as duplicitous and dangerous.

Perhaps the most transgressive fictional account of a female investor is Olive Christian Malvery's 1908 novel, *The Speculator*. In 1904, the Indian-born Malvery dressed in various guises to explore the lives of the London poor, especially working women, and wrote about her experiences in *The Soul Market* (1906).[87] Malvery was also a novelist, and in *The Speculator*, her heroine Helen March disguises herself as the Greek stockbroker Otto Martini in order to gain entry to the Stock Exchange and earn money for her family. Men have let Helen down: her father ruined himself by speculating and her husband, British Consul in a remote Arabian port city, does not earn enough money to support the

[84] *Saturday Review*, 53 (25 March 1882), 375.

[85] Patricia Thomas Srebrnik argues that Victorian middle-class class prejudices against trade and the City—especially among the university-educated literary class that published and reviewed the literature of the period—accounted for the increasingly hostile tone adopted by reviewers of Riddell's work. See 'Mrs. Riddell and the Reviewers: A Case Study in Popular Fiction', *Women's Studies*, 23 (1994), 69–84.

[86] Oscar Wilde, *An Ideal Husband* (1895; London, 1992), 345.

[87] Historian Judith Walkowitz has explored this aspect of her life and work. See 'The Indian Woman, the Flower Girl and the Jew: Photojournalism in Edwardian England', *Victorian Studies*, 42 (1998–9), 3–46.

family. As Helen studies the 'science of finance', she complains: ' "A woman is handicapped in the race of life. She is never given any business training, nor taught the value of money." '[88] As Otto, Helen is particularly successful in helping female investors who 'seemed born into the world to be the victims of any adventurous scoundrel'.[89]

Her quest for money leads this high-born young woman with two children living in a Surrey cottage into the opium dens of London and into anarchist plots, international financial conspiracies, and traffic in women. She conceals her activities from her husband, whom she rightly suspects would find them repugnant. When he discovers the truth, he is crushed: ' "The shame of it! His beautiful, dainty Helen masquerading as some wretched foreigner among the coarse crowds of the City." '[90] His attitude is contrasted to that of Helen's long-suffering friend Paul Heyward, who loves and supports her through all that she does. Eventually, however, her husband forgives her 'immodest and unwomanly' behaviour and domestic harmony is restored.[91] For her part, Helen regrets leaving her work in the City, 'with all its strenuousness and [the] strange adventures', but consoles herself that she has 'the children's careers to plan'.[92]

The novel is a melange of Victorian genres. Helen's encounters with the London poor recall Margaret Hale's encounters with the industrial workers in *North and South*. The anarchist conspiracy reminds us of Conrad's *Secret Agent* (1907), and the colonial scenes in which her husband puts down a Bedouin insurrection are reminiscent of late Victorian boys' adventure fiction. *The Speculator*'s central plot, however, is financial, and by staging the domestic, genteel world as geographically separate from the public, financial world, Malvery dramatizes the possibilities, limitations, and dangers of a woman's crossing from one to the other. At war within the novel are the values of female independence and of domesticity: of good business and earning power on the one hand and the 'higher' values of wife and motherhood on the other.

Throughout the nineteenth century, many women survived on the income of money safely invested in the Funds. Others could afford to be more speculative. As a middle-class domestic ideology seemed to restrict women's opportunities outside the home, purchasing shares and collecting dividends were activities in which they could participate and which could be a means to increased wealth and independence. Similarly, women had equal access to knowledge about their investments in the newly emerging financial press.[93] Hence Emily Brontë could make herself 'mistress of the necessary degree of knowledge' by reading 'every paragraph & every advertisement in the news-papers that related to rail-roads',

---

[88] Olive Christian Malvery, *The Speculator* (London: Werner Laurie, 1908), 32.
[89] Ibid. 42.   [90] Ibid. 288.   [91] Ibid. 302.   [92] Ibid. 288.
[93] See Mary Poovey, 'Writing about Finance in Victorian England: Disclosure and Secrecy in the Culture of Investment', *Victorian Studies*, 45 (2002), Special Issue on Victorian Investments, ed. Cannon Schmitt, Nancy Henry, and Anjali Arondekar, 17–42.

and Charlotte Riddell could astonish readers with her 'fearful and wonderful knowledge of matters financial'.[94]

Representations of female investors in Victorian fiction provide evidence of conflicted attitudes toward more ostentatious incursions into the world of finance, but from Aunt Glegg's cargoes to Mrs Cheveley's Argentine canal shares, many Victorian characters would not allow social disapprobation to inhibit their speculative instincts. Historians are now beginning to investigate the role that female shareholders played in nineteenth-century business and finance, and as we learn more, we will come to a better understanding of a 'culture of investment'—a model that incorporates rather than separates the public and private, as well as the literary and financial spheres.

[94] *The Letters of Charlotte Brontë*, i. 390; John Ashcraft Noble, Review of *Mitre Court*, *The Academy* (5 Dec. 1885), 372.

7

Literary Realism in the Wake of Business Cycle Theory: *The Way We Live Now* (1875)

Tara McGann

What causes the reversal of fortune for Augustus Melmotte, the financial villain of Anthony Trollope's novel *The Way We Live Now*? Chairman of the English Board of Directors of the South Central Pacific and Mexican Railway, newly elected to Parliament, and host of a banquet for the Emperor of China, he tumbles from this financial, political, and social pinnacle to bankruptcy and suicide. Following the same course as the speculative bubble centred on this railway company, his power, influence, and wealth inflate—'becoming greater and greater in every direction—mightier and mightier every day'.[1] And then, as we expect, he bursts, but what brings about the *peripeteia*?

Not until *The Way We Live Now* does such a reversal become problematic in the British novel rather than preordained because given by a predetermined narrative trajectory: speculative bubbles burst and, more to the point, financial villains reap the wages of sin. With *The Way We Live Now*, however, finance becomes problematic, that is, a phenomenon to be explored rather than one fixed in meaning by literary convention and cultural assumptions. Yet the innovative dimensions of the novel have largely escaped notice, as critics have followed Trollope in regarding it as solely delivering a stern rebuke to 'the commercial profligacy of the age'.[2] Fifty years ago, A. O. J. Cockshut pronounced the novel's unifying theme to be 'the collapse of standards and of social order before new methods of finance'.[3] Commenting more recently, Patrick Brantlinger views it as 'close to Augustan criticism of the "money'd interest": Melmotte represents counterfeit forms of wealth—above all, stock market speculation—not tied to land or to Britain's aristocratic traditions'.[4]

---

[1] Anthony Trollope, *The Way We Live Now* (Harmondsworth: Penguin, 1994), 267. Subsequent references will be cited parenthetically within the text.

[2] Trollope, *An Autobiography* (Oxford: Oxford University Press, 1980), 353. Subsequent references will be cited parenthetically within the text.

[3] A. O. J. Cockshut, *Anthony Trollope: A Critical Study* (London: Collins, 1955), 204. Subsequent references will be cited parenthetically within the text.

[4] Patrick Brantlinger, *Fictions of State: Culture and Credit in Britain, 1694–1994* (Ithaca: Cornell University Press, 1996), 171.

While Brantlinger strenuously distances himself from such an allegedly Augustan attitude, his and Cockshut's readings of the novel as a conservative response to finance agree. While they correctly identify a central theme, they over-simplify in reducing the novel to this theme. In any case, the subject proves formulaic, for what Victorian novel finds in financial speculation anything other than a sign of social corruption, and which takes a stance other than stinging indictment?[5]

If restricted to the elaboration of this theme, *The Way We Live Now* would only stand out for its spleen: Robert Polhemus calls it 'the most vitriolic satire of the Victorian era and one of the most powerful satires on capitalism ever written.'[6] Yet more interesting than either the vitriol or adeptness of its satire is the way the novel curiously moves back and forth between conforming to the conventions by which Victorian novels treat finance and undoing them. With *The Way We Live Now*, these conventions crack under the burden of representing high finance, to which they prove inadequate, while a realist novel of finance emerges from those fissures.

A CERTAIN CLASS OF DISHONESTY

Reading the novel against the grain of literary conventions as well as against its critical reception, my account runs the risk of distortion. If *The Way We Live Now* exposes the reader to the amoral complexities of finance, it also represents financial speculation in conventionally condemnatory terms. Certainly, Melmotte fulfils every stereotype of the financial villain, and the success of the railway company he directs as well as his entrance into society and Parliament serve as indices of degeneration: his wealth gives him a passport to enter where his vulgarity, dishonesty, and presumed Jewishness should bar him. Then again, the treatment of another Jewish character, Ezekiel Breghert, tempers the anti-Semitism, as he exemplifies integrity in both his commercial and private affairs. His probity contrasts with the corruption of mercenary, social-climbing society, which courts Melmotte even as it believes him to be a cheat. 'People said of him that ... he had swallowed up the property of all who had come in contact with him, that he was fed with the blood of widows and children—but what was all this to Lady Carbury?' (61). Unconcerned by his alleged misdeeds, Lady Carbury worries only about whether others accept invitations from him. Roger Carbury bitterly complains, 'No one pretends to think that he is a gentleman. There is a consciousness among all who speak of him that he amasses his money, not by honest trade, but by unknown tricks—as does a card sharper' (117). Thus

---

[5] For more on speculation and fiction, see Francis O'Gorman, 'Speculative Fictions and the Fortunes of H. Rider Haggard', below 157–72.

[6] Robert M. Polhemus, *The Changing World of Anthony Trollope* (Berkeley: University of California Press, 1968), 187. Subsequent references will be cited parenthetically within the text.

society, the 'We' of the title, takes the brunt of Trollope's ire. The entrance of Jews into society still represents social decline. Edgar Rosenberg rightly points to the limitations of this only seemingly more enlightened viewpoint: 'he makes it painfully clear all the same that he means Melmotte's conquest of London to point up the fatal corruption of a society which tolerates and makes common cause with Jewish opportunists on the order of Melmotte; in a way, the terms are as insulting as they have every been.'[7]

As with other Victorian novels, the perennial collapse of standards hastened by speculation remains a central concern. Trollope observes in *An Autobiography* (1883) that he was instigated to write *The Way We Live Now* by reflecting on the ways the 'great speculator' threatened his society:

a certain class of dishonesty, dishonesty magnificent in its proportions, and climbing into high places, has become at the same time so rampant and so splendid that there seems to be reason for fearing that men and women will be taught to feel that dishonesty, if it can become splendid, will cease to be abominable.   (355)

What he scourges as deceitful, counterfeit, and profligate amount to species of speculation:

I went beyond the iniquities of the great speculator who robs everybody, and made an onslaught also on other vices,—on the intrigues of girls who want to get married, on the luxury of young men who prefer to remain single, and on the puffing propensities of authors who desire to cheat the public into buying their volumes.   (355)

Again, with other Victorian novels, *The Way We Live Now* traces the proliferation of speculation—into politics, the marriage market, the literary world, gatherings of fashionable society, and a gentlemen's club, where IOUs circulate in lieu of cash to cover gambling debts. Among such worthless scraps of paper, we can include Felix's vapid letters to Marie, his signed promise to Melmotte to drop his pursuit of her, the tickets to the ball for the emperor, the puff reviews of Lady Carbury's book, *Criminal Queens*, and the railway shares, once their value plummets. Paper substitutes for cash, and further dematerializing money, words then substitute for paper, as the bemused narrator comments: 'under the new Melmotte régime, an exchange of words was to suffice' (36). As ever, speculation signifies the bleeding of the economic sphere past its supposedly proper boundaries as well as the reign of sign over substance, the abandonment of honest work for gambling, and the eclipse of true worth by its simulacra.

Roger Carbury, the idealized representative of the squierarchy, who regards Melmotte and all associated with him as 'false, fraudulent, and ruinous' (108),

---

[7] Edgar Rosenberg, *From Shylock to Svengali; Jewish Stereotypes in English Fiction* (Stanford, CA: Stanford University Press, 1960), 142. Subsequent references will be cited parenthetically within the text.

exemplifies this posture towards speculation. Despite Trollope's obvious attachment to Carbury, the reader cannot collapse his perspective with the narrative perspective, reducing the novel to his tirade against the collapse of standards, which Melmotte signifies: 'A failure! Of course he's a failure, whether rich or poor—a miserable imposition, a hollow vulgar fraud from beginning to end—too insignificant for you and me to talk of, were it not that his position is a sign of he degeneracy of the age' (423). His invective sounds scripted by Thomas Carlyle while Trollope, in his discussion of this novel from *An Autobiography*, counters such Carlylean gloom: 'If he be right, we are all going straight away to darkness and the dogs. But then we do not put very much faith in Mr. Carlyle,—nor in Mr. Ruskin and his other followers' (354). In fact, the narrative perspective is both less sclerotic and far more ambiguous than Roger Carbury's.

For all that it might now seem to exemplify an unambiguously conservative response to finance, the novel takes a stance at turns disgusted, jaundiced, wry, and irate, undoubtedly chagrined, yet resigned to examining the actual.

IT WAS ASSERTED IN ABCHURCH LANE

The commitment to comprehend the actual in *The Way We Live Now* extends to social phenomena that earlier novels had taken to be set in meaning. Charles Dickens's *Little Dorrit* (1855–7), for instance, understands the trajectory from a speculative boom to bust within a pre-scripted moral framework of transgression, followed by the ineluctable consequences of such transgression. Merdle's joint-stock bank necessarily collapses: based on fraud, hence lacking substance and a legitimate basis, it must fail. Correlatively, Merdle, the great speculator, self-immolates sooner than later because he 'was simply the greatest Forger and the greatest Thief that had ever cheated the gallows'.[8] Ideology produces story logic: a speculative craze, assumed to be indistinguishable from a swindle, leads unavoidably to financial ruin, as fraud often will. Given this story logic, questioning why a financial villain experiences a reversal of fortune would be meaningless, as the reversal represents a defining characteristic.

The Way We Live Now poses this hitherto tautological question and then extends the surprising un-moralized answer that Melmotte simply experiences a cash flow problem, and just when his credit dries up. Written in 1873 and published in 1875, the novel attempts to account for the business cycle theory emerging during the late 1860s and 1870s, which looked to impersonal factors such as fluctuating credit, liquidity crises, and time to understand what produced sharp downturns in the money market, of the sort that crush Melmotte. His

---

[8] Charles Dickens, *Little Dorrit* (Oxford: Oxford University Press, 1999), 594.

vicissitudes of fortune, proceeding from relative stasis to an excited state, to a panic, and then to financial crisis, resemble those of a business cycle, if in miniature. Then again, the fortunes of financial villains always trace an arc from mania to crisis, yet tightening credit strangles Melmotte, not the hand of Providence, which creates a new narrative arc.

Victorian economists and financial journalists began to see the swing from cheap and plentiful, to dear or even unattainable money as periodic, hence characteristic of the business cycle, specifically at the point leading up to a crisis.[9] The outline, if not the mechanism, of the nineteenth-century business or trade cycle was becoming all too apparent. From experience, they recognized its periodicity, and from close description of its events, they distinguished its contours, such as the relaxing or tightening of credit and concomitant lowering or raising of interest rates. Once they appreciated its periodicity, they no longer experienced surprise at the recommencement of what they now understood to be a ten-year cycle, nor did a speculative craze appear to erupt without precedent, for they discerned a pattern whereby, as financial journalist H. R. Fox Bourne wrote in 1871, after the lull of a year or two following a crisis, 'speculative energy revives and steadily gains force during seven or eight years, until it develops into a mania, lasting for about a year, and ending in another panic'.[10] For that reason, the Victorian social scientist and economist John Mills concluded that speculation 'is not an ultimate fact'.[11]

By subjecting the phenomena of manias and panics to rational analysis, even such nascent understandings of the business cycle unseated the providential explanation that they court and then deliver penalty for individual or social sin. As well, business cycle theory demoted the crisis in favour of the wave: an alternating, repeating phenomenon. With that conceptual shift, the role of the crisis diminishes to an episode, a scene, even if the most dramatic one in the cycle. The terminology of a cycle had been used previously to business cycle theory to characterize economic fluctuations. The banker, economist, evangelical, and parliamentarian Samuel Jones Lloyd, Lord Overstone, described what he termed a trade cycle in his 1837 text, *Reflections suggested by a Perusal of Mr. J. Horsley Palmer's Pamphlet on the Causes and Consequences of the Pressure on the Money Market*. In it, Overstone described the trade cycle as starting 'in a state of quiescence, — next improvement, — growing confidence, —

---

[9] For studies of the ten-year business cycle of the nineteenth century with reference to Great Britain, see François Crouzet, *The Victorian Economy*, trans. Anthony Forster (New York: Columbia University Press, 1982); W. W. Rostow, *British Economy of the Nineteenth Century* (Oxford: Clarendon Press, 1948); A. D. Gayer, W. W. Rostow, and A. J. Schwartz, *The Growth and Fluctuation of the British Economy, 1790–1850* (Oxford: Clarendon Press, 1953); and R. C. O. Matthews, *A Study in Trade-Cycle History: Economic Fluctuations in Great Britain* (Cambridge: Cambridge University Press, 1954).

[10] H. R. Fox Bourne, *The Romance of Trade* (London: Cassell, Petter, and Galpin, 1905), 328.

[11] 'On Credit Cycles and the Origin of Commercial Panics', *Business Cycle Theory: Selected Texts, 1860–1939*, i, ed. Harald Hagemann (London: Pickering & Chatto, 2002), 57.

prosperity,—excitement,—overtrading,—convulsion,—pressure,—stagnation, —distress,—ending again in quiescence.'[12] His model awards the central dramatic role to the crisis.

Were one to create a diagrammatic representation of Overstone's notion of the trade cycle, it would readily map on to Gustav Freytag's pyramidal model of the structure of a tragedy.[13] What provides the inciting moment? The financial villain forms the joint-stock company and floats shares. What supplies the rising action? The mania commences. The complication? Whispers of fraud and insolvency. The climax leading to reversal of fortune? The bubble bursts. Catastrophe? Bankruptcy for the villain and morally delinquent. Moment of last suspense? The suicide of the villain. The financial crisis stands at the apex, as the climax of this drama. Financial catastrophe produces dramatic catastrophe.

The trade cycle as conceived by Overstone has all of the requisite dramatic elements of tragedy, or as regards novels, of tragicomedy. Given the conventionally dramatic structure of the trade/business cycle as understood by early and even mid-Victorians, it can easily be understood why it furnishes the plot structure for so many novels. Of course, its topicality explains as well why it features so prominently within them. More significantly, Victorian novels shared with such an understanding of economic fluctuations not only a conviction of the central importance of crises but also an emphasis on the individual moral agent. In other words, manias tempt the moral agent while panics administer justice to the sinful and warnings to the morally lax.

Business cycle theory, however, dissevers any causal relationship between individual moral agents and economic fluctuations. Mills recognized in his famous speech, 'On Credit Cycles and the Origin of Commercial Panics,' delivered to the Manchester Statistical Society in 1867, that his analysis of business cycles chafed against the beliefs of his society: 'To some, who have been accustomed to denounce the sinister action of a class of freebooters and wreckers in the financial world as the true cause of Panics, the idea of forces essentially independent of such action, and following a course normal of development, will be specially unwelcome' (84). His analysis fatally wounds the cultural and literary figure of the financial villain by examining the effects 'of forces essentially independent' of the wicked deeds of individuals. Even more corrosive to accepted beliefs, hence 'unwelcome,' the 'forces' identified by Mills act independently of any individual, villainous or virtuous.

Such forces include liquidity crises and contracting credit, both of which beset Melmotte. 'It was asserted in Abchurch Lane that ... he had allowed himself to become hampered by the want of comparatively small sums of ready money' (663). The collective wisdom of the financial quarter of London (for that is what

---

[12] Quoted in Boyd Hilton, *The Age of Atonement: The Influence of Evangelicalism on Social and Economic Thought, 1785–1865* (Oxford: Clarendon Press, 2001), 134.

[13] See Gustav Freytag, *Technique of the Drama*, trans. E. J. McEwan (Chicago: Scott, 1894).

would be asserted in Abchurch Lane) passes this judgement. Those who make the assertion understand the financial workings of this quarter, the City, which they express in a kind of verbal shorthand. The assertion reflects the language and assumptions of high finance: these experts identify not the lack of cash *per se* as the problem but the lack of foresight that would allow one to 'become hampered' by its want. Neither strangers to, nor opponents of, borrowing, for their business concerns financial markets, they mean (were they to use verbal longhand) that Melmotte found himself in need of a loan at the very moment that his credit receives a crushing blow. Had his credit not disintegrated, and along with it, his access to cash, he could have withstood the various storms that batter him without capsizing. For those who conduct business in Abchurch Lane, he acted imprudently—the question of his villainy occupies no part of their calculations.

That confident, cosmopolitan assertion voiced in Abchurch Lane marks a sea change. The novel imparts an understanding of finance that sharply diverges from literary conventions and from what the imagined public holds to be true, one freshly probing the phenomenon of high finance. The reader apprehends potentially unfamiliar, perhaps unwelcome concepts, which if known to financial insiders, uncomfortably confront financial outsiders, for instance that wealth need not be in hand nor even take tangible form to exist. *The Way We Live Now* sets out to enlarge knowledge, even when the presumed sympathies of the reader and avowed sympathies of the author militate against that task. It enlarges knowledge about finance, not in the manner of a text of political economy, but by holding questions in unresolved suspension and thereby unsettling assumptions. Melmotte's bankruptcy and the issues it raises without settling—whether or not he possesses the wealth with which rumours have credited him, whether or not the shares in the railway company are worthless or valuable, and whether or not the railway company is a sham—press the attentive reader to reconsider received notions about finance, economic value, and wealth, and to re-evaluate literary conventions, such as the stereotype of the financial villain.

In short, Trollope writes a realist novel about finance, which while it does not entirely cast aside the verities and conventions of preceding novels, calls them into question. Financial events bear a sequential, causal relationship to each other instead of merely being required by story logic and given by a predetermined narrative trajectory. Further, finance occupies a far larger narrative role in *The Way We Live Now* than in earlier Victorian novels and is represented with greater specificity.

Melmotte had not always occupied the centre stage. The advance layouts for the novel found in Trollope's manuscript notes demonstrate that the original plan for it centred on Lady Carbury as the chief character and her speculative writing and marriage schemes as the main plot elements.[14] As originally envisioned, the novel would not have departed from the conventional way Victorian novels treat

---

[14] Michael Sadleir, *Trollope: A Commentary* (London: Constable, 1945), 422.

financial speculation. Nevertheless, as the novel took form in the summer of 1873, it focused on Melmotte and his large-scale, complex financial schemes, shifting its focus from the topos of the wheel of fortune (and the title of Lady Carbury's next literary venture) to a very different kind of cycle.

HOW DELICATE A THING IS CREDIT

A scheme of financial speculation concerning the rather shady South Central Pacific and Mexican Railway Company, and the 2,000 miles of rail stretching from San Francisco, California to Vera Cruz, Mexico that may or may not ever actually be built, lies at the heart of *The Way We Live Now*. Melmotte, Chairman of the English Board of Directors, and those who serve on its Board make money by selling shares allotted to them at a premium or anticipate making money by selling shares they hope will be allotted to them. No matter how dubious these services or the flotation of the shares may be, the reader can arrive at no definitive judgement about whether the company is a thorough scam, whether the shares have value, or whether Melmotte's wealth is bogus. He runs into trouble because while share prices exponentially rise after he starts up the company, they even more precipitously fall when he becomes the subject of devastating rumours, which burst the bubble.

Melmotte needs to explain to his prospective son-in-law, Lord Nidderdale, why the shares in the railway company have recently plummeted in value in order to convince him that although diminished for a time, his wealth remains secure. Melmotte's antagonists, a cabal of newspaper editors who opposed his candidacy for a seat in Parliament, published rumours about him, thereby widely assailing his reputation: 'They couldn't get their man in, but they could and did have the effect of depreciating my property suddenly by nearly half a million of money. Think what that is!' (566). When the dim-witted Nidderdale fails to comprehend the effect of such knocks to his reputation on share prices, Melmotte exasperatedly spells out how the articles eroded the confidence of the public, and how share prices fluctuate with people's confidence.

> 'Because you don't understand how delicate a thing is credit. The effect upon shares which I held was instantaneous and tremendous. The Mexican railway were at one hundred and seventeen, and they fell from that in two days to something quite nominal—so that selling was out of the question. Cohenlupe and I between us had about eight thousand of these shares. Think what that comes to!' Nidderdale tried to calculate what it did come to, but failed altogether. 'That's what I call a blow—a terrible blow ...'
> 'Will they never go up again?'
> 'Oh yes—perhaps higher than ever. But it will take time.'   (566)

The public associates the company so closely with Melmotte that the value of shares rises or falls with its perception of his wealth. Melmotte must convince

Nidderdale, not only to retain this aristocrat as a son-in-law, but also because any loss of confidence holds fatal consequences for him. If only credit were not so delicate! Melmotte complains to Paul Montague, 'Gentlemen who don't know the nature of credit, how strong it is—as the air—to buoy you up; how slight it is—as a mere vapour—when roughly touched, can do an amount of mischief of which they themselves don't in the least understand the extent!' (312).

Right before Trollope began writing *The Way We Live Now*, Walter Bagehot, had elucidated the *delicate* nature of credit in the widely read and influential *Lombard Street, a Description of the Money Market*, published in April 1873. Equipped with the knowledge of the delicacy of credit, non-experts could 'comprehend the inevitable vicissitudes of Lombard Street'—that is, of the money market.[15] Bagehot hoped that promoting an understanding of its periodic volatility and fragility could help keep the precarious house of cards from tumbling, for during the 'period of reaction and adversity, just even at the last instant of prosperity, the whole structure is delicate' (78). *Lombard Street* attempts to clarify the reasons for this delicacy, the pressures that 'make our credit system much more delicate at some times than at others' and which produce the 'periodical seasons of delicacy' (61).

It is impossible to know if *Lombard Street* directly influenced Trollope when writing *The Way We Live Now*, but the thinking expressed in *The Economist*, stirred up in Lombard Street, and asserted in Abchurch Lane certainly made an impression on him. Trollope, notes Norman Russell rightly, 'had thought carefully about the rapidly advancing importance of credit in commerce'.[16] Further, he recognized, as Bagehot demonstrated, that the complexities of credit undid simple oppositions between intrinsic, real value on the one hand and the smoke and mirrors of finance on the other. Bagehot would agree with Melmotte that the value of something like shares in the South Central Pacific and Mexican Railway Company depends significantly on how others act, which in turn depends on their predictions of how yet others will act, an insight that leads one in an infinite regression away from concepts of true and false riches: indeed, it makes them untenable. Credit, for Melmotte, as well as for Bagehot, concerns another's propensity to believe and to make conjectures about the future. It refers to perceptions, and as a result, Bagehot notes, 'Credit—the disposition of one man to trust another—is singularly varying' (64). Because subjective, ephemeral, and insubstantial, credit necessarily oscillates according to whether the public feels disposed towards being happy, hence credulous, or suspicious. Bagehot writes,

[15] Walter Bagehot, *Lombard Street: A Description of the Money Market* (Homewood: Richard D. Irwin, 1962), 78. Subsequent references will be cited parenthetically within the text.
[16] Norman Russell, *The Novelist and Mammon. Literary Responses to the World of Commerce in the Nineteenth Century* (Oxford: Clarendon Press, 1986). Subsequent references will be cited parenthetically within the text.

All people are most credulous when they are most happy; and when much money has just been made, when some people are really making it, when most people think they are making it, there is a happy opportunity for ingenious mendacity. Almost everything will be believed for a little while, and long before discovery the worst and most adroit deceivers are geographically or legally beyond the reach of punishment. But the harm they have done diffuses harm, for it weakens credit still farther. (78)

Credulity benefits unworthy investments, just as distrust dooms worthy ones, which explains Bagehot's hostility to speculation and profound antipathy towards figures like Melmotte, since they make the money market that much more unstable. Nevertheless, such instability, born of the inevitable vicissitudes of Lombard Street, prevents our concluding that Melmotte's difficulties in obtaining credit prove his insolvency, for if the mendacious can obtain credit during credulous seasons, even the honourable experience difficulty doing so during suspicious ones.

Does Melmotte tell the truth when he claims his financial distress to be temporary? Influenced by cultural assumption as well as literary conventions, the Victorian reader would have felt disinclined to grant his words any truth, even if the narrator did not intone, 'Of course every word he had said to Nidderdale had been a lie, or intended to corroborate lies' (567). However, those who frequent Abchurch Lane conclude differently:

The crushing blow to him, so said Herr Croll, had been the desertion of Cohenlupe—that and the sudden fall in the value of the South Central and Pacific and Mexican Railway shares, consequent on the rumours spread about the City respecting the Pickering property. It was asserted in Abchurch Lane that had he not at that moment touched the Pickering property, or entertained the emperor, or stood for Westminster, he must, by the end of the autumn, have been able to do any or all of those things without danger, simply as the result of the money which would then have been realized by the railway. But he had allowed himself to become hampered by the want of comparatively small sums of ready money, and in seeking relief had rushed from one danger to another, till at last the waters around him had become too deep even for him, and had overwhelmed him. (663)

Paying for the banquet and ball for the emperor while running for a seat in Parliament dangerously drains his cash reserves, which prompts him to raise money on the Pickering property, which he has purchased without having paid for yet, which in turn compels him to forge the signature conferring the title deed to him. The City does not condone the forgery—'dat vas nasty—very nasty' (663). So says Herr Croll, especially as Melmotte took the liberty of forging his name to another document. Neither does the City form the judgement that the forgery confirms Melmotte's wealth to be fraudulent. It reaches the verdict that an unfortunate confluence of events brought him down, and that if he cannot be blamed for Cohenlupe's embezzlement and flight, in it was inexcusable folly to incur substantial expenses while purchasing an estate, and right when the railway had absorbed all of his cash.

Then again, the voice of the City proclaims no oracular truth, for sometimes it does no more than amplify rumour, such as when it puffs Melmotte up: 'It was very generally said in the City about this time that the Great South Central Pacific and Mexican Railway was the very best thing out. It was known that Mr Melmotte had gone into it with heart and hand' (170). Nonetheless, Mr Broune, the respectable and knowledgeable newspaper editor, who understands the financial workings of the City, also thinks it likely that Melmotte, in the language of Abchurch Lane, 'allowed himself to become hampered by the want of comparatively small sums of ready money'. Correcting Lady Carbury when she declares that if the dreadful rumours are true, '[t]hen he can't be rich at all,' Broune responds, 'Even that would not follow. He has such large concerns in hand that he might be very much pressed for funds, and yet be possessed of immense wealth' (490). Because one can be pressed for funds while still wealthy, not his cash flow problems, inability to obtain credit, or subsequent bankruptcy answer the conundrum of his actual fortune.

My aim lies not in mustering sympathy for the devil but with pointing out unanswered questions surrounding Melmotte's wealth, the railway, and the value of the shares, which oblige the reader to engage new concepts—precisely those set forth by Bagehot in *Lombard Street*. W. W. Rostow emphasizes that Bagehot drew readers' attention to the factors that produced crises, both to 'the so-called "psychological factors"' as well as to factors such as demands for liquidity.[17] Bagehot wished to minimize the psychological determinants of crises, and thus to contain the contagiousness of panics, by educating his readers about the pressures to which the credit system is subject, such as how floating capital, once bound up in fixed capital (like a railway), remains unavailable for a time for other uses. As Rostow shows, Bagehot was concerned that liquidity crises prompted uneducated investors to stampede and hoped that once readers understood how 'the forms of fixed investment ... take time to mature,' they might not increase pressures on the credit system by assuming, thus producing, crises where none need exist (164–5). Abchurch Lane demonstrates that it already has absorbed this lesson when it asserts that by the end of the autumn Melmotte would have been able to handle outlays of money, 'without danger, simply as the result of the money which would then have been realized by the railway.' Demonstrating the validity of their assertion, the narrator comments, 'When Melmotte's affairs were ultimately wound up there was found to be nearly enough of property to satisfy all his proved liabilities' (707).

Critics have tended to view Melmotte as a typical financial villain, hence deeming his wealth a sham and the railway a swindle. As evidence that the railway will never be built, they point to a passage in which the scandalized Paul

---

[17] W. W. Rostow, *British Economy of the Nineteenth Century* (Oxford: Clarendon Press, 1948), 162. Subsequent references will be cited parenthetically within the text.

Montague, a financial outsider and reluctant business partner to Hamilton K.
Fisker and then Melmotte, listens to Fisker's plans for the railway:

The object of Fisker, Montague, and Montague was not to make a railway to Vera Cruz,
but to float a company. Montague thought that Mr Fisker seemed to be indifferent
whether the railway would ever be constructed or not. It was clearly his idea that fortunes
were to be made out of the concern before a spadeful of earth had been moved   (68)

When the reader recognizes that this passage is focalized from Montague's perspective (note the tag clause 'Montague thought'), its ambiguities can be gauged.
Montague assumes that Fisker's indifference to the railway being constructed
indicates he never intended for a 'spadeful of earth' to be moved. Should the
reader join him in making that leap? Montague, a stand-in for the reader, has
difficulty digesting that the railway itself amounts to no more than a means for
Fisker to realize profit through the flotation of shares. But of course the projects
to which capital flows only ever supply a means to realize profit and remain
ancillary to that object, for capitalism aims ever and only at capital accumulation.
From the perspective of a financial insider such as Fisker or Melmotte, if fortunes
can be made before shovelling earth or even without having to go to the trouble
of shovelling any, *tant mieux*. But this does not mean that they never intended to
build the railway. Rather, the railway itself holds little interest for them. Before
such an attitude is labelled aberrant or villainous, it needs to be recalled that
capital always seeks flexibility and resists being bound up. Fisker and Melmotte
act like rational capitalists in feeling indifferently towards the railway.

If Fisker displays indifference towards the construction of the railway, his
enthusiasm for the joint-stock company batters Montague and the reader.
Bearing 'brilliantly printed programmes' for the unbuilt railway, he arrives in
Liverpool pronouncing that in the time it took to travel from San Francisco to
there, ' "I've no doubt we've an office open already in Mexico and another at Vera
Cruz" ' (68–9). He sails to England to launch the joint-stock company, which
will provide the necessary capital for the railway scheme, and takes the brash
venture to London, the financial capital of the world, in order to spark a fever for
the shares, as he explains while cunningly drawing in Melmotte: 'you don't want
me to teach you, Mr Melmotte, that nothing encourages this kind of thing like
competition.' As Melmotte asks questions, 'Fisker understood perfectly that Mr
Melmotte did not ask the question in reference to any value that he might attach
to the possession of such lands, but to the attractiveness of such a prospectus
in the eyes of the outside world of speculators' (72). For Fisker and Melmotte,
the railway represents no more than an engine to generate capital and personal
wealth—an unpleasant drought for a reluctant speculator such as Montague to
swallow. Even worse for him, the railway can generate profits even if it fails, as
Fisker clarifies: 'There's more to be got out of the smashing up of such an affair
as this, if it should smash up, than could be made by years of hard work out of
such fortunes as yours and mine in the regular way of trade' (75).

Confirming the assumptions of many readers, the South Central Pacific and Mexican Railway Company operates in an undeniably underhand manner. Melmotte selects as members of the Board men possessing neither capital nor acumen but titles, idle men who at overly brisk meetings unanimously approve all he proposes. Encountering resistance in Montague, Melmotte dodges him when he tries to find out just how much scrip has actually been issued. Montague persists in asking, 'what is being done with the shares', but Melmotte, as well as the novel, remains unresponsive on this score (285). Melmotte's dealings with Sir Felix Carbury might indicate more clear-cut skulduggery. Sir Felix wants to purchase one thousand pounds worth of shares from what Dolly Longestaffe owes him from gambling debts. When the two visit the surprisingly agreeable Melmotte, Dolly signs a number of documents, yet Sir Felix never receives his shares. Does Melmotte cheat Sir Felix or subtly refuse to exchange valuable scrip for meaningless IOUs?

> The great man … had told Sir Felix that the shares were his. Sir Felix had been not only contented, but supremely happy … It was only after the reflection of a day or two that he found that he had as yet got nothing to sell … Sir Felix was but one among hundreds. In the meantime the bills in Grosvenor Square were no doubt paid with punctuality—and those bills must have been stupendous.   (268)

The passage only amplifies uncertainty. Has Melmotte taken the money of hundreds without issuing shares, and should the reader deduce that he embezzles the money of unwitting dupes to cover the stupendous bills? If so, then how are shares being bought and sold? One could chalk up the inconsistency to carelessness on Trollope's part or to the demands of the competing tendencies in the novel. The Victorian financial novel must render him a mere swindler, a move the emergent realist novel stymies. As well, we could ascribe the uncertainty to the way the novel teasingly holds back reliable information. Far from omniscient, the narrator only guesses that the almost certainly tremendous bills 'were no doubt paid with punctuality'. The novel repeatedly thwarts resolution of questions concerning Melmotte's wealth, the railway, and the shares.

Tracking down the associations the fictional railway would have created for the reader of the mid-1870s will not resolve these questions, for such associations both support the sense of the railway as a con and complicate that assumption. Undoubtedly, readers of the mid-1870s associated the fictional railway company with the scandal surrounding the collapse of the venerable London credit house of Overend, Gurney & Company in 1866, which echoed Melmotte's predicament. Mismanagement by its partners led to severe losses, which when the company went public required the Gurney family to sell off assets to make up for the losses. Bagehot comments, 'It was the publicity of their losses which ruined them. But if they had continued to be a private partnership they need not have disclosed those losses: they might have written them off quietly out of the immense profits they could have accumulated' (134). Selling off estates devastated the company's credit by attracting unwanted attention: 'their visible ruin destroyed the credit of the concern ... if the great losses had slept a quiet sleep in a hidden ledger,—no one would have been alarmed' (135). He subversively insinuates that public panic led to irreversible financial ruin, not the reverse: the loss of public confidence doomed this credit house.

Finally the dishonest business practices of the South Central Pacific and Mexican Railway Company—even Melmotte's crimes of forgery—present, in plot terms, elaborate red herrings. To understand what pulls down Melmotte, 'forces essentially independent' of the actions of financial villains, forces beyond the intervention of any individual, need to be examined. Even a villain shrinks in importance, deprived the role of agent.

After Melmotte takes prussic acid, Fisker once more travels from San Francisco to London, just when Montague, again standing in for the reader, has assumed the utter collapse of the joint-stock company. Fisker quickly disabuses him of that notion:

> 'Bust up at Frisco! Not if I know it. Why should it be bust up? D'you think we're all going to smash there because a fool like Melmotte blows his brains out in London?'
> 'He took poison.'
> 'Or p'ison either. That's just not our way. I'll tell you what I'm going to do; and why I'm over here so uncommon sharp. These shares are at a'most nothing now in London. I'll buy every share in the market. I wired for as many as I dar'd, so as not to spoil our own game, and I'll make a clean sweep of every one of them. Bust up! I'm sorry for him because I thought he was a biggish man—but what he's done'll just be the making of us over there.' (702–3)

He buys up the shares on the London exchange for a bargain, in order to maintain their high price in the United States—so much for the shares being worthless scraps of paper. Returning at the close of the novel to comment on Melmotte's actions in the manner of a Chorus, he challenges received notions about speculative ventures and financial villains. He regards the forgery as a sign of Melmotte's ineptness, which, combined with being swindled by Cohenlupe, indicates Melmotte was not the 'biggish man' Fisker took him for: 'I call it damn clumsy from beginning to end; damn clumsy. I took him to be a different man' (702). When he buys up the shares, he definitively severs Melmotte from the South Central Pacific and Mexican Railway, for the corporation survives this withered financial villain and, if we believe Fisker, even flourishes.

The novel undermines cultural assumptions that were confused with causality, striking a tuning fork to hollow literary conventions that prove inadequate to grasp the complexities of high finance. As the novel retreats to the terrain of the comic pastoral, winding up with a series of weddings, Fisker and the voice of the City call attention to unanswered questions, such as what instigates Melmotte's *peripeteia*. Neither his frauds, even if as extensive as his detractors claim, nor his considerable imprudence precipitate his downfall. The lavish banquet and ball for the emperor, the run for Parliament, purchase of an estate, and even forgery

furnish no more than proximate causes. Though a swindler, crook, and profligate
spender, Melmotte falls due to the evaporation of credit. According to Broune,
Melmotte thought he could 'obtain universal credit. He very nearly succeeded
too' (647). Embedded within his analysis of the collapse of standards, Cockshut
uncovers the same cause: 'In outline Melmotte's story is the great traditional
story of fortune's wheel, the rise, the grandeur, and the fall of a great man. But
the treatment has unique features ... Credit makes him and loss of credit breaks
him' (205). More incisively, Russell writes, 'Melmotte is destroyed by lack of
credit, by the inability to raise immediate cash when it is required ... It is wrong
to imagine that he was "ruined": he died not really through lack of money,
but through lack of time' (157). Actually, Melmotte has far too much time; it
hangs heavy on his hands and collects in puddles about him. His downfall occurs
through the slowdown of narrative speed.

MR MELMOTTE IS PRESSED FOR TIME

Entitling a chapter of *Lombard Street* 'Why Lombard Street is Often Dull, and
Sometimes Excited,' Bagehot instructs his readers to conceptualize the business
cycle in terms of movement, sensation, excitement, and speed. Throughout the
chapter, he compares good credit to swiftly moving time and bad credit to the
idling of time. Trollope, too, in trying to understand 'how delicate a thing
is credit', understands its vicissitudes in terms of fluctuating speed—narrative
speed, for accelerated narrative speed corresponds with good credit and slow with
bad. Melmotte feels the first pinch for cash in Chapter 45, entitled 'Mr Melmotte
is Pressed for Time'. At this busy time his credit stands at its apex: 'It was part of
the charm of all dealings with this great man that no ready money seemed ever
to be necessary for anything. Great purchases were made and great transactions
apparently completed without the signing even of a cheque' (345–6). But Dolly
Longestaffe wants the money Melmotte owes for Pickering Park in cash, and
not a bill payable in six or even three months. Unlike his father, Adolphus
Longestaffe senior, he refuses to be put off or awed into submission. The squeeze
is on, and from this moment, narrative speed falters.

By narrative speed I am, to adopt and adapt Gérard Genette's term, discussing
the relationship between the amount of time covered by the situations and events
recounted in the novel and the length of the narrative as measured in pages and
chapters. The novel facilitates tracking narrative speed precisely as it provides
abundant evidence to date chapters accurately, most notably letters, lest one
forgets Trollope's career as a senior civil servant in the post office. Further aiding
the endeavour, the dates in the novel map exactly on to the calendar year of
1873. 'The title was meant to be taken literally, in that the story is set firmly
in the year of its creation, 1873' (Hall, 384). Trollope begins writing the novel
on 1 May 1873 and continues until December while the novel begins on 25

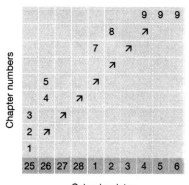

Fig. 7.1. 25 February–6 March

February and ends at the beginning of September: writing and setting were nearly contemporaneous (384, 393).[18]

The first nine chapters span ten days; taking up sixty-six pages, they average between seven and eight pages per chapter, an average that remains constant throughout the novel even as narrative speed oscillates. The sixth chapter is excluded from the chart (see Figure 7.1) as it analeptically looks towards events that precede the 'present' time of the narrative. In the chart, calendar dates run horizontally (the x axis) and chapter numbers run vertically (the y axis). Regarding the first nine chapters, expressing as a ratio the relationship between the amount of time covered by the narrative and the length of the narrative measured in chapters, one finds roughly 1:1, represented by the line $x = y$. Let me demarcate its slope as Genette's 'the hypothetical reference zero' from which deviations will be considered either 'slowdowns' (a line $x < y$) or 'accelerations' (a line $x > y$) of narrative speed.

Fisker meets Melmotte at the end of the ninth chapter, on 6 March. From 7 March to 15 April, no chapters are set. During this non-narrated period, Fisker and Melmotte accomplish the considerable work of setting up the English Board of Directors of the South Central Pacific and Mexican Railway and float shares. At the end of this fallow period (only fallow in terms of the narration, for outside the boundaries of the narrative much activity takes place), 'the company was fully launched in England, with a body of London directors, of whom Mr Melmotte was the chairman' (73). As the financial plot resumes with Chapter 15, so too does the narrative speed designated as the reference. Between Chapters 15 and 23, the ratio between time covered by the narrative

---

[18] Mark W. Turner has also considered the writing of Trollope in relation to time. See ' "Telling of my weekly doings": The Material Culture of the Victorian Novel', *A Concise Companion to the Victorian Novel*, ed. Francis O'Gorman (Oxford: Blackwell, 2005), 113–33. Subsequent references will be cited parenthetically within the text.

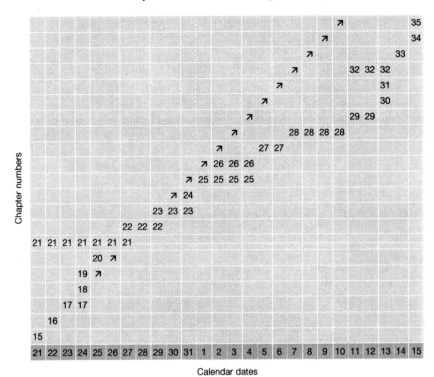

Fig. 7.2. 21 May–15 June

and length of narrative as measured by chapters returns to the ratio 1:1, and the chapters hug the slope of the line $x = y$ (see Figure 7.2). Following Chapter 23, as share prices take off and Melmotte's credit appears limitless, narrative speed accelerates, deviating sharply from the reference, describing a line $x > y$. Then, in the chapters leading up to the middle of the novel, narrative speed slows down, and just as cash flow problems beset Melmotte. Chapters 37 to 45 stack up on each other while narrative speed would be represented by the line $x < y$, all while the average of nearly eight pages per chapter stays constant (see Figure 7.3). What occurs during this time? Melmotte first suffers demands for cash in Chapter 45 ('Mr Melmotte is Pressed for Time'), both for the Pickering property and from Sir Felix, who now wants either his scrip or cash for the IOUs. The latter presents a mere irritant, but the former endangers him, for Dolly Longestaffe threatens to engage his lawyer, Mr Squercum. However, the slowdown of narrative speed precedes this chapter, as do pressures on Melmotte. He first meets an impediment in Paul Montague in Chapter 37, who as a member of the board demands to know how much scrip has been issued. This loss of confidence (erosion of credit) as yet remains restricted. 'Normal' narrative

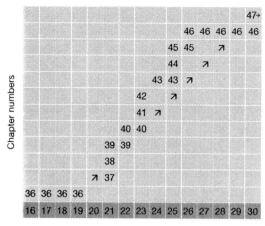

Fig. 7.3. 16–30 June

speed returns between Chapters 46 and 56. No imminent shipwreck menaces Melmotte, who rights himself, but he cannot much longer defer paying for Pickering Park.

The reader waits until Chapter 53 to find out how Melmotte withstands the pressure, as Chapters 46 to 52 switch focus to story-lines only indirectly related to the railway company and his mounting financial distress. The first page of Chapter 53 returns immediately to Melmotte's pressing concerns: 'At this especial point in his career ready money was very valuable to him' (404). Reports travel about the City 'that Mr Melmotte must be much pressed for money' (412); meanwhile Dolly Longestaffe has engaged Mr Squercum to obtain payment. Having renewed the mortgage of £30,000 on the property, Melmotte still must pay the £50,000 owed jointly to Adolphus Longestaffe senior and junior, or at least the minimum of £25,000 to satisfy Dolly. As he cannot relinquish the title deed, having already mortgaged the property, everything now depends on obtaining that £25,000. Melmotte charges Cohenlupe with the desperate task on the afternoon of Friday, 5 July. The ball and dinner for the emperor take place on Monday, 8 July, and on the following day the election falls. Before he can obtain the cash, rumours concerning Melmotte billow out of the City the morning of that fateful Monday and are carried in newspapers controlled by his political rivals. Right at this point, narrative speed grinds to a halt (see Figure 7.4). The flow of time becomes viscous following Chapter 56 and even moves in reverse (see Chapters 60, 66, 78, 79, and 80).

Had Cohenlupe successfully procured the £25,000, all danger would have been averted, and with a successful reception for the emperor and election to Parliament, his credit, after recovering from this wobble, would have stood

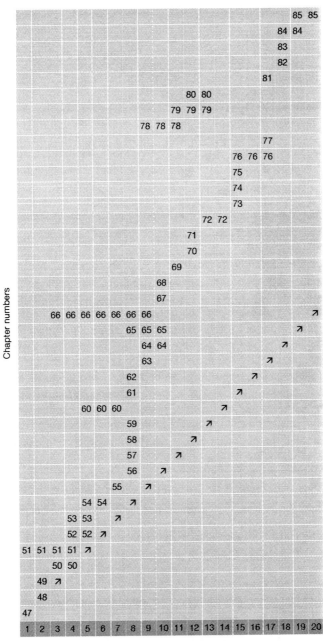

Calendar dates

Fig. 7.4. 1–20 July

higher than ever, but those rumours wreck him. To mortgage Pickering, he forged Dolly's name to the title deed, for Dolly refused his signature until he received payment, and now, due to Squercum, 'the word forgery was whispered by more than one pair of lips' (442). Squercum lacks the power, in fact, to elevate whispers into rumours, for he 'had been at work for above a week' without gaining the interest of the City in this 'little matter'. Then Cohenlupe dumps shares of the South Central Pacific and Mexican Railway to raise money. Taking notice of this and 'other facts coming to light', such as Melmotte's mortgaging of Pickering, and some irregular real estate speculations that have come to light, the City doubts his solvency and therefore gives credence to Squercum's charge (447). The rumours rapidly gust about the City, blow into the House of Commons, and wind towards the West End of London, causing share prices as well as the tickets to the emperor's ball to drop precipitously in value. Hearing the rumours, many invited guests declare themselves 'defaulters' (448). Much more significantly, the rumours capsize Melmotte's credit when he has most need of it.

The rumours have as yet no proof. If Dolly adamantly maintains he never signed over the title deed to Melmotte, he also admits to his 'propensity to be "tight"'. Nonetheless, the signature 'was not like the scrawl of a drunken man' (446). Even the reader does not know for sure until fifteen chapters after the rumours about forgery first disseminate that Melmotte had 'with his own hand traced Dolly Longestaffe's signature' (557). In the meantime he manages to brazen the rumours out; all still hinges on whether he can get hold of enough cash, and in time. That he cannot do. On Wednesday, 17 July (Chapter 75), the Longestaffe lawyers force him to agree to pay £50,000 by Friday at noon. That evening (Chapter 77), his daughter refuses to sign over to him the settlement he had created in order to draw on in case of emergency, and which would more than cover what he owed the Longestaffes. At the end of Chapter 83, before the morning of that Friday, with his assets tied up in depressed stocks and unable to raise the cash to meet this pressing obligation—disasters compounded by Cohenlupe's flight and embezzlement—he poisons himself.

The two weeks between 5 July (Chapter 53), when he knows he must produce £50,000, to 18 July (Chapter 83), when, failing that, he commits suicide, span thirty chapters and stretch over nearly a third of a novel set over a period of six months, all while the average of almost eight pages per chapter remains steady (see Figure 4). Between these chapters narrative speed, expressed by the line $x < y$, deviates significantly from that designated as the reference. This extreme slowdown of narrative speed creates the opposite of pleasurable expectancy. Slowing down narrative speed heightens tension, especially when we know a bomb (or speculative bubble) will explode. Alfred Hitchcock famously illustrates suspense as occurring when the viewer of a film (the reader could be substituted) knows a bomb will detonate in fifteen minutes; then, the dilation of time only builds tension. The potential victim, however, must not know of the impending disaster.[19] As the reader observes Melmotte struggling vainly to diffuse his own ticking bomb, the tempo established in these chapters—the agonizing slow motion of nightmare—provokes discomfort. Why would Trollope risk courting the reader's displeasure?

With narrative speed Trollope conceptualizes credit as an impersonal agency that drives financial markets and takes account of the significance of time as an economic factor. Poor credit—slow time—bedevils Melmotte. The slow time of the novel represents the slow time of downturns of the business cycle. True, the forgery ties his hands by preventing him from declaring bankruptcy and treating the Longestaffes like other creditors. Nonetheless, the underlying problem is that, foolishly incurring huge out-of-pocket expenses while his capital remained tied up, 'he had allowed himself to become hampered by the want of comparatively small sums of ready money'. Hence Fisker's disappointment that he was not a 'biggish man'. While he can face down rumours and silence his enemies, he remains powerless to prevent the feedback effect of rumours on credit. Further, his imprudence and arrogance deliver him into the pincers of that most impersonal agency against which his bluster means nothing—time. Unable to propel the narrative forward to the end of autumn, when he would have realized money from the railway company, he would have done well to heed Bagehot: 'Our current political economy does not sufficiently take account of *time* as an element in trade operations' (62, emphasis added). Instead, Melmotte acted obliviously with reference to what economists call turnover time—the time requisite to realize profit—and recklessly in terms of how his cash-flow difficulties would impinge upon credit.

THE FINANCIAL VILLAIN TAKES A BOW

Because the reader cannot ascribe his ruin to the ineluctable consequences of his villainy, Melmotte's *peripeteia* becomes problematic rather than preordained by providence, truism, or literary convention. At the same time, the financial villain, ceding agency to impersonal forces, becomes an irrelevant figure lacking any explanatory purchase. The choice of name signals Trollope's interest in the fate of this figure, for it evokes literary forebears: first, John Melmoth, the demonic villain of Charles Maturin's gothic novel *Melmoth the Wanderer* (1820), who unsuccessfully searches for someone with whom to contract the devil's bargain of a soul in exchange for omnipotent power; and second, the John Melmoth of Balzac's comic–gothic novella, *Melmoth reconcilié* (1835). Updating the story by transplanting John Melmoth to Paris during the time of the restoration, Balzac's novella comically suggests that Melmoth would readily have found willing

---

[19] See François Truffaut, with the collaboration of Helen G. Scott, *Hitchcock* (London: Secker and Warburg, 1968).

partners had he gone to the Parisian stock exchange. Augustus Melmotte, whose last name amounts to a French version of Melmoth, arrives in London from Paris. Yet this third iteration of Melmoth, if equipped with financial acumen and force of will, lacks demonic powers. After all, the deathblow comes from his daughter: this villain fails to compel the obedience of even his puny child.

With Merdle, Dickens had already begun to take apart the literary figure of the financial villain. As he turns out to be an almost feeble figure, society emerges as the guilty party instead of victim. Still his narrative trajectory remains predetermined, as does the narrative arc of the speculative bubble to which he is linked. Trollope, concerned with credit cycles, dismantles this figure much further[20] and lends Melmotte both magnificent and pathetic qualities, giving him a complexity and interiority rather than reducing him to a cipher, like Merdle. Falling victim to the myth of his insuperable greatness, he loses track of his limits and grows careless in trying to scale the heights of society with the dinner for the emperor, planned marriage of his daughter into the aristocracy, run for Parliament, and purchase of the estate. 'But there had grown upon the man during the last few months an arrogance, a self-confidence inspired in him by the worship of other men, which clouded his intellect, and robbed him of much of that power of calculation which undoubtedly he naturally possessed' (404). His hubris, harnessed to a pathetic desire to be taken for a gentleman and to ally himself with the aristocracy, delivers him over to unforgiving financial forces. Significantly, Fisker and Marie will avoid such missteps, as Croll declares, praising Marie to Fisker as 'her father's own daughter': 'He vas passionate, and did lose his 'ead; and vas blow'd up vid bigness ... 'E bursted himself, Mr Fisker. 'E vas a great man; but the greater he grew he vas always less and less vise. 'E ate so much that he become too fat to see to eat his vittels ... But M'me'selle—ah, she is different' (747). Revealing the inadequacy of pinning the cause for recurrent economic fluctuations on financial villains, the novel directs its reader's attention instead to forces over which they exercise no control.

With this text, Trollope attempts to escape literary convention, including those concerning his fiction. Sadleir contends that he turned his focus to financial events in London so as not to be dismissed as out-of-date. 'The critics were beginning to contrast his leisured comedies of country manners with the glorious actuality of business ... He was declared to represent a moribund and frumpish Eng[land]' (387). Yet he needed to do more than change the setting and plot from Barsetshire to the City, for, as Kermode remarks, 'In a London that was the world's chief financial market, and for the past twenty years or so habituated to enormous share issues, there was no great novelty in the idea of a

---

[20] Trollope claimed not to have read *Little Dorrit*, and Sadleir, on this basis, dismissed any thought that Trollope had Dickens's novel in mind when writing *The Way We Live Now*. Trollope's claim has subsequently been debunked. See Russell, 150.

big-time swindler.'[21] The conventional baiting of finance was spent, especially in the face of the growing financialization of the British economy; the mythical categories of true and tangible *versus* false, ephemeral and speculative riches were collapsing of their own dead weight, lacking explanatory power. Looking at *The Way We Live Now*, George Levine sees 'no evidence of a struggle to find new ways to get stories told'[22], but I disagree. Understanding phenomena such as high finance required new narratives, new narrative devices, new modes of narration, and a new narrative arc—not the singular catastrophe plotted by Freytag's pyramid but the wave plotted by the business cycle.

High finance emerges as a phenomenon in need of exploration. The novel refuses pre-given meaning by declining to resolve certain questions and instead complicating concepts hitherto thought to be unproblematic. Among all of the conflicting reports, what should the reader believe about Melmotte's wealth and the railway company? The reader, held in suspense as to whether Melmotte will 'pull through,' learns that the 'world at large' is 'inclined' to think he will, although the acute Mr Squercum, the lawyer who doggedly uncovers the forgery of the title deed, firmly believes the opposite. But then the narrator unsettles (without overturning) his supposition: 'Squercum was quite sure that Melmotte was not a falling, but a fallen star—perhaps not giving sufficient credence to the recuperative powers of modern commerce' (570). This noncommittal narrator, although extradiegetic and seemingly omniscient, often makes undependable statements, whether because swayed by gossip or because the narrator passes on another's limited, prejudiced view. When Montague visits Mr Ramsbottom to learn the truth about Melmotte and the railway, the reader only receives hearsay, which in any case is focalized from Montague's standpoint: 'Mr Ramsbottom did not believe in it, nor did Roger Carbury. He himself did not in the least believe in Fisker, and Fisker had originated the railway' (319). Neither Roger Carbury nor Montague possesses a privileged access to truth. The pervasive use of free indirect discourse makes the judgements the reader receives much more unreliable, for it distributes narrative perspective widely while undercutting the truth of the perception, rendering narrative judgements limited rather than true within the terms of the narrative: 'The bloated swindler, the vile City ruffian ... this surfeited sponge of speculation, this crammed commercial cormorant' (184–5). These devastating epithets hurled at Melmotte voice the rage of the debauched Sir Felix that Melmotte should scorn his mercenary proposal of marriage to Marie Melmotte.

As a result, neither the effulgent worship nor bitter condemnations have a ground in anything other than a limited, subjective perspective or other than in rumour. Indeed, rumours precede Melmotte wherever he goes, and the reader first encounters him by way of rumours: 'It was at any rate an established fact that Mr Melmotte had made his wealth in France. He no doubt had

21 Frank Kermode, 'Introduction', *The Way We Live Now*, p. xi.
22 George Levine, *The Realistic Imagination* (Chicago: University of Chicago Press, 1981), 185.

had enormous dealings in other countries, as to which stories were told which must surely have been exaggerated.' The rumours protest ironically for their truthfulness—'an established fact' and 'no doubt'—but then propel themselves towards exaggeration. 'It was said that he had made a railway across Russia, that he provisioned the Southern army in the American civil war, that he had supplied Austria with arms, and had at one time bought up all the iron in England' (31). And the reader discerns how rumours will eventually stalk Melmotte.

By withholding from the reader a touchstone to assess the judgements received, the novel forces a reassessment of assumptions and the discarding of empty conventions. As such, *The Way We Live Now* stands as the first realist novel about finance in the British novel tradition, yet it holds this distinction precariously, for competing tendencies destabilize its realism. The first is the Victorian financial novel, whose conventions it undermines while still partly adhering to them. The second is an embryonic naturalist novel positing social forces over which humans exercise no agency. For all that this novel angrily censures the collapse of standards it also tries to conceptualize the impersonal agency driving financial markets, which not only renders the literary figure of the financial villain obsolete but also displaces the individual moral agent and even human agency. One could argue that dissemination of business cycle theory compels novels to adhere more to the real in their treatment of finance, as villains and poetic justice can hardly be considered hallmarks of realism, yet the individual moral agent is precisely such a hallmark, undeniably so for the Victorian novel. To contend that the individual's abandonment of moral responsibility inflates a speculative bubble coheres with realism. Indeed, this way of regarding economic fluctuations mirrors assumptions about moral action, free will, agency, and causality that underpin literary realism. For this reason, Trollope's realist endeavour to uncover the mechanisms of the business cycle takes this novel curiously close to naturalism, for we hardly expect that in a realist novel impersonal forces, in no way shaped by individuals, would determine their fate.

Nonetheless, Trollope's achievement went unappreciated by both the actual readers of the 1870s, who largely ignored the poorly selling novel, which remained out of print for many years, and by its critics, both then and now. The novel failed to produce its ideal readers. Resuscitated by Sadleir and subsequently appraised as one of Trollope's finest texts, it has since been viewed nearly exclusively as delivering a blistering condemnation of the financial developments of the period and their degrading effects on Victorian society rather than as offering a new understanding of high finance, hence of the way they lived then. The demands of grasping the dynamics and implications of high finance and of the business cycle, I suggest, however, forge a new kind of financial novel.

8

Speculative Fictions and the Fortunes of H. Rider Haggard

Francis O'Gorman

The novels of Henry Rider Haggard (1856–1925) glitter with the possibilities of wealth. Famously, there are diamonds in plenty—but also gold and ivory, other riches of empire. In the *She* novels (*She* (1887), *Ayesha: The Return of She* (1905), and *Wisdom's Daughter* (1923)), the chance of vast prosperity arises for those who could discern the secret of immortality. The man who learned it, Haggard's narrator wildly speculates in *She*, 'could no doubt rule the world. He could accumulate all the wealth in the world, and all the power'.[1] But wealth, and indeed power, is at the same time often decentred in major early tales. Where one plot tendency is towards earthly prosperity, other worthier motives for action usually have precedence. Sir Henry Curtis in *King Solomon's Mines* (1885) is uninterested in wealth when he inaugurates the journey towards the diamond fields but in finding his lost brother. Allan Quatermain is not looking for anything more than financial security (certainly not vast riches) in joining him and, later, barely has a reason other than distraction from grief over his lost son for embarking on the adventure narrated in *Allan Quatermain* (1887). Horace Holly is fulfilling a commitment to a friend in beginning the journey in *She* and has little thought of making his fortune; Leonard wants to obtain money in *The People of the Mist* (1894) but his quest is partly altruistic in that it will restore the fortunes of his family and honour a pledge he made to his departed brother. Likewise, Colonel Quaritch hopes to find a lost fortune in *Colonel Quaritch, V. C.* (1888) so that he can save another family from ruin (and, it is true, marry the daughter). Harmarchis will, certainly, obtain prosperity if he succeeds in acquiring the ancient throne of Egypt in *Cleopatra* (1889) but his first aim is to fulfil the summons of history and restore a legitimate ruler to his kingdom. Rider Haggard's most important early tales give to riches, from the comfortable annual income to the unimaginable prosperity glimpsed at the heart of King Solomon's mines, allure. But the texts also, in many cases, endeavour to avoid

---

[1] H. Rider Haggard, *She* (Oxford: Oxford University Press, 1991), 120. In the absence of a standard edition of Haggard's works, I am obliged to cite a range of editions.

proclaiming money as the first priority of their heroes. At the heart of this duality is, I think, a clue to anxieties in Haggard's life as an author. Making money, especially money that one has not earned by orthodox hard labour, or which is crazily disproportionate *to* one's labour, is a matter that concerns empire and, to borrow a modern formulation, the discourses of gentlemanly capitalism. But, more importantly for my purposes, Haggard's authorial nervousness and sense of the problematic value of his work, commercial and cultural, and its chances of lasting, define those ambivalent financial representations.

Wealth is as captivating in Haggard's early romances as it is decentred. *King Solomon's Mines* was spurred by reading Stevenson's *Treasure Island* (1885) but it has, symptomatically, a sharply different conclusion about the acquisition of treasure (Quatermain comes away with only a handful of the diamonds that are now lost for ever). Yet despite the equivocation about prosperity and where to place it as a motive, Haggard's early tales were at a pragmatic level about the business of making money. Their interest in fortunes, and the difficulties with them, related to an obvious personal situation. Returning from his military and legal career in South Africa, and the unsuccessful attempt at farming on the *veldt*, Rider Haggard took to the law as a reasonably safe source of income for his new wife and family. But writing took more of his time. Haggard held no university degree: his prospects of reaching the high levels of the legal profession were slight. Yet money might be obtained from a runaway success with a book. His first, the non-fiction *Cetawayo and his White Neighbours* (1882), was important but not lucrative. *King Solomon's Mines*, three years later, was both. Appropriately, it began as a bet (that Haggard could write something half as good as *Treasure Island*) and its publication was hedged with a gamble. Cassell's offered him £100 for the copyright or 10 percent royalty on the published price. Haggard initially asked for the down payment: such a sum was large for a man of limited means. But, as he later recalled, a clerk, while Haggard was waiting for his contract to be drawn up, advised him to take the royalties. It might have been a fool's counsel but Haggard followed it and the novel, selling 31,000 copies in the first year in England, transformed his and his family's fortunes in the 1880s, which the publication of *She* confirmed.[2] The story of that financial gamble was a tale Haggard liked to tell and, in a sense, this chapter explores the reasons why he did. Writing afterwards was to be Haggard's principal occupation and primary source of money. Its success, Haggard's career as an author of romance, began with a speculation, a choice between a cheque and an uncertain amount of money. His plots of unpredictable occurrences, dangerous guesses, and improbable turns of fortune were strange echoes of that successful first adventure with the fickle world of literary fortunes.

---

[2] Figures from Morton Cohen, *Rider Haggard: His Life and Works* (London: Hutchinson, 1960), 95.

On the completion of *She*, which Haggard had written at high speed, he took the manuscript to his newly obtained literary agent, A. P. Watt. Throwing down the pages on Watt's desk, he said, he later recalled, 'There is what I shall be remembered by'.[3] Being remembered was different from the attainment of money (though money he needed), and being remembered for a romance, seemingly the transient froth on the surface of serious literature, was an expression of remarkable confidence in the genre's contested place. Haggard had a good deal more to say in public on the value of his chosen medium that made it a worthy vehicle of a writer's legacy. In a feisty article in the *Contemporary Review* for February 1887 (later he judged it unwise), he was starkly explicit about romance's durability. Surveying the amount of fiction published yearly and denouncing 'most of this crude mass' as 'worthless', he claimed instead the value of the well-finished romance as 'perhaps the most difficult art practised by the sons of men'.[4] Such a claim was plainly ridiculous in its pitching of romance against all other forms of late century writing, let alone against all other forms of human labour (with, he curiously notes, the exception of sculpture). Yet the acclamations of 'About Fiction' were, in their intemperate polemic, a hyperbolic expression of the author's real self-assurance—and a nervous sign of something like its opposite.

Looking back in the preface to his autobiography, *The Days of My Life* (1926), Haggard observed, in words not wholly out of temper with his repudiated *Contemporary Review* essay, that the firmest index of a book's value was its capacity to remain a living force among readers. When Father Butler in James Joyce's short story 'An Encounter' (from *Dubliners* (1914)) deplores the Wild West romance Leo Dillon is reading, he calls the man who wrote it doubtless 'some wretched scribbler that writes these things for a drink'.[5] Joyce, not averse to a drink himself, was making fun both of modern romance and over-reactions to it. But Father Butler's response was as distant from Haggard's ambitions as could be. What, Haggard would later reflect in *The Days of My Life*, would futurity make of his work? To what extent had he achieved more than prosperity—more than merely a drink—from the products of his imagination? The answer to his question was modest but certain:

Now, although it may seem much to claim, my belief is that some of my tales *will* live. Possibly this belief is quite erroneous, in which case in years to come I may be laughed at for its expression. It is obvious also that a great deal of what I have written is doomed to swift oblivion, since, even if it were all equally good, in the crowded days that are to come, days even more crowded than our own, posterity will not need much of the work of any individual. If he is remembered at all it will be by but a few books. The present

³ H. Rider Haggard, *The Days of My Life: An Autobiography*, ed. by C. J. Longman, 2 vols (London: Longman, Green, 1926), i. 246.
⁴ H. Rider Haggard, 'About Fiction', *Contemporary Review*, 51 (1887), 172.
⁵ James Joyce, *Dubliners* (London: Grafton, 1917), 17.

question is, What chance have I of being so remembered, and I can only hope that my belief in the vitality of at any rate some of my books may be justified.[6]

The balance of money against memory, the weighting of a fortune while living against a future beyond the grave, seemed answered here. Longevity, perceived as the guarantor of high cultural status long before Leavis made it a requirement for entry into the great tradition, is that now chiefly coveted. 'I can remember', said Walter Besant in his primer for would-be writers *The Pen and the Book* (1899), 'no single instance, in literary history, of the survival of a bad writer'.[7] Rarely at the end of the nineteenth century was the argument between financial prosperity, which Haggard needed, and literary survival, which he understood with Besant as the arch-marker of literary worth, so consequential on the imaginative fabric of a popular author's productions.

When Haggard declared that *She* was the novel by which he would be remembered, he was voicing an ambition that shaped a range of narrative tropes in his early work and which, in different ways, disclosed the peculiar finance-related tensions of his position. Reproducing a letter from Robert Louis Stevenson in *The Days of My Life*, Rider Haggard confessed his bafflement. The letter obviously refers to *King Solomon's Mines* so it must, he remarked, date from that time. But its legal language and its apparent request for a donation to an unspecified cause were, looking back decades later, beyond comprehension. It is, Haggard says, 'an enigma to me. I have not the faintest idea to what it refers.'[8] Why, then, did Haggard bother to publish it in his autobiography? Partly, to be sure, because, at the plainest level, the letter helped re-enforce his reader's sense of Haggard's friendship with the celebrated author of *Treasure Island* and *Kidnapped* (1886). But that letter's presence was also the result of an imaginative reflex, a moment in the autobiography that followed by long habit an impulse from the romances to privilege strange and enigmatic documents. Haggard's early tales find their embarkation points in the meanings of fragmentary papers and a fascination with curious, half readable words was hard to relinquish. The adventure of *King Solomon's Mines* commences after Quatermain's revelation of the map long ago drawn by José da Silvestra, a sparse attempt at cartography, together with the dying words of Silvestra himself, written in his own blood on a rag. The faded fabric of another man's text that has managed to survive three hundred years is the first guide of Curtis, Good, and Quatermain to the marvellous land of the Kukuanas. *She* is inaugurated with the stories that are more or less decipherable from the contents of old Vincey's casket, particularly the so-called sherd of Amenartas, with its strange legend communicated by Leo Vincey's 'remote ancestress'.[9] Old Vincey's letter accompanying the sherd, only a few years old, is itself, symptomatically, like a returning voice from the dead.

---

[6] H. Rider Haggard, *The Days of My Life*, i, p. xxiii.

[7] Walter Besant, *The Pen and the Book* (London: Burleigh, 1899), 35.

[8] Haggard, *The Days of My Life*, i. 236.   [9] H. Rider Haggard, *She*, 45.

'I stretch out my hand to you across the gulf of death', the younger Vincey reads, 'and my voice speaks to you from the unutterable silence of the grave.'[10] Old Vincey's letter, hinting that there is more than silence beyond the tomb, clinches the text's broader interest in forms of human intention that have not been entirely effaced by time.

Early on, taking a step back, Haggard parodied his fascination with documentary survival. The persistence of a man's intentions in a form of writing is the half comic, half satirical plot of *Mr Meeson's Will* (1888). The principal aim of this account of the best-selling author in the nightmare of contemporary literary marketplace is to make a point—it is not a subtle work—about the vampiric relations of publishers with authors. It is a novel that belongs, if only in theme, with George Gissing's *New Grub Street* (1891) and Marie Corelli's *The Sorrows of Satan* (1895). Written alongside the major early romances, the novel relates how the heartless publisher, Mr Meeson, dies on a desert island. In the absence of any other suitable material, the only way in which he can record a codicil to his will, reversing a decision to disinherit his son, is to have it tattooed on the back of Augusta Smithers, his best-selling and most abused author who, coincidentally, happens to have been shipwrecked with him. The novel makes somewhat savage humour out of this transformation of an author into a legal document and satirizes a bleak capitalist plot that sees a large sum of money made *by* authors passed on *through* one but not *to* one.[11] Beyond this, however, the story raises an amused eyebrow at Haggard's own imaginative attraction to the doubtful survival of human intentions in forms of writing. Against all likelihood, Augusta does in fact survive, and she does escape the island; back in the law court at home, the codicil is, unexpectedly, accepted as an authentic document, despite being written on a lady's back. Narrating the survival of an absurdly vulnerable text which seems at first to have little chance of preserving intentions, *Mr Meeson's Will* does, at last, enact the plot of a lucky survival.

The documents of Haggard's early fiction have a habit of lasting, even against the hardest of circumstances, like the manuscript of *Allan Quatermain* that is miraculously conveyed from the land of Zu-Vendis where Sir Henry and Good are permanently inured. Survivals hint at Haggard's mental preoccupation with endurance as a cultural marker of literary worth—but they also reveal his debts. Though the documents are readable as strange yet successful survivals, they are also inseparable from the material base of Haggard's popular fiction and circuit the reader back to the fiscal issues that haunted Haggard's ambitions from the start. Almost inevitably, the fragile indestructible texts are what lead the adventurers to glimpses, or actual possession, of wealth, and their survival often means the recovery not only of lost human intentions but long-hidden

---

[10] Ibid. 27.

[11] It ought to be added that, in fact, the younger Mr Meeson, a man of principle, has long been in love with Augusta, whom he weds at the end. Augusta thereby becomes the beneficiary of her own generosity in allowing the codicil to be written on her body.

riches. Money may not always be the absolute first motives of heroes, but it is conspicuous nevertheless. Silvestra's map is a treasure map, mirroring that acquired by the Jim Hawkins, Dr Livesey, and Squire Trelawney in *Treasure Island*; Augusta Smither's back is marked with a codicil that secures her lover's (and eventually her own) prosperity; the enigmatic paragraph written in Sir James de la Molle's 1611 Bible just before his execution is that which, once understood centuries later, directs the hero to the discovery of long-lost gold, buried in gothic fashion, at the end of *Colonel Quaritch*. These forms of lingering, cryptic texts, setting underway adventures that lead to the sight if not the possession of riches, are expressions of the impulse to make the written word pay; they brightly comment on, and stand as models for, Haggard's novels, which, in narrating adventures, reach out for longevity *and* financial prosperity, for future celebrity and present security.

Documents avoid destruction in Haggard's peculiar worlds—and so do some people. The endurance of a manuscript or a piece of rag suggested, in part, authorial longing about the *terra incognita* of tomorrow, but Haggard's bewitchment with reincarnation was a more sensational element of the same thinking. Yet, like the persistence of documents that were as much related to money as to durability, the reincarnated figures of the early romances were also double. They revealed two sides of another dilemma, related to the broader question of literary value and financial solvency, about writing in the new environment of late Victorian popular fiction, and ways in which the material situation of publishing determined the life of the imagination. Cradled in Haggard's interest in reincarnation and the manner in which history replays its own past was, in the first place, the notion of the indestructibility of a plot. In tension with Haggard's apparent Christianity, this theological fascination suggested a form of endurance that was, prima facie, consolatory. The values of Haggard's Tory imperialism were, as Carolyn Burdett usefully remarks, supplemented by his Theosophical interests and preoccupation with reincarnation. His 'imagined worlds', she says, 'seek to incarnate the past, and to reimpose a world in which authentic hierarchy holds fast against the vulgarizing forces of democracy'.[12] Central to Haggard's interests in immortality was indeed a faith in the preservability of greatness and his books muse admiringly, with a displaced political hope, on the ideally lasting nature of men and women of heroic stature. He helped construct terms which high Modernism would privilege further. But the plots of reincarnation were also in touch with a popular author's abiding ambition about the indestructibility of tales.

She, and its succeeding narratives, concentrated on the returning of Ayesha, She-Who-Must-Be-Obeyed, and the re-performance of her ancient love for

---

[12] Carolyn Burdett, 'Romance, Reincarnation and Rider Haggard' in Nicola Bown, Carolyn Burdett, and Pamela Thurschwell (eds) *The Victorian Supernatural* (Cambridge: Cambridge University Press, 2004), 232.

Kallikrates with its inevitable tragedy. *When the World Shook* (1919) sees the recall to life of Oro and Yva after a quarter of a million years in a crystal tomb. *The Yellow God: An Idol of Africa* (1909) is about an indestructible spirit named Little Bonsa whose powers to deal riches and death are unchangeable through time and are part of a system of religious belief; *King Solomon's Mines* offers Gagool, either a reincarnation or extraordinarily old, who plays out the same role across centuries and is a kind of community memory before she is destroyed; *Wisdom's Daughter* is spoken by the recurring spirit of Ayesha herself, who, in telling the story of her early life, outlines the plot which she is compelled to re-live. 'A story that began more than two thousand years ago', remarks Holly at the end of *She*, 'may stretch a long way into the dim and distant future'.[13] Haggard could have been speaking of aspirations for his own work. The reprise of the past, the robustness of tales, hints at the cyclical nature of Haggard's plots, the returns to the narratives of returns, the recapitulation of that which by nature seeks its own repetition, and the aspiration for a literary legacy that endured into the 'dim and distant future'.

'"Then you think that we live again upon this earth?"' asks Arbuthnot, suggestively, in *When the World Shook* of the resuscitated Lady Yva: '"Again and yet again"', she replies, '"until the time comes for us to leave the earth for ever"'.[14] That 'again and yet again' was a quality Haggard had once ascribed to romance itself as a '[work] of fancy' which appeals, 'not to a class, or a nation, or even to an age, but to all time and humanity at large.'[15] Yet the apparent optimism in the permanence of plots and the lasting nature of romance disguised dissatisfaction with writing for the popular market and one the ways in which that market put in jeopardy literary value and the possibilities of imaginative growth. Just as the fascination with ineradicable stories was consolatory, Haggard's engagement with reincarnation and repetition also echoed with alarm about how romance writing was inclined to become uninventive and that tired reprise was the mark of a popular writer's entrapment by an audience who demanded a reliable commodity 'again and yet again'. Invested with hopes about literary endurance, the interest in permanent stories also disclosed apprehension about inspiration that was impeded not so much by an abstract failing muse but by the publishing conditions in which Haggard materially worked. He made of repetition the substance of a career, but imaginatively it came close to ruining him. Even early this was visible. *Allan Quatermain* re-ran much of *King Solomon's Mines* whose central characters it set again on a journey to a strange land while *Ayesha* proclaimed in its subtitle that it was the *Return of She*, revealing the half-truth that, in its plot repetitions, it was also the 'return of *She*'. *Wisdom's Daughter* re-narrated the foundational tale of Kallikrates and repeated adventures

---

[13] H. Rider Haggard, *She*, 316.

[14] H. Rider Haggard, *When the World Shook: Being an Account of the Great Adventure of Bastin, Bickley and Arbuthnot* (New York: Ballantine, 1978), 286.

[15] H. Rider Haggard, 'About Fiction', 180.

with Leo Vincey while *Allan's Wife* (1889) overlapped with *Allan Quatermain*. *The World's Desire* (1890), written with Andrew Lang, was as much preoccupied with a plot of the return of the dead as any of Haggard's single-authored books (and it was also a more curious form of plot return insofar as it was offered as a palimpsest of the *Odyssey*). Haggard's reincarnational stories figured a relocated hope of the survival of plots but also an anxiety that repetition enfeebled. There is 'no new thing under the sun', Arbuthnot wearily remarks at the beginning of *When the World Shook*, and that 'with certain variations it is the same thing over and over again'.[16] Wryly, Haggard could easily have used the same words to declare that the business of prolific romance writing, the transformation of literary work into a commodity that risked far too much the impoverished narrative *rechauffé*.[17]

The financial circumstances surrounding Haggard's romances, and chiefly the post-Romantic friction between forms of value, enter areas of his imaginative world. Money and fame are agents in the shaping of this writing, and forces which colour its representational fabric: Haggard's romances are in part stories not only *for* but *about* the Victorian popular fiction market. In a critical climate that has recently emphasized the suspicions of high culture writers about the value of popular culture,[18] Haggard's fiction discloses that which is easily forgotten: the imaginative consequences of such suspicion on a writer endeavouring to propose the validity of his own popular form while steeling himself against doubts about it. The relationship between the economic circumstances of Haggard's life and the broader financial culture of the late nineteenth century were more than this, however, and they involved a larger question about why Haggard was so widely read, and a much ampler cultural and fiscal issue about the place of risk, and its representation, in the modernity of the late nineteenth century.

Haggard's novels were predicated on hazard; his heroes were exceptional takers of risks. They spoke, in this respect, to the new domains of empire which offered, at the most superficial level, opportunities for adventure unavailable at home.[19]

---

[16] H. Rider Haggard, *When the World Shook*, 23.

[17] Sometimes Haggard makes a quiet joke of his own lack of imagination. Trying to find a credible start to the adventure narrated in *Allan Quatermain* defeated him, and he offered amusing self-recognition in Good's words, as Good agrees to the adventure: '"I'll go into training at once. By all means let's go to Mount Kenia and the other place with an unpronounceable name, and look for a white race that does not exist. It's all one to me"' (20).

[18] See, for instance, John Carey, *The Intellectuals and the Masses: Pride and Prejudice among the Literary Intelligentsia, 1880–1939* (London: Faber, 1992); Linda Dowling, *The Vulgarization of Art: The Victorians and Aesthetic Democracy* (Charlottesville: University Press of Virginia, 1996); Patrick Brantlinger, *The Reading Lesson: The Threat of Mass Literacy in Nineteenth Century British Fiction* (Bloomington: Indiana University Press, 1998).

[19] Sustained considerations of Haggard and imperial fiction include Wendy R. Katz, *Rider Haggard and the Fiction of Empire: A Critical Study of British Imperial Fiction* (Cambridge: Cambridge University Press, 1987); Joseph Bristow, *Empire Boys: Adventures in a Man's World* (London: Unwin Hyman, 1991); and Laura Chrisman, *Rereading the Imperial Romance: British Imperialism and South African Resistance in Haggard, Schreiner, and Plaatje* (Oxford: Oxford University Press, 2000).

Yet Haggard's fictions are too preoccupied with money, in their local habits and their broader imaginative shapes, to be wholly innocent of financial concerns even in their identity as novels about the outcomes of an enthusiasm for taking chances. My suggestion here is that they can be placed, as novels interested in accident, vulnerability, and luck, in an oblique relationship with a financial practice about which Haggard thought hard and which, for many commentators, helped define the economic identity of late Victorian capitalism: speculation. Read as texts in indirect connection with this practice of high capitalism, as partakers in a shared discoursal environment, Haggard's novels suggest, at the least, a distinctive interchange between late Victorian finance and culture, a creditable instance of the circulation of common patterns of thought between fields centred on the representation and privileging of risk. The romances also, beyond this, implied an unspoken and censored truth about a hazardous element of British fiscal life just as they offered to the *fin de siècle* a new hero—a literary inscription which responded to as much as it helped shape a discourse from the domains of modern wealth acquisition—who was neither producer nor consumer but, triumphantly, adventurer.

Speculation was not, of course, new in the late nineteenth century. But its level so increased in the second half of Victoria's reign that it was for many a marker of modernity, an embodiment for both economists and literary artists of late Victorian capitalism itself. The remembered appeal of the (in many cases temporary) wealth created by the 1840s railway boom, the subsequent development of the stock market, the expansion of joint-stock companies, and legislation on limited liability in the 1850s, in 1862 and 1867, and related acts including the 1879 Companies Act which helped banks deal with limited liability, encouraged wider participation in speculative schemes.[20] Disinflationary pressure played a part too, alongside that critical tendency of legislation to protect, at least to a point, the assets of the speculator and the interests of companies. The results were a growth of speculative ventures and widening public debate about how to regard them. As one contemporary put it in the mid-1870s, there were around him 'floods of new schemes'[21] and the fascination and distaste for speculation, usually carefully distinguished from 'investment',[22] gradually moved to the centre of discussions about the motors of modern economic development at the end of the nineteenth century. The now well-recognized dependency of economic growth on speculative ventures was, in this environment, struggling to

[20] Timothy L. Alborn's *Conceiving Companies: Joint-Stock Politics in Victorian England* (London: Routledge, 1998) is the most important of recent studies of Victorian joint-stock companies. See also Donna Loftus, 'Capital and Community: Limited Liability and Attempts to Democratize the Market in Mid-Nineteenth-century England', *Victorian Studies*, 45 (2002), 93–120.

[21] Anonymous, 'Stockbroking and the Stock Exchange', *Fraser's Magazine*, 14 (1876) reprinted in Mary Poovey (ed.), *The Financial System in Nineteenth-century Britain* (New York; Oxford: Oxford University Press, 2003), 149–73, 151

[22] See David C. Itzkowitz, 'Fair Enterprise or Extravagant Speculation: Investment, Speculation, and Gambling in Victorian England', *Victorian Studies*, 45 (2002), 121–47.

make itself apparent in the face of cultural suspicion which came, not least, from literary representations.

An anonymous writer in 1876 perceived the 'gambling fever which has in recent years more and more pervaded all classes of society'[23] and, in one obvious way, such a business entered literature in the second half of the period in the form of a typical character, the speculator-as-villain, as much deserving of obliquity as the reckless gambler whose identity was habitually imagined as synonymous with his. The fall of Trollope's Ferdinand Lopez in *The Prime Minister* (1875–6) was modern in this respect and a restatement of a censoriously treated figure from diverse Victorian financial representations. Oscar Wilde's *A Woman of No Importance* (1893) was surprising only in making a woman, Mrs Cheveley, the principal player in a financial swindle rather than a man such as Richard Cumberland (in Frank Smedley's *Frank Fairleigh* (1850)) or Merdle (in Charles Dickens's *Little Dorrit* (1855–7)).[24] Abroad, the text that came most grimly to signify the way in which the *tragedy* of the modern was bound up with financial speculation was Zola's *L'Argent* (1891), the eighteenth of the Rougon-Macquart cycle. There, Zola handed to the arch speculator Saccard the potent description of his business at the heart of the contemporary:

Comprenez donc que la spéculation, le jeu est le rouage central, le cœur même, dans une vaste affaire comme la nôtre. Oui! il appelle le sang, il le prend partout par petits ruisseaux, l'amasse, le renvoie en fleuves dans tous les sens, établit une énorme circulation d'argent, qui est la vie même des grandes affaires. Sans lui, les grands mouvements de capitaux, les grands travaux civilisateurs qui en résultent, sont radicalement impossibles ... C'est comme pour les sociétés anonymes, a-t-on assez crié contre elles, a-t-on assez répété qu'elles étaient des tripots et des coupe-gorge! La vérité est que, sans elles, nous n'aurions ni les chemins de fer, ni aucune des énormes entreprises modernes, qui ont renouvelé le monde.[25]

Words like these at the end of the nineteenth century could express sincerely a belief in how a national economy could grow. But Zola's frame of mind was different. With a greater impatience even than his English counterparts—Dickens and Wilde, Ruskin and Trollope—he declined to regard any of speculation's potentially generative power in state economies. Instead, *L'Argent* bitterly revealed

---

[23] Anonymous, 'Stockbroking and the Stock Exchange', reprinted in Poovey (ed.), 159

[24] For an argument about the hidden manner of *The Way We Live Now*'s interrogation of this stereotype, see Tara McGann, 'Literary Realism in the Wake of Business Cycle Theory: *The Way We Live Now* (1875)', above 133–56.

[25] Émile Zola, *L'Argent* (Paris: Gallimard, 1980), 164: 'Understand then that speculation, gambling, is the central wheel, the heart itself, in a vast business such as ours. Yes! it calls the blood, it takes it from everywhere by small brooks, amasses it, sends it back in rivers in all directions, and establishes an enormous circulation of money, which is the very life of great businesses. Without this, the great movements of capital, the great civilizing works that result, are radical impossibilities ... It is the same with joint-stock companies. There has been enough of an outcry against them; it has been repeated enough that they are gambling dens and cut-throat institutions. The truth is that, without them, we should have no railways, nor any of the enormous modern enterprises which have renewed the world' (my translation; ellipses original).

that such apparently appealing words existed in modernity only as a temptation and deadly rhetorical trap. Saccard's discourse of a European nation's economic progress was only conceivable as a cover for financial deception and a language built over the crevasses of disaster.

Henry Rider Haggard knew what it meant to speculate. He had once tried a small business venture himself and later he speculated, as even Marx did, in the stock exchange. On the eve of his marriage, Haggard had raised funds for a plan to rear ostriches close to Newcastle, two hundred miles outside Pretoria. His brother, hearing of the attractive financial possibilities, declared that the 'speculation is a thoroughly sound one'—but he turned out to be wrong.[26] Haggard, recovering, remained intrigued by the possibilities of what might be won and lost in speculative ventures but this time only as a shareholder. Such speculating was despite the fact that his family history provided him with discouragement: Haggard's father had lost a substantial portion of his wife's money on marriage by putting it into land, as Haggard later said, 'just at the commencement of its great fall in value'.[27] It was a melancholy history that lay behind the narrative of failing land prices and the miraculous discovery of lost family fortune in the story of wise and unwise investment, *Colonel Quaritch, V. C.* Returning to England from Egypt in 1888, Haggard found himself tempted by the stock exchange and put at jeopardy some of his new-found prosperity—from *King Solomon* and *She*—in up-and-coming London schemes. But, as he remarked later, 'the investments suggested by kind friends connected with the City were apt to prove disappointing'.[28] The 'kind' was not unequivocal.

Haggard's fiction involved literal plots of speculation as he registered and analysed the prominence of this financial activity in the modern world. He was, superficially, not inclined to critique the familiar trope of the speculator–villain which had appealed widely elsewhere and to which D. Morier Evans had given such monumental support in his *Facts, Failures & Frauds: Revelations Financial Mercantile Criminal* (1859).[29] The most extensive literal speculation plot in Haggard's early fiction was the strange mixture of pantomimic comedy, financial analysis, and supernatural adventure, *The Yellow God: An Idol of Africa*, a novel which looked squarely at the speculators who, as Zola would have it, thought themselves at the heart of '[*les*] *énormes entreprises modernes*'.[30] Sir Robert Aylward and the aptly-named Mr Champers-Haswell are London speculators on the verge

[26] Quoted in Cohen, *Rider Haggard: His Life and Works*, 53.

[27] H. Rider Haggard, *The Days of My Life*, i. 27.

[28] Ibid. i. 250. It was accidental but nonetheless appropriate that Haggard should have been returning from Egypt at this point for, in the mid-1870s, the country had become associated precisely with the sort of financial jeopardy that Haggard was about to experience on a small scale, thanks to what England regarded as the Khedive's disastrous fiscal imprudence.

[29] D. Morier Evans (1819–74), financial journalist and historian of financial panics.

[30] For other speculators in Haggard, see, for instance, the failed speculation in Chapter VIII of *Beatrice: A Novel* (London: Longmans, Green, 1890) and the decline of Sir Junius into failed speculations in the Quatermain story, *The Ivory Child* (London: Cassell, 1916).

of a duplicitous scheme called 'Sahara Limited' which will be the glory of their career and the ruin of others. Their business partner, Alan Vernon, dislikes the plan and is particularly appalled by Haswell's indifference to the investing public—'the speculative parson, and the maiden lady who likes a flutter' who are the 'props of modern enterprise'[31]—and the money they will ultimately lose. Vernon abandons it but, unfortunately, happens to be engaged to marry Barbara, Haswell's niece. While she regards her uncle and Sir Robert as 'no better than thieves',[32] her lover's resignation leaves them without enough money on which to marry.

The plot then changes country and, after noting the apparent success of the Sahara scheme—'Sir Robert and my uncle have made millions', Barbara remarks, 'I wonder how long they will keep them'[33]—recounts the half comic adventures of Alan and his manservant Jeekie. In West Africa, they endeavour to make Alan's fortune by what the novel encourages its reader to see as more legitimate means than financial speculation. Alan eventually comes away, following some supernatural adventures, with fifty-three cases of gold—given to him rather than stolen, at least—which, together with a necklace, provide him with £100,000. It is enough, he notes laconically of such a huge sum, 'to begin our married life upon'.[34] By this stage, the expected 'fearful smash'[35] of the Sahara scheme has occurred: its victims are many, not least because it precipitates a fatal heart attack for Barbara's uncle. The novel sets side by side the relatively laborious activity of making money by risky African exploration and the attempt to procure wealth by even more risky speculation and asks its reader to be in no doubt about which deserves approval.

The Yellow God, with a near-theological belief in earned reward, looks askance at the business of speculation and deploys the familiar trope of the speculator–scoundrel. Yet that does not constitute the whole picture of the relationship between Haggard's early fiction and practices of financial speculation. His romances more widely shared with contemporary and high-profile fiscal activity a fascination with the yields of risk and the profits which may come from playing substantial odds. Cultural and literary critics are familiar with the explanatory power and the limits of George Levine's notion of 'one culture' in relation to Victorian imaginative writing and science, and there are obvious objections to invoking such a model for the relationship between forms of Victorian fiction and the more recondite narrative paradigms of high finance. Yet ideas about speculation moved in prominent and visible locations—journals, musical halls, newspapers, popular novels—and not merely in the elite, inaccessible spaces of the City and they left, unexpectedly, more creative marks on responsive, contemporary imaginative textures than merely negative representations of swindlers. Haggard's writing, musing on the nature of jeopardy and the

---

[31] H. Rider Haggard, *The Yellow God: An Idol of Africa* (London: Cassell, 1911, reset 1919), 16.
[32] Ibid. 47.   [33] Ibid. 88.   [34] Ibid. 241.   [35] Ibid. 226.

precarious adventures of financial obtainment, was—even as it tried to make money secondary to more noble motives—in contact with the culture of financial speculation as it struggled to articulate its national advantage at the end of the nineteenth century. Haggard's work transacted with its discourses in more engaging ways than the irritation of *The Yellow God* suggests. His romances may not belong in any generalist 'one culture' of finance and popular fiction, but the tales share in a contemporary fascination, a conceptual privileging, that was a recognizable currency between the two. The texts opened up a space in which the motivations, the hidden appeals of profiting from a willingness to take risks, were, despite Haggard's disapproval in *The Yellow God*, glimpsed in a relocated but identifiable way; they were fictional narratives that belonged in, as they helped created, an environment intrigued by the revenues of danger.

The central motor of Haggard's plot excitement—and his plots are far more excitable than those of their most prominent predecessors such as Frederick Marryat (1792–1848), Charles Kingsley (1819–75), R. M. Ballantyne (1825–94), and R. D. Blackmore (1825–1900),—is the tense guess against the future: a question of whether heroes will succeed even as the reader knows they will. Page-turning apprehension is their essence; adventure with the improbable hope of success their impulse. Can heroes make it across a waterless desert, or leap an apparently impossible gap, or survive a terrible fall into a ravine, or fight successfully against an army of overwhelming odds, or escape from what looks like an entirely sealed cave, or survive encounters with the supernatural? The reader's experience, enthralled by the narrative dynamic of spectacular gambles in harm's way, is one of pleasing anxiety which resolves almost always into triumph as if the texts were protected by a kind of aesthetic limited liability. Observing gambles, the reader is invited to experience something like a gambler's pleasure aestheticized while being safe in the knowledge that the odds are stacked entirely in his or her favour. Risk's pleasurable transformation into reward—both literal rewards for the heroes and the reader's reward of pleasure—is at the heart of Haggard's literary mode. As such his romances offer a distinctive version of the cognate privileging of the precarious that was claiming, in a different location, to be newly necessary in the growth of modern economies.

The most substantial recent work on Victorian representations of risk contests the commonplace assumption—represented by Anthony Giddens, Niklas Luhmann, Marshall Berman[36]—that modernity is defined by a unique acceptance of the continual presence of hazard. Elaine Freedgood argues that 'the "modern" attitude to risk is distinguished from past attitudes more by its strategies of containment than by a new acceptance of the inevitability of risk'.[37] *Pleasure* in Victorian accounts of risk-taking, Freedgood continues, must in turn be signed,

---

[36] See 'Selected Bibliography'.
[37] Elaine Freedgood, *Victorian Writing About Risk: Imagining a Safe England in a Dangerous World*' Cambridge Studies in Nineteenth-century Literature and Culture (Cambridge: Cambridge University Press, 2000), 2.

in imaginative and non-fictional prose, as dangerous because pain has to be given the last word, 'ensuring that risk takers, in fiction and in the culture at large, are morally entitled to their rewards'.[38] While this may be an apt description of the texts of early Victorian political economy, mountain climbing, ballooning, and African exploration that Freedgood examines, it is importantly not the case for the scenes of jeopardy in Haggard's writing and his transformation of peril into narrative reward. Haggard's work suggests a feature of risk that Freedgood's thesis cannot countenance. The refusal to privilege pain in the activities of the venturesome and in the reader's experience of romance constitutes both a fundamental description of the adventure genre in Haggard's hands and, at the end of the Victorian period, a hint of a culturally censored element in narratives of speculation.[39]

Risk for Haggard is constructed in a way that ensures things will usually work out, but more prominently in a manner that celebrates and encourages, *pace* Freedgood, a readerly enthusiasm for, an addiction to, the chancy. Reading Haggard at his best, before the repeated plot formulae bled him of much of his power, is to experience in gratifying form the tensions of something like a gamble on the turns of fortune. A tense moment in *Eric Brighteyes* (1891) as the hero is caught in a turbulent river—'A fathom from him was the corner of Sheep-saddle. If he may grasp it, all is well; if not, he dies'[40]—is a basic unit of suspense for countless repetitions and variations. These romances offer simultaneously a consoling alternative to the histories of precarious financial speculation because things are inclined to work out. But they also make enthralling the experience of jeopardy, which, in another field, in other ways, high finance increasingly knew it needed however much it was still far from publicly celebrating the 'appetite for risk'[41] in the exultant manner of Peter Bernstein's late twentieth-century account of speculation as the engine room of economies in *Against the Gods: The Remarkable Story of Risk* (1996). Haggard's tales of 'very venturesome people',[42] nonetheless, allowed the pleasures of that appetite to slip momentarily through cultural barriers in traditional nineteenth-century representations of 'the rotary motion of Dame Fortune's wheel', as D. Morier Evans called the money markets,[43] and to appear in the undercurrents of popular fiction.

Critics and historians have explored in detail the emergence of consumer culture in late Victorian England: the societal cartography of Walter Benjamin's

---

[38] Freedgood, *Victorian Writing About Risk*, 96.

[39] On more general issues of narrative fiction and the reader's experience as like that of a gambler, see Gillian Beer, 'The Reader's Wager: Lots, Sorts and Futures', *Essays in Criticism*, 40 (1990), 99–123; reprinted in Beer, *Open Fields: Science in Cultural Encounter* (Oxford: Clarendon Press, 1995), 273–294.

[40] H. Rider Haggard, *Eric Brighteyes* (London: Longman, Green, 1916), 33

[41] Peter Bernstein, *Against the Gods: The Remarkable Story of Risk* (New York: Wiley 1996), 105.

[42] H. Rider Haggard, *Allan Quatermain*, 51.

[43] D. Morier Evans, *Speculative Notes and Notes on Speculation: Ideal and Real*, Reprints of Economic Classics (1864; New York: Kelley, 1969), 51.

Charles Baudelaire: Ein Lyriker im Zeitalter des Hochkapitalismus (1955) continued to be significant for studies by, for instance, David Amigoni, Rachel Bowlby, Geoffrey Crossick and Serge Jaumain, Regenia Gagnier, and Erika Diane Rappaport.[44] The consumer figure, whether the literal shopper in the new(ish) department store or the Paterian aesthete figuratively consuming the experience of art, have become familiar terms of late Victorian studies. But Rider Haggard offers, I suggest, the outlines of a different kind of economic identity at the end of the century which has been occluded not only by the emphasis on the consumer but also by the more local consideration of Haggard's romances in terms of imperial subjectivities.[45] The heroes of his tales are neither easily recognized as consumers (unless it be that they 'consume' excitement) nor fully as producers (unless in the sense that they 'produce' excitement). More or less excluded from both these two major terms of nineteenth-century economic analysis, they are, rather, quintessential adventurers—men who risk themselves and their possessions in the hope of reward. As such they are both fantasies of masculinity and simulacra of a different sort of modern economic man. With heroes animated by desire for rewards which are the result not of traditional productive labour but of the readiness to take risks, Haggard's novels salute the adventurer and allow a glimpse of that thrilling element of risk-taking that was hard to disclose in the Victorian period. Haggard's romances are enthralled by, and allow the reader to feel a little of the pulse provided by, the act of gambling and in so doing they turn into fictional pleasure an underlying narrative of the speculator's experience.

Rider Haggard called Chapter X of *She* 'Speculations' and the title referred to Holly's philosophical reflections on how much man should know about the future. But Haggard's early fiction was in a layered relationship with a different sort of speculative culture at the close of the Victorian period. Offering momentary

---

[44] See David Amigoni, 'Sincerity in Every Department? Masks, Masculinity, and Market Forces in Eighteenth-century English Men of Letters' in Francis O'Gorman and Katherine Turner (eds), *The Victorians and the Eighteenth Century: Reassessing the Tradition* (Aldershot: Ashgate, 2004), 182–202; Rachel Bowlby, *Just Looking: Consumer Culture in Dreiser, Gissing and Zola* (London: Methuen, 1985); Geoffrey Crossick and Serge Jaumain (eds), *Cathedrals of Consumption: The European Department Store, 1850–1939* (Aldershot: Ashgate, 1999); Regenia Gagnier, *Idylls of the Marketplace: Oscar Wilde and the Victorian Public* (Stanford, CA: Stanford University Press, 1986) and *The Insatiability of Human Wants: Economics and Aesthetics in Market Society* (Chicago: University of Chicago Press, 2000); Erika Diane Rappaport, *Shopping for Pleasure: Women in the Making of London's West End* (Princeton, NJ: Princeton University Press, 2000).

[45] Influential in the recent investigations of Haggard and imperialism has been Joseph Bristow's *Empire Boys: Adventures in a Man's World* (London: Unwin Hyman, 1991), a book with much to offer but which is a little heavy-handed in its reading of racial and sexual politics in Haggard's fiction: *Empire Boys* implicitly supports the problematic view that Haggard's popular romances are ideologically unitary and that complications are not their business. See also Wendy R. Katz, *Rider Haggard and the Fiction of Empire: A Critical Study of British Imperial Fiction* (Cambridge: Cambridge University Press, 1987) and Laura Chrisman, *Rereading the Imperial Romance: British Imperialism and South African Resistance in Haggard, Schreiner, and Plaatje* (Oxford: Oxford University Press, 2000).

and subversive disclosure of the lure that could not be easily associated with chance and luck in the moral programmes of Victorian representations; providing a tempting mirror image of risk-taking by ensuring that profit was always secured; finding it impossible, at the same time, to do without rebuking the actual speculator as a scoundrel and unprincipled gambler destined to fail: Haggard's novels occupy a strikingly multiple position in accounts of the relationship between high capitalism and literature in the late nineteenth century. Haggard's fiction silently transformed speculation's narratives into aesthetic delight even while, at the level of plot, loudly censoring its workings. In such ambivalence, the modern reader may glimpse a faultline in late Victorian capitalism as the moralizing discourses of the past, and the literary representations they sustained, began—uncomfortably, ambivalently—to recognize the cautious claims of a new and potentially vibrant financial energy.

Playing out aspirations for cultural longevity and hope for financial reward in his romances, Haggard offered his readers—even in fiction that was itself a commodity needing to be consumed—heroes, 'adventurers to the backbone',[46] who constituted an alternative to the consumerist subjectivities conspicuous on the High Street and in the high culture aesthetic theories of the *fin de siècle*. Speculation, even by Haggard's own account, was, from the beginning, bound up with his literary success in that gamble over the future of *King Solomon's Mines*. At the very close of his career, he was still banking on his work's future performance only now exclusively in terms of cultural return, speculating, in connection with the literary reward of longevity, that 'some of my tales *will* live'. Always interested in speculation, Rider Haggard's work constitutes, apart from anything else, a remarkable covert and complicated transaction between the popular literary imagination at the end of the century and the emerging temper of the City. H. G. Wells satirized the 'romance of modern commerce'[47] in *Tono-Bungay* (1909), a novel explicitly impatient with the deceptions of consumerism. But Rider Haggard's fiction, looking at a different feature of financial modernity, offered a more unexpected way of glimpsing, with its tales of venturesome heroes and the rewards of risk, not only the excitement of imperial exploit but the secret romance of the another form of economic man who was beginning to make claims—such as those which Zola severely rebuked—for his lively role in the development of the modern capitalist system.

---

46 H. Rider Haggard, *Allan Quatermain*, 51.
47 H. G. Wells, *Tono-Bungay* (London: Collins, 1953), 141

9

Cultural versus Financial Capital: Defining Literary Value at the *Fin de Siècle*

Josephine M. Guy

Oscar Wilde's biting definition of a cynic in *Lady Windermere's Fan* (1892) as someone who knows 'the price of everything and the value of nothing' could also stand as one of the most pithy comments on the opposition between art and capital.[1] Yet the relationship between literature and money in Wilde's own career was both intimate and formative, for ironically it was the art industry which was Wilde's main source of income. Moreover, his favourite past-time, what he called in *De Profundis* 'feasting with panthers', turned out to be exceptionally expensive, involving a dissipated and extravagant lover, luxury hotels, costly gifts, sexual tourism in the Mediterranean, frequent travel, and (eventually) lawyers' fees and bankruptcy. The purist attitude towards creativity which Wilde so often celebrated in his critical essays was thus not one which he could afford to adopt in his own life: he had to make art that would sell, and sell well. Price mattered to Wilde: in his negotiations with publishers he invariably argued for his works to be priced as highly as possible, and in so doing his principal aims were to increase his royalties and mark off his books as expensive art-objects in themselves.[2] The question which I wish to explore in this chapter, one which the details of Wilde's career so usefully focus, is whether a recognition of the economic dimensions of late nineteenth-century literary production—that is, of the financial transactions inevitably involved in bringing literature into the public domain—affects our understanding and more particularly our evaluation of the literary value of particular works. To put this question even more simply: how does the knowledge that, say, *The Importance of Being Earnest* was a written for the commercial West End theatre at a time when Wilde was technically almost bankrupt and was negotiating hard to obtain the highest royalties, bear on our

---

[1] Oscar Wilde, *Lady Windermere's Fan*, ed. Ian Small (London: Black, 1999), 67.

[2] This aspect of Wilde's career is explored more fully in Josephine M. Guy and Ian Small, *Oscar Wilde's Profession: Writing and the Culture Industry in the Late Nineteenth Century* (Oxford: Oxford University Press, 2000). The extent of Wilde's 'sexual tourism' was recently laid bare in Neil McKenna's provocative and revisionist biography *The Secret Life of Oscar Wilde* (London: Century, 2003).

appreciation of that play today? More abstractly, perhaps, can such information *ever* form part of our judgements about a work's literary value? It will be easier to understand the force of this last question by examining the ways in which an interest in the economics of late nineteenth-century literary production has developed in recent years.

Seeing literary works as material objects whose value can be understood—at least in part—in relation to the ways in which they are produced and consumed is not in itself a particularly new activity: Marxist critics would probably claim that it has long been one of their central concerns, and it is now commonplace to argue for a connection between, say, the commercial interests of nineteenth-century literary institutions such as circulating libraries and the conservatism (both formal and ideological) of much of the realist fiction written specifically for them. What *is* new, though, is the kind of scrutiny to which the late nineteenth-century literary market is now being subjected, particularly by historians of the book trade. The interests of these historians are often quite at odds with those of literary historians, and recently (and perhaps most significantly) their work has begun to produce a new vocabulary and a new set of concepts for understanding late nineteenth-century literary production. So the 'old' Marxist model of literature, which was broadly speaking divided between that which appealed either to a mass or an elite readership (and the politics underlying that division), has given way to what has been termed 'cross-over' fiction, works which addressed both popular and 'high' taste simultaneously, as authors attempted to maximize both cultural and financial capital. We are now encouraged to see all late nineteenth-century literary works (even those of the most rarefied tastes) as being the product of market forces, aspects in the early development of what is now termed a 'consumer culture', that culture where everything had its price, where literature was just another commodity, and where success in selling one's work in an ever more complex and diverse market place can be much more tellingly described as a form of literary professionalism.[3]

---

[3] It is worth noting in passing here that terms such as 'consumerism' and 'commodity culture' have begun to appear in accounts not just of the late nineteenth-century literary market (where most economic historians would place them), but also those of the eighteenth century (and, on occasions, of even early periods of literary history): mass popular publishing clearly means different things to different historians. As James Raven has argued, it is certainly the case that there had been a late eighteenth-century commercial revolution in publishing, with a 'take-off' in publication totals from the 1740s reflecting an expansion in distribution networks and increased institutional demand. But these developments were of a different order to the transformations in printing capacity that took place in the 1820s and 1870s, and which were driven by technological advances, improvements in transport, and cheaper raw materials. It has been estimated, for example, that between 1846 and 1916 the volume of publications quadrupled while the average price of books was halved; and it was the economics of this level of production which fuelled the fast turn-over of titles, aggressive selling techniques, and immense print-runs associated with late nineteenth-century consumerism. It is thus important to maintain this distinction between late nineteenth-century and earlier forms of what is called consumerism. See James Raven, *The Commercialization of the Book: Booksellers*

An interest in the development of professional authorship has in its turn generated an investigation into the mechanisms and institutions of publishing. This has produced a virtual roll-call of agents and agencies affecting literary culture. The list includes phenomena such as the introduction of royalty payments, the net book agreement, developments in copyright law (particularly the 1891 Chace Act), the growth and diversification of publishing houses and changes in their management (such as the conversion in the 1880s and 1890s of private or family-owned businesses into limited-liability or joint-stock companies), the 'rise' of the literary agent, and the influence of trade journals such as *The Bookman*. It is argued that all of these had significant influences on late nineteenth-century literary production because they brought about fundamental changes in the relationships between writers, makers, and sellers of books.[4] More particularly, and in distinction to many Marxist influenced histories, there has been an acknowledgement that some happy consequences flowed from the particular disciplines which the market enforced, that the decisions of publishing-house readers, periodical editors, and actor–managers—all of whom have traditionally been considered as possessing a censoring role, one which curtailed authorial creativity—could have had a positive influence, restraining self-indulgence and prolixity.

Running parallel to this new historiography there has been, of course, a continuing interest in reading late nineteenth-century literary works in terms of their engagement with contemporary ideologies of class, race, gender, and especially of capitalism; of valuing those works in relation to what Jonathan Rose has referred to as their 'adversarial' role.[5] However, this stress on the political function of literary representation, on its potential to act as a form of cultural critique—what Terry Eagleton once rather pompously if vainly referred to as 'human emancipation'[6] —is not at all easy to reconcile with a recognition of the commercial nature of the late nineteenth-century publishing industry, and of the constraints as well as the opportunities which participation in the literary market inevitably imposed on writers. It is perhaps worth reminding ourselves here that, as book-historians such as James Nelson have demonstrated, even those small-scale, minority publishers (such as, say, John Lane or Leonard Smithers) who seemed to encourage the kind of *risqué* works turned down by

---

and the Commodification of Literature in Britain, 1450–1900 (Cambridge: Cambridge University Press, 2005) and Alexis Weedon, *Victorian Publishing: The Economics of Book Production for a Mass Market, 1836–1916* (Aldershot: Ashgate, 2003).

[4] A cogent overview of many of these developments in nineteenth-century publishing can be found in James Raven's 'The Promotion and Constraints of Knowledge: The Changing Structure of Publishing in Victorian Britain', in Martin Daunton (ed.), *The Organisation of Knowledge in Victorian Britain* (Oxford: Oxford University Press, 2005), 263–86.

[5] Jonathan Rose, 'Was Capitalism Good for Victorian Literature?', *Victorian Studies*, 46 (2004), 489–501.

[6] He made this case most forcefully in his popular *Literary Theory: An Introduction* (Oxford: Blackwell, 1983).

more commercial houses like Macmillan or Chapman and Hall, still had to make
money. They did so by trading explicitly on the higher prices which a work's
rarity (or 'naughtiness') could demand. So elitism, far from signifying a rejection
of market values, might be better interpreted as just another strategy for exploiting
them.[7] There have also been studies which have shown that arch-modernists like
Conrad, who have traditionally been thought to have held themselves aloof from
the market, from what Wilde termed 'trafficking their wares', were in practice
shrewd literary entrepreneurs, carefully placing their works in order to maximize
their income.[8]

Surprisingly, perhaps, this tension between attending to the economic aspects
of literary works on the one hand, and to their political functions on the other,
has only recently begun to surface. As I will argue, it is particularly glaring in
the case of accounts of Oscar Wilde, for it seems to produce quite incompatible
explanations of his motives and purposes as an author: one kind of historiography
emphasizes the subversive qualities of his work and his standing as an oppositional
writer; the other shows him to have been deeply implicated in the very values
which it is claimed he is criticizing. In this last view, to be too critical of the
culture industry would have involved biting the hand that was feeding him so
lavishly. That this consequence matters more for Wilde than for some other late
nineteenth-century authors derives from the fact that his biography has had, and
continues to have, a particularly tenacious hold on readers' imaginations. It is
virtually impossible, even for the most strictly formalist of critics, to see in Wilde's
works only text, for any talk of his 'intentions', even if the critic means only the
manifest intentions of an implied author, inevitably invokes the spectre of the
'real' man. This in turn might also explain why modern appreciations of Wilde's
writing are so frequently based on exhibiting and stressing its adversarial qualities.
The question which is overlooked here is whether predicating a different or more
complex intention behind his works (that Wilde wished to make money from
his writing just as much as wished to 'épater les bourgeois') changes the way we
interpret and evaluate them.

The failure to address this issue has been largely because histories which attend
to the material aspects of literary production—to detailing the transactions
of publishing houses, the costs of book production and sales, the contractual
arrangements between authors, publishers, and printers, and so forth—almost
never focus on critical interpretation. By the same token, the critic concerned
with the way works replicate or interrogate contemporary ideologies is unlikely

[7] See, for example, Nelson's *The Early Nineties: A View from the Bodley Head* (Cambridge,
Mass: Harvard University Press, 1971), and his two later works: *Elkin Mathews: Publisher to Yeats,
Joyce, Pound* (Madison, Wis.: University of Wisconsin Press, 1989) and *Publisher to the Decadents:
Leonard Smithers in the Careers of Beardsley, Wilde, Dowson* (University Park: Pennsylvania State
University Press, 2000).

[8] See, for example, Peter D. McDonald, *British Literary Culture and Publishing Practice,
1880–1914* (Cambridge: Cambridge University Press, 1997).

to be familiar with the empirical data which concern historians of the book, the sort of information which Wendell Harris has laconically described as 'the driest of facts'.[9] A better way of identifying this difference might be to say that a great deal of recent research into the economics of the late nineteenth-century literary publishing industry presupposes the agency of authors in creating works, even if it is to explain how that agency is compromised, curtailed, or superseded by the interests of other agents, such as publishers or readers. By contrast many currently fashionable modes of critical interpretation tend to marginalize the concept of authorial agency in favour of linguistic or formalist models of textuality. They seem to have relatively little time for the idea that information about the 'real' author as 'historical-person' can be relevant to what is said about the implied author, or how we construct a concept of an implied author from the text, even when (as in the case of most readings of Wilde's works) a pre-existing and virtually ineradicable conception of the real author is quite clearly informing the notion of the implied author.

These observations prompt a number of further questions: the first is whether 'economic' and 'political' understandings of literary works *need* to be brought more closely together. After all, it has long been a tradition in English Studies for different paradigms of literary interpretation and historiography, with their different ways of understanding text, to pursue their activities side by side, even though they produce radically incompatible explanations of the same work. Moreover, although for some this theoretical pluralism has been an indication of disciplinary weakness, for others it has been a cause for celebration, testimony to the intellectual vibrancy and diversity of the discipline. A second question, then, is what exactly is to be accomplished by an accommodation of the economic and the political? Can the information provided by historians of the book enrich our appreciation of the literary qualities of particular works, rather than simply help us to understand their place within a publishing history, or within a history of taste? Establishing connections between the economics of literary production and *nineteenth-century* definitions of literary value is a relatively straightforward task, even if it is also a relatively unimportant one for establishing grounds for our appreciation of late nineteenth-century literary works today. For example, the anxieties about mass taste that are so common in *fin de siècle* critical discourses are self-evidently a consequence of mass popular publishing. As Samuel Smiles disarmingly put it in his 1891 memoir of the publisher John Murray: 'Cheap bookselling, the characteristic of the age ... has been accompanied by a distinct deterioration in the taste and industry of the general reader. The multiplication of Reviews, Magazines, manuals, and abstracts, has impaired the love of, and perhaps the capacity for study, research,

---

[9] Harris used this term (and others, such as 'unglamorous') in a review article (in *Victorian Studies*, 40 [2003], 88–91) when commenting on the kind of research undertaken for books like *Oscar Wilde's Profession*.

and scholarship on which the general quality of literature must depend'.[10] Regardless as to how one interprets Smiles's comments (as evidence of snobbery, nostalgia, or, perhaps, of plain common-sense), they have no *necessary* relationship with a modern reader's appreciation of what is perceived as the literary qualities of the self-same works, a circumstance which we can see clearly by briefly considering some of the general ways in which this new understanding of the late nineteenth-century literary market place is being used to enable a re-assessment of the canon.

The most obvious consequence of a recognition of the inevitably commercial nature of late nineteenth-century literary production is that it provides new grounds for assessing the careers of writers of popular fiction, a category which (in the nineteenth century) often includes women writers.[11] Thus figures such as Marie Corelli and Ouida, for many years routinely dismissed for the derivative and formulaic qualities of their work, and their often reactionary politics, can now be celebrated for their entrepreneurial skills and commercial acumen, for their ability to recognize and exploit changes in the nineteenth-century literary market place. The near-unanimous contempt with which their 'best-sellers' were treated by contemporary critics—their novels generated some of the most negative notices received by any writer as reviewers gleefully listed the factual errors in their over-exuberant prose—all of this can be dismissed by some as a form of professional 'jealousy'.[12] Such an approach is in marked contrast with earlier revaluations of popular fiction which tended to require scholars to demonstrate that works contrived to entertain a mass audience could nevertheless possess a subversive or 'adversarial' element, even if it was one not necessarily appreciated by contemporary readers, nor fully realized in the work itself. And in this way the contrast between the politics of 'popular' works and their canonical cousins tended to be eroded. So, for example, Marlene Tromp explains how Mary Elizabeth Braddon's 'astoundingly popular' *Aurora Floyd* (1863) 'indirectly' exposes the tensions underlying attitudes towards female aggression

---

[10] Samuel Smiles, *A Publisher and His Friends: Memoir and Correspondence of the Late John Murray*, 2 vols (London: Murray, 1891), ii. 56–7; quoted in Raven, 'The Promotion and Constraints of Knowledge', 264.

[11] It is perhaps worth noting in passing here the subtle influence of this historiography on our view of writers who did not sell well. So it is probably no accident that two recent fictionalized treatments of the life of Henry James—Colm Tóibín's *The Master* and, more particularly, David Lodge's *Author, Author*—take as a central motif the dismal and, for James, traumatizing reception of *Guy Domville*, his abortive attempt to write for popular West End theatre audiences.

[12] Talia Schaffer, for example, refers to Ouida's 'jealous critics' in her account of the novelist in Chapter IV of *The Forgotten Female Aesthetes: Literary Culture and Late-Victorian England* (Charlottesville and London: University Press of Virginia, 2000), 123; see also Annette R. Federico, *Idol of Suburbia: Marie Corelli and Late-Victorian Culture* (Charlottesville and London: University Press of Virginia, 2000). It is perhaps worth drawing attention here to the awareness paid to publishing history, and to its economics, in the University Press of Virginia's 'Victorian Literature and Culture Series'—a circumstance which in turn relates to the interests of one of its general editors, Jerome J. McGann.

in contemporary debates about the Contagious Diseases Acts.[13] What we should notice here is the way in which an attention to a writer's professionalism can redirect questions about the politics of literary representation to that of the politics of a writer's engagement with the literary establishment: so Ouida and Corelli can be championed not so much because of any radicalism in their works, nor for the quality of their writing, but rather for the tenacity with which they battled with an upper middle-class, male-dominated, literary-critical industry, and thus (by implication) challenged that interest group (including dear old Samuel Smiles) who had most agency in defining literary taste.

Refreshing though these sorts of reappraisals might be, they possess an obvious limitation: it is one which brings into stark relief the contrast between the kind of literary history constructed by historians of the book and the interests of many literary critics. Admiring Ouida's astute understanding of the marketplace, and her dogged determination (like that of Corelli) to be taken seriously as—to use Talia Shaffer's term—'a producer of "art"',[14] will not necessarily stimulate anyone to read her works a century or more later (except perhaps for historical reasons). Such information, that is, provides neither necessary nor sufficient grounds for a modern appreciation of Ouida's work, except as a historical phenomenon. On the contrary, and as I have hinted, there is a danger that attending to a writer's professionalism, to his or her ability to 'sell', can also be a way of avoiding or deflecting judgements about literary value. So recognizing that there may have been an element of class and gender prejudice in contemporary reviewers' criticisms of Ouida's tremendously popular representations of aristocratic lifestyles does not make a work such as *Under Two Flags* any 'better', when 'better' is understood in relation to the tastes of the modern reader. Shaffer may be correct in supposing that it was 'positively offensive for a single woman from a provincial town to invent the sayings and doings of European royalty', but so what? Those sayings and doings *were* largely invented, and those inventions (particularly when they involved spoken French) were laughably inaccurate.[15] Here a critical judgement is being avoided by eliding

---

[13] Marlene Tromp, *The Private Rod: Marital Violence, Sensation, and the Law in Victorian Britain* (Charlottesville and London: University Press of Virginia, 2000), 103–52.

[14] See Schaffer, 123.

[15] Ibid. 123, 152. To be fair to Schaffer, her willingness to applaud a writer who could appeal to 'mass-cultural consumers', especially when those consumers were middle-class women, is not the sole, nor even the principal grounds for her reappraisal of Ouida's work. She is also at pains to establish Ouida's role as 'pioneer' of the aesthetic novel (and thus as an influence on Wilde and James), stressing that her main achievement was imagining a 'new female identity' through her invention of 'the female aesthete ... one of the strongest female characters in Victorian fiction' (150). Regardless as to whether one agrees with these claims (and it is noticeable that Schaffer feels obliged to find an 'adversarial' element in Ouida's work), they do not address the stylistic infelicities in Ouida's writing that make her novels barely readable today. By contrast, Shafquat Towheed's recent reappraisal of Kipling's *The Naulahka* is refreshingly honest in acknowledging that the novel is 'unloved' and 'artistically weak'; its chief claim on our attention, in his view, lies in its 'importance in defining our understanding of the contingent realities of writing for Kipling in the

the distinction between poor writing which is a consequence of unavoidable compromises made to ensure that a work sells, and poor writing which particular market conditions enable to be 'passed off' as art, or to claim for itself the status of art, whether by clever packaging or by an appeal to popular taste.

If literary critics are to be persuaded of the relevance of that 'driest' of research into the economics of the late nineteenth-century publishing industry, then its details need to be connected much more directly to questions of literary critical evaluation. How exactly do market forces shape style? If they do play the formative role that is sometimes assumed, why is it that writers working under exactly the same commercial conditions, and equally intent on earning money, can nonetheless produce very different sorts of works. What kind of agency do market forces possess if they can simultaneously produce *both* the novels of Corelli and Hardy, or *both* the dramas of Elizabeth Robins and of Wilde? Even if we could answer that question it would not help us to understand why most modern readers prefer to read Hardy and Wilde and not Robins and Corelli.

These questions bring into focus what is actually a very old controversy, dating back at least as far as the debates conducted in the very first numbers of *Essays in Criticism* between F. R. Leavis and F. W. Bateson over the role of what was then called the 'social context' of literary works. Bateson's proposition was that an 'essential requirement' of judgements about a work's literary value—about whether we are 'able to use it, to live ourselves into it'—was 'an understanding' of its 'original social context', for it was only in relation to that context that 'the values implied [in the work] become explicit, and its relative goodness or badness declares itself'.[16] Leavis's response was that 'context', however defined, was always a construction placed on the past by the historian. More importantly, for the modern reader it was a prior judgement or judgements about a work's literariness which determined the limits and relevance of the historical information that one brought to bear on it. It was not, as Bateson implied, the other way round. By re-casting this argument in more up-to-date terms, we can see that what is being contested here is the *nature* of the relationship between knowledge of the historical circumstances (however defined) in which a given work is situated and an attribution of literary identity and literary value. As I shall argue below by using examples from Wilde's *oeuvre*, it turns out that information of the kind currently being brought to our attention by historians of the late nineteenth-century literary book-trade has a strong bearing on judgements about a work's literary value when, and only when, that information also changes our

1890s ... demonstrating the effects upon him of a bibliographical environment radically different from our own' (Towheed, 'Rudyard Kipling's Literary Property, International Copyright Law and The Naulahka', *English Literature in Transition*, 48 (2005), 420–35.)

[16] F. W. Bateson, 'The Function of Criticism at the Present Time', in *Essays in Criticism*, 3 (1953), 1–27; quoted in F. R. Leavis, 'The Responsible Critic, or The Function of Criticism at the Present Time' (1953), in Leavis (ed.), *A Selection from Scrutiny* (Cambridge: Cambridge University Press, 1968), ii. 294.

conception of a work's identity. Significantly, though, such a change—as I shall also show—seems to occur relatively infrequently. And it is for this reason that I would hazard to predict (as Leavis certainly would have done) that the recent expansion of our sense of what a 'social context' can include (so that it now embraces the economics of literary production) will have a relatively small impact on the canon. My fundamental proposition, then, is that information about the late nineteenth-century book trade will probably serve mainly to consolidate or to enhance (rather than to challenge) our view of a work's literary value.

I suggested above that an attention to the 'economic' as opposed to the 'political' or 'ideological' nature of literary works has produced what seem to be incompatible explanations of Wilde's motives for writing. Conveniently enough, we can best glimpse that tension in the ways in which critics have discussed Wilde's attitudes towards capital. The oldest and most deeply entrenched view of what are taken to be his 'anti-capitalist' politics can be traced back at least as far as George Woodcock's 1949 monograph *The Paradox of Oscar Wilde*. Woodcock saw 'The Soul of Man Under Socialism' as the key work in Wilde's *oeuvre*, one which established his anarchist credentials, a theme which was still being rehearsed nearly half a century later by critics as diverse in their interests as Christopher Lasch and Sos Eltis.[17] In this tradition Wilde's hostility towards capitalist modes of production is to be seen in the ways in which his works articulate a critique of various capitalist institutions such as charity and philanthropy (portrayed as activities which merely ease the consciences of the rich and justify enormous inequities in wealth); private property (shown to be deleterious of personal development by identifying worth with possessions); and the Victorian marriage-market (whose primary function is the policing of class boundaries). A contempt for the vulgarities, carelessness, and immorality of the rich, and a corresponding sympathy for the exploited poor, might seem to provide the thread linking an otherwise diverse *oeuvre*, connecting early works such as 'The Canterville Ghost' and 'The Happy Prince' to *The Picture of Dorian Gray*, to essays such as 'The Soul of Man Under Socialism', to the later society comedies, and finally to *De Profundis* where Wilde rails (probably unfairly) against what he sees as the obscene extravagances of his lover, Lord Alfred Douglas.[18]

A second and rather different way of thinking about Wilde's engagement with capitalism, associated in particular (though not exclusively) with the work of Regenia Gagnier, has been to focus on Wilde's response to consumerism,

[17] See George Woodcock, *The Paradox of Oscar Wilde* (London: T. V. Boardman, 1949), Christopher Lasch, *The Revolt of the Elites and the Betrayal of Democracy* (New York & London: Norton, 1995), and Sos Eltis, *Revising Wilde: Society and Subversion in the Plays of Oscar Wilde* (Oxford: Clarendon Press, 1996).

[18] In the commentary to his recent edition of *De Profundis*, Ian Small provides evidence to suggest that Wilde probably exaggerated the amounts of money which he spent on Douglas—certainly both men's recall of that expenditure was significantly different. See Small (ed.), *The Complete Works of Oscar Wilde*, ii: *De Profundis: Epistola in Carcere et Vinculis* (Oxford: Oxford University Press, 2005).

understood as a mode of evaluation explicitly associated with a capitalist society.[19] The advantage of this line of research was that it seemed to produce an account of Wilde that was more sensitive to the details of his lifestyle, particularly to those parts of his personality which sat uneasily with his image as socialist or anarchist. Thus his publicity-seeking and posing, his apparent attraction to an acquisitive life style, lavish spending, and to the conspicuous consumption of the very class he satirized, could be reinterpreted as a prescient attempt to create himself as a media personality, under the guise of which he was better enabled to manipulate and subvert the emerging 'society of the spectacle'. Here Wilde is still cast in an adversarial role, but rather than critiquing the evils of capitalism as defined by socialism—such as its manner of wealth creation and class politics—he is revealed as a critic of capitalist (or market-driven) modes of evaluation, his works holding up for inspection what are termed consumerist (rather than productive) models of value.[20]

There are some obvious tensions between these two lines of research, most notably, perhaps, in the ways they understand Wilde's interest in individualism. For earlier critics it was seen as part of his commitment to anarchism, and thus evidence of his opposition to the normative character of bourgeois society. But for those (like Gagnier) who locate Wilde's oppositional politics in his critique of markets, individualism means something rather different: as the ideological justification of consumer choice, individualism is a defining characteristic of a 'market-society' and is thus a concept to be rejected by Wilde in favour of 'the more substantive value of the earlier Victorians'.[21] These sorts of interpretative variations are significant, though they are of a different order to that which exists between both of them and evidence which has emerged concerning the actual finances of Wilde's career. As I noted earlier, an attention to the material as opposed to the symbolic value of money, and to economics considered as a matter of profit and loss, rather than of discourse, reveals that the attitudes which critics have been attributing to Wilde via his texts are radically different from those with which he operated when making and publishing his works. In matters of literary production, Wilde was fully a capitalist, concerned as much (if not more) with the financial bottom line as with literary integrity, refusing (at a

[19] See, for example, Gagnier's *Idylls of the Market Place: Oscar Wilde and the Victorian Public* (Stanford, CA: Stanford University Press, 1986).

[20] It is perhaps worth noting in passing that one limitation of this line of research, particularly as developed in Gagnier's later monograph, *The Insatiability of Human Wants: Economics and Aesthetics in Market Society* (Chicago: University of Chicago Press, 2000), concerns the agency it ascribes to late nineteenth-century economic theorists (especially William Stanley Jevons) whose work neither Wilde nor his readers were likely to have read (certainly there is no concrete evidence to suggest as much). There are also certain methodological difficulties involved in appropriating the specialist language of late nineteenth-century economics (particularly that of marginal utility theory) to describe general cultural values and concerns.

[21] Gagnier, 'Is Market Society the Fin of History?', in Sally Ledger and Scott McCracken (eds), *Cultural Politics at the Fin de Siècle* (Cambridge: Cambridge University Press, 1995), 305.

certain point in his career) to write what he termed 'speculative work'—that is, material for which he had not been offered payment in advance. Does any of this information matter to the literary critic? Does it have any bearing on the sorts of literary critical differences to which I have alluded, such as those concerning Wilde's understanding of individualism?

As I have already suggested, Wilde's 1891 essay 'The Soul of Man Under Socialism' has in the past been central for those critics who wish to establish his 'oppositional' credentials. Yet the piece can hardly be described as his most successful work if we think of success in terms of style and structure, and it is certainly not the most widely read of his works today. (Though modern readers can probably quote a number of its aphorisms, relatively few would be able accurately to recapitulate its argument, a situation which holds for much of Wilde's other critical prose as well.) 'The Soul of Man Under Socialism' has also proved rather troublesome for literary critics, because although it seems to promise a kind of intellectual seriousness—provocatively critiquing cherished Victorian institutions such as private property and philanthropy—its tone makes it difficult to know quite how its claims are to be taken. As Lawrence Danson has cogently put it, there is a 'fine line ... between satire and silliness' and it is one which 'The Soul of Man Under Socialism' unfortunately 'occasionally crosses'.[22] As a first step to answering the question of the relationship between book history and critical evaluation, I shall briefly rehearse the main details of how this work was made and sold in order to consider whether those details can have any bearing on how we interpret and value it.

Unlike his other long critical essays (those collected in *Intentions* and 'The Portrait of Mr W. H.') there is little evidence that Wilde paid much attention to 'The Soul of Man Under Socialism' after he had written it for publication in 1891 in the *Fortnightly Review*. Although it was reprinted (without Wilde revising it) in book form in 1896, that publication was a very minor affair, involving only fifty modestly priced copies that were probably bought by (or distributed among) Wilde's friends and sympathizers.[23] These circumstances may seem surprising for a piece which has so often been assumed to have been central to Wilde's political philosophy. The editor of the *Fortnightly* in 1891 was Frank Harris who, by that time, was a fairly close friend of Wilde, meeting him regularly for lunch. He had already published work by Wilde, and on one occasion at least had (unsuccessfully) requested a further contribution from him, apparently because

[22] Lawrence Danson, *Oscar Wilde's Intentions: The Artist in his Criticism* (Oxford: Clarendon Press, 1997), 152.

[23] The evidence for Wilde's lack of involvement in the book publication of 'The Soul of Man Under Socialism' is too complex to discuss here; a pivotal issue, however, is the fact that a paragraph which was misplaced in the periodical version remains misplaced in the book version, a circumstance which strongly indicates that Wilde did not see proofs of the book version of his essay, or if he did, that he no longer cared about it. Full details of the textual history of this work can be found in Josephine M. Guy, '"The Soul of Man Under Socialism": A Con-Textual History', in Joseph Bristow (ed.), *Wilde Writings: Contextual Conditions* (London: University of Toronto Press, 2003), 59–85.

he saw Wilde as an author in possession of 'prodigious notoriety' whose 'sayings and doings were eagerly canvassed from one end of society to another'—in short, Wilde, in Harris's view, could sell copy.[24] There are relatively few variants between the only (incomplete) extant manuscript of 'The Soul of Man Under Socialism' (which was used as printer's copy for the *Fortnightly* and which is currently held in the Berg Collection at the New York Public Library)[25] and the version of the essay which appeared in that periodical. This suggests that Harris (in marked distinction to some other periodical editors with whom Wilde worked, such as James Knowles of the *Nineteenth Century*) was not a strongly interventionist editor, and that Wilde was not in any significant way constrained or censored by the publication process.[26] At the same time, though, he was still a jobbing journalist and could not afford to have work turned down. His finances in the winter of 1890–1, when he probably wrote most of 'The Soul of Man Under Socialism', were reasonably secure, but he was by no means a wealthy man. He had yet to receive significant income from any of his plays, though he was beginning to place longer pieces in periodicals, and had a couple of new books in the pipe line.

Taken together, these details point us in the direction of thinking about 'The Soul of Man Under Socialism' as a piece of journalism—certainly that is the form in which most nineteenth-century readers would have encountered the text. They indicate that we should identify it more closely with Wilde's occasional, uncollected pieces, rather than with his book publications, those works to which he himself seemed to have assigned a higher literary value.[27] Moreover, identifying the essay as journalism, rather than as 'literature', can in turn direct us towards contextualizing it rather differently; to use terms familiar to Leavis and Bateson, to construe its 'relevant' social context as that of contemporary periodical writing (of other essays written for the commercial

[24] Frank Harris, *Oscar Wilde: His Life and Confessions* (London: Privately Printed by the Author, 1916); repr. as *Oscar Wilde: His Life and Confessions. Including the hitherto unpublished full and final confession by Lord Alfred Douglas and My Memories of Oscar Wilde by Bernard Shaw* (New York: Garden City Publishing, 1930), 81.

[25] This manuscript only recently came to the attention of the academic community when it was sold at public auction in the spring of 2004. I am grateful to the curator of the Berg Collection, Isaac Gewirtz, for providing me with a microfilm of it, and to Merlin Holland for giving permission for the copy to be made.

[26] When discussing disagreements about the aphorisms published as a 'Preface to *Dorian Gray*' in the March 1891 issue of the *Fortnightly Review*, Harris claimed that he had been happy to let 'the final judgement' rest with Wilde, and there is every reason to believe that he took the same attitude regarding other works of Wilde that he published (*Oscar Wilde*, 85). By contrast, Wilde and Knowles had had a bitter disagreement over excisions which Knowles had made to 'The Critic as Artist', apparently without Wilde's full consent.

[27] There is evidence that Wilde had, at one time, considered including 'The Soul of Man Under Socialism' in a new edition of *Intentions*, substituting it for 'The Truth of Masks', a piece he had never been very happy with. But these ambitions were not realized in his life time. More significantly, perhaps, there is no mention of 'The Soul of Man Under Socialism' in the contract which Wilde drew up with the Bodley Head in 1893, and which contained a number of works in his 'back-catalogue', including a book publication of 'The Portrait of Mr. W. H.'.

press), rather than a tradition of philosophical writing encompassing the work of, say, Herbert Spencer, Ralph Waldo Emerson, and the fourth century BC Chinese mystic Chuang Tzû (a translation of whose work Wilde had reviewed in February 1890). The result of such a process is that we come to see how closely Wilde's argument mirrors the terms of other pieces published around the same time and which were also debating the merits of Socialism and Individualism, and of philanthropy and charity. It also helps us to see that the term Individualism may have had (for Wilde's contemporary readers at least) a quite specific set of political connotations, and that these had little to do either with anarchism or, indeed, with the marginal utility theory of contemporary economic theorists of consumerism.[28] In this context, then, it is not the originality nor 'daring' nature of the essay which strikes us so much as its irreverent good humour: the casual wit with which it plays with arguments that would have been largely familiar, and which in other contexts had been treated very much more seriously. In other words, the 'silliness' that worried Danson seems more comprehensible and even admirable in a piece written with the aim of entertaining its readers—written, as one contemporary commentator put it, 'merely to startle and provoke talk', rather than as a work of serious political philosophy.[29] Here, then, we have an example of how an attention to the economics of literary production can propose different grounds for evaluating a work by changing (or modifying) the way we identify it. That said, it is still a moot point whether 'The Soul of Man Under Socialism' possesses a greater or lesser *literary* value when viewed as a piece of exemplary popular journalism rather than as a flawed and relatively unimportant piece of political theory. Moreover, we might also add that drawing attention to its topicality, to the ways in which it engages with specific areas of late nineteenth-century political debate, fails to provide a compelling reason for modern readers to open it.

Another area of Wilde's *oeuvre* which has puzzled modern critics is his poetry, particularly his 1881 volume *Poems* (which was republished in 1892). This work is probably the least read, and least highly regarded, of all Wilde's writings; even the editors of the most recent and fullest edition of his poems do not make any particular claim for their literary merit.[30] It is unnecessary to rehearse in detail

---

[28] As far back as 1975, the historian Edward Bristow drew attention to the political meanings of the term Individualism, explaining its association in the late nineteenth century not with anarchism but with right-wing pressure groups such as the Liberty and Property Defence League (see Bristow, 'The Liberty and Property Defence League and Individualism', *Historical Journal*, 18 (1975), 761–89), His research, however, seems to have been largely ignored by literary historians, with the exception of M. W. Taylor's *Men Versus the State: Herbert Spencer and Late Victorian Individualism* (Oxford: Blackwell, 1992). I make a more sustained case for identifying 'The Soul of Man Under Socialism' with Wilde's uncollected prose in ' "The Soul of Man Under Socialism": A Con-Textual History'.

[29] The comment appeared in a review in *The Spectator* (7 Feb. 1891); it is quoted in Stuart Mason [Christopher Millard], *Bibliography of Oscar Wilde* (London: T. Werner Laurie, 1914), 73.

[30] In his Introduction to Bobby Fong's and Karl Beckson's edition of Wilde's poetry Ian Small acknowledges that 'to judge Wilde's literary achievement against that of contemporaries such as

the kinds of criticisms that have been directed towards Wilde's poetry, except
to note that they have tended to centre on its derivative qualities and perceived
lack of sincerity. Significantly, however, Nicholas Frankel, who has made the
most ambitious attempt to challenge this judgement, begins with an account of
how Wilde's *Poems* was marketed—with the decision by John Lane and Elkin
Mathews of the Bodley Head to acquire the unbound sheets of the proposed
'fifth' edition of *Poems* which had laid in 'limbo' for nearly a decade following
the bankruptcy of David Bogue, the work's original publisher.[31] Frankel argues
that the Bodley Head's beautifully presented, highly expensive (it was priced at
15 s.), signed, limited-edition of *Poems* is a work of key 'historical significance',
for it 'marks a sea change in the world of 1890s publishing; and it marks a sea
change in Wilde's own publishing arrangements'. Frankel then moves beyond
the familiar terrain of book-history to the altogether more arresting assertion that
the 'historical questions raised by the volume ... compel us to examine *Poems*
(1892) as a *literary text*, both as a work of poetry and as a book, in ways that
Harold Bloom's dismissal of Wilde's poetry as the epitome of "the anxiety of
influence" ... has tended to stifle'.[32] Here a concern with the economics of literary
production, and with decisions (some of which were clearly finance-driven) about
how a book was to be produced and sold, seems to be directly prompting issues of
literary-critical interpretation. Frankel's work may thus seem to undermine my
earlier comments about the limited relevance of 'economic' accounts of literary
works.

Frankel's argument centres on the proposition (adapted from the works of
theorists such as Jerome J. McGann) that the design of a book—in the case of
the 1892 *Poems*, its elaborate binding and cover device by Charles Ricketts, and
the inclusion of Wilde's signature on the page facing the title-page—constitute
a 'sign system in its own right', one which can 'alter the meaning of the poetry'.
More particularly, he argues that the 'self-conscious materiality of Ricketts's
designs for the volume', that is, the deliberately anachronistic (and expensive)
choice of a hand-carved woodcut for the title page, has the effect of 'ironizing'
the mechanical typography of the poetic text. This in turn, according to Frankel,

Thomas Hardy and W. B. Yeats, who made poetry their central creative activity, inevitably tends
to reflect poorly on him. It is much more appropriate to evaluate Wilde's poetry in relation to his
own development as a writer—to see it in the context of the successful author he became in his
criticism, fiction, and drama'. (See Fong and Beckson (eds), *The Complete Works of Oscar Wilde*, i:
Poems and Poems in Prose (Oxford: Oxford University Press, 2000), p. x.)

[31] The second and third 'editions' of *Poems* had been made up from unsold copies of the first
edition; by contrast, the fourth edition, which had appeared in 1882, *was* a new edition in that it
incorporated Wilde's revisions to some of his poems. However, this edition did not sell particularly
well either, and the proposed 'fifth' edition was to have been made up from the same print-run
as the fourth. Ian Small thus concludes that the many editions which *Poems* went through was
evidence not of the work's 'popularity', but rather the opposite, of Bogue's desperate attempt to
'boost sales' (see the 'Introduction' to ibid).

[32] Nicolas Frankel, *Oscar Wilde's Decorated Books* (Ann Arbor: University of Michigan Press,
2000), 110–11 (my emphasis).

'creates a historical frame' by which we read the poems, particularly those in the opening section 'Eleutheria': 'it puts quotation marks around Wilde's political sonnets, throwing the full pretentiousness of their attitudinizing into sharp relief and exposing them for what they really are: social comedies.' Frankel sees similar consequences following from Ricketts's 'magnificent binding' which, he claims, 'almost single-handedly ... lifts Wilde's poetry into the decadent 1890s', despite the fact that the composition of the individual pieces in *Poems* 'predate the decadent movement in strict historical terms' (some, we might add, were written as early as the mid-1870s). In this way the bibliographic codes 'create the conditions' for the 'resurrection' of a 'difficult' poem such as 'Charmides'; though 'vilified' on first publication, it can be re-read in *Poems* (1892) as a work whose tendency towards 'visual ornamentation' mirrors the decorative qualities of the book as object.[33]

Although he does not quite put it in these terms, Frankel's argument amounts to the claim that decisions about the materiality of *Poems* (1892), which from one perspective at least can be seen simply as 'a cunning business manoeuvre'[34] designed to re-sell *Poems* (1892), had the effect of changing the identity (and therefore the value) of the works embodied therein. So, for example, the allegation of insincerity which was once held to mar Wilde's 'political' sonnets can now be neatly set aside when they are re-labelled 'social comedies', and the Romantic persona behind the lyrics transformed into the cynical 'detachment' of the decadent. Ingenious though this argument is, it has a very obvious limitation, one which is, moreover, a direct consequence of the ways in which the volume was originally marketed. Frankel's argument requires the reader to have an intimate connection with the book itself, with one of those 220 copies which were freshly bound: we need to 'pick up the book physically and turn it around in our hands'.[35] How many readers today can possibly hope for such a privilege? Even if they had the huge amounts of money which Wilde's first editions command, there are still not enough copies to go around. Failing this, they have to have the time and resources to visit the special collections of a university or copyright library. If *Poems* (1892) was rare when it was first published, then it is very much rarer today. The interpretations which Frankel so carefully adduces are thus available only to the tiniest of scholarly elites or rich connoisseurs. To his credit, Frankel is partly aware of this dilemma, and he acknowledges that *Poems* (1892) conveys its meanings 'privately', and that the 'interdependence' of the book's linguistic and bibliographic codes 'calls attention to itself as a time-bound artefact, speaking its difference from incarnations ... that came before it as well as

[33] Ibid. 127–30.

[34] Ibid. 124. As Frankel acknowledges, this is the perspective most likely adopted by book historians such as Nelson. In *Oscar Wilde's Profession*, Ian Small and I calculated that trade sales of *Poems* (1892) probably realized around £125 for Matthews and Lane, with Wilde receiving somewhere between £45 and £60 (see *Oscar Wilde's Profession*, 149–50).

[35] Frankel, *Oscar Wilde's Decorated Books*, 117.

from those that have succeeded it'.[36] To this observation, the cynical literary critic
might respond that so long as the vast majority of readers continue to experience
Wilde's poetry (as they do most nineteenth-century poems) in cheap paper back
editions, then knowledge of its production history must remain irrelevant as to
how it is valued, and therefore to its place in the canon. Moreover, even those
reprints of 1890s texts, which faithfully reproduce the bibliographical codes of
the printed pages, but not the binding, cannot hope to recover the conditions of
existence of that 'time-bound artefact'. Far from safeguarding its literary status, as
Wilde had presumably hoped, the material exclusivity with which *Poems* (1892)
was marketed, and to which Frankel is so attentive, has produced a valuation of
the work which makes it virtually impossible for any of us, in Bateson's terms, to
be 'able to use it, to live ourselves into it'.

For my last example from Wilde's oeuvre, I will concentrate on a work which,
in contrast to both *Poems* and 'The Soul of Man Under Socialism', has a much
more secure place in the literary canon. *The Importance of Being Earnest* is
Wilde's best known, and probably most highly valued work. Yet there have been
disagreements among some critics as to which version of it—the three-act play
produced by George Alexander in 1895 and published by Leonard Smithers
in 1899, or an earlier, four-act drama which exists in various manuscript and
typescript forms, the latest of which is dated October 1894—has the greater
literary merit.[37] As one might expect, the reduction of a four-act play into a
three-act work inevitably involved extensive revisions, including the wholesale
deletion of some passages. Of these, the most controversial is what has come
to be known as the 'Gribsby' episode, a long scene in which the eponymous
solicitor interrupts the domestic comedy of the society drawing-room to serve
Algernon with a writ for unpaid debts owed to the Savoy Hotel. The intrusion
of such details about how the 'real' world operates—the way in which Algernon
is threatened, however jokingly, with incarceration in Holloway Prison—seem
uncannily reminiscent of tensions which would soon overtake Wilde's own life,[38]

---

[36] Frankel, *Oscar Wilde's Decorated Books*, 130.

[37] The four-act version of the play was first made available in a transcription by Sarah Augusta
Dickinson of Wilde's manuscript draft of August 1894 which was published in 1956; this in
turn formed the basis of what is described as a 'reconstruction' of the four-act version of the play
published in the 1957 edition of the perennially popular Collins *Complete Works* edited by Vyvyan
Holland; that text was retained in the 1994 revised edition co-edited by Merlin Holland. For many
years, then, the four-act play was the version with which most readers would have been familiar.
Other editions of the plays, such as The New Mermaids *The Importance of Being Earnest* edited by
Russell Jackson and first published in 1980, or the Oxford World's Classics *The Importance of Being
Earnest and Other Plays* edited by Peter Raby and first published in 1995, reproduce the three-act
version.

[38] For example, an often cited reason for Wilde's initiation of the disastrous libel suit against
Lord Queensberry was an unpaid hotel bill. Wilde claimed that had he not been detained in London
at the Avondale Hotel, on account of owing the management a sum of some £140, he would have
'been happy and free in France'. He would, that is, have been far away from a goading Douglas,
and from any temptation to instigate legal proceedings. Two days before his own trial began the

and it is therefore unsurprising that critical debate about the two versions of the play has often been framed in terms of a language of censorship. Where the four-act version is preferred it is because it is argued to be the more subversive or dangerous work, one which is closer to Wilde's 'intentions' as an oppositional author. The issue which I should like briefly to consider is whether a knowledge of the economic circumstances which underlie the production of this work—that it was written, as I suggested earlier, at a time when Wilde himself was technically almost bankrupt—bears on our critical evaluation of the two versions of the plays.

Initially it might seem that the answer to this question is yes, for attention to the details of Wilde's financial arrangements with George Alexander, and the ways in which they determined the power relations between the two men—in short, financially speaking, Wilde needed Alexander much more than Alexander needed Wilde[39]—would suggest that Wilde was not in much of a position to have resisted Alexander's proposition that the play would work 'better' if it were shortened, even if that meant excising what was arguably the most controversial material in the play.[40] What, though, are we to make of Wilde's later decision, when he published the play, to retain the three-act version? There are a number of equally plausible scenarios which explain this situation. When preparing the text for book-publication Wilde no longer had his typescript of the four-act version to hand, and had to work from Alexander's prompt copy. Four years on from the performances of his play, he may simply have forgotten the details of the excised scene, or found them too difficult or time-consuming to reconstruct.

entire contents of his family home in Tite Street were sold at public auction to pay his debts. (For a discussion of these issues, see Merlin Holland (ed.), *Irish Peacock & Scarlet Marquess* (London: Harper Collins, 2003), pp. xv–xliii.)

[39] The fraught nature of Wilde's relations with Alexander, which dated back to the staging of *Lady Windermere's Fan*, were first revealed by Joel Kaplan in 'A Puppet's Power: George Alexander, Clement Scott, and the Replotting of *Lady Windermere's Fan*', *Theatre Notebook*, 46 (1992), 59–73; they are also discussed by Joseph Donohue in Donohue (with Ruth Berggren) (eds), *Oscar Wilde's The Importance of Being Earnest: The First Production* (Gerrard's Cross, Bucks: Colin Smythe, 1995), pp. xlii–xliii, and by myself and Ian Small in *Oscar Wilde's Profession*, 125–34, 244–57. What is important to note here is that Wilde's initial decision to offer a new play to Alexander (which would become *Earnest*) was based largely on the expectation that he would be given a hefty advance for it; but Alexander had been dissatisfied with an initial scenario, and no money had been forthcoming. He and Wilde had then quarrelled over who should have the American rights to the finished work. And as a result of all this, Wilde offered *Earnest* to another producer, Charles Wyndham, and it was Wyndham (apparently at the instigation of Wilde) who later sold the British rights back to Alexander following the unexpected failure of Henry James's *Guy Domville* which in turn had left a gap in Alexander's programming. Wilde's desire to have his play returned to the St James's theatre seems to have been financially motivated: Alexander could offer him an earlier run, and thus earlier income, than Wyndham.

[40] It is worth noting here that Alexander's decision to cut the Gribsby episode may not necessarily have been because he judged it to have been too controversial and thus likely to alienate audiences; Joseph Donohue, for example, has argued that he may have been trying to save on an actor's salary, as well as increasing the prominence of his own part in the play (he took the role of Jack Worthing); see Donohue, ibid.

Alternatively Wilde may have decided, with the benefit of hindsight, that the three-act version was in fact the 'better' work, that the play had been improved by, say, Alexander's superior sense of theatre and of the importance of a consistent dramatic tone. Then again, perhaps it was the case that the circumstances of Wilde's own life, following his trials and imprisonment, made bankruptcy a topic that was just too painful to revisit. Finally there is the possibility that the profit motive may once again have reared its head: that Wilde (and/or Smithers) thought it would be easier to sell the version of the play which had been so successful on the stage, and which would presumably have still been in the memories of potential customers for the book.

The point which I wish to stress here is how speculative all these narratives are: the available 'facts' about the economics behind the initial staging and first publication of *The Importance of Being Earnest* are capable of a variety of interpretations, and can be appropriated to support quite different conceptions of Wilde's creative intentions. At one end of the spectrum, he can be seen as a writer prevented by powerful commercial interests, which his own perilous finances made it impossible for him to resist, from fully realizing the political potential in his play. At the other end, he is a willing participant in capitalist accumulation, pleased to go along with which ever version of *Earnest* would make him the most money. That both these views seem equally reductive indicates how crude a measure economic value is if it is used to ascertain literary worth. More to the point, perhaps, wherever we 'sit' on the question of the extent to which financial considerations entered into the reduction of *Earnest* from a four- to a three-act play, we get no nearer to establishing grounds for evaluating which is the 'better' version. So it is possible to argue that the three-act play is formally the superior work and that, say, the exchanges in the Gribsby episode merely repeat earlier jokes, while also acknowledging that Wilde himself was bullied, for commercial reasons, into endorsing it. Likewise, the proposition that Wilde willingly discarded his four-act version is not incompatible with the judgement that the inclusion of the Gribsby episode produces a more richly-textured play because it allows for the development of themes only glancingly mentioned in earlier acts. That few critics would bother to argue any of these cases is because the contextual evidence does no work for them; or rather the work which it does do is oddly perverse, suggesting that Wilde himself was unable to judge the value of his own writing. Why would a critic bother to invoke evidence about a 'real' author's intentions if they run counter to those of an implied author? And it is for this reason that an appeal to the economic factors involved in the writing of *Earnest* seems incapable of resolving critical differences about the various texts of the play. It is rather the other way round: once again, a prior judgement about the intrinsic merits of the three- or four-act versions will determine both the weight and interpretation which we give to that 'social context'.

Few twenty-first century readers would hold to the view that only great men can make great art, and we are more likely to applaud than condemn Wilde for wanting to make (and for succeeding in making) money out of works which criticized the profit motive. At the same time, however, those critics who *are* disturbed by evidence that creativity and commerce were often intimately connected, might take some comfort from the fact that recent scrutiny of the financial transactions underlying the nineteenth-century book trade, though of crucial importance in constructing a history of taste, is unlikely to have a significant bearing on why the vast majority of modern readers continue to read the works which that trade produced, on the literary (as opposed to the historical) value which they have for us.[41]

[41] The most direct link between literary evaluation and an attention to the economics of the book trade is probably to be seen in the work of text-editors, a topic which the constraints of space have prevented me from exploring. Numerous factors can feed into text-editors' choices about copy-text—about the version of a work which they exhibit to the reader for literary judgement—and these typically include all those issues, including commercial ones, which are seen as impacting on the 'agency' of the author. It is also the case that literary historians may bring to our attention works which, in their view, have been marginalized because the book-trade under-valued or 'mis-sold' them. In this case, though, knowledge of the economics of the late nineteenth-century publishing industry is limited to offering works for literary judgement; it is not providing the criteria by which they are to be judged.

Selected Bibliography

Full references to all cited publications are given in footnotes to individual essays. But the following provides readers with a guide to recent significant works related to the subject of this book. Where more than one essay in a collection is relevant, the collection itself is listed alone. This bibliography does not include a list of primary literary texts nor a detailed account of earlier Marxist literary criticism.

Alborn, Timothy, *Conceiving Companies: Joint-stock Politics in Victorian England* (London: Routledge, 1998).

Altick, R. D., *The English Common Reader: A Social History of the Mass Reading Public, 1800–1900* (1957; Chicago: Chicago University Press, 1967).

Austin, Linda M., *The Practical Ruskin: Economics and Audience in the Late Work* (Baltimore: The Johns Hopkins Press, 1991).

Bagehot, Walter, *Lombard Street: A Description of the Money Market* (London: King, 1873).

Barnes, James J., *Authors, Publishers and Politicians: The Quest for an Anglo-American Copyright Agreement, 1815–1854* (London: Routledge & Kegan Paul, 1974).

Beck Ulrich, *Risk Society: Towards a New Modernity*, trans. Mark Ritter (London: Sage, 1992).

Beer, Gillian, 'The Reader's Wager: Lots, Sorts and Futures', *Essays in Criticism*, 40 (1990), 99–123.

Benjamin, Walter, *Charles Baudelaire: A Lyric Poet in the Era of High Capitalism*, trans. Harry Zohn (London: Verso, 1983).

Berman, Marshall, *All That is Solid Melts into Air: The Experience of Modernity* (London: Verso, 1983).

Bernstein, Peter, *Against the Gods: The Remarkable Story of Risk* (New York: Wiley 1996).

Besant, Walter, *The Pen and the Book* (London: Burleigh, 1899).

Bigelow, Gordon, *Fiction, Famine, and the Rise of Economics in Victorian Britain and Ireland* (Cambridge: Cambridge University Press, 2003).

Birken, Lawrence, *Consuming Desire: Sexual Science and the Emergence of a Culture of Abundance, 1871–1914* (Ithaca: Cornell University Press, 1988).

Blaug, Mark, *Ricardian Economics: A Historical Study* (New Haven: Yale University Press, 1958).

Bourdieu, Pierre, *Outline of a Theory of Practice*, trans. Richard Nice (Cambridge: Cambridge University Press, 1977).

_____ *The Field of Cultural Production: Essays on Art and Literature*, ed. Randal Johnson (Cambridge: Polity Press, 1992).

Bowlby, Rachel, *Just Looking: Consumer Culture in Dreiser, Gissing and Zola* (London: Methuen, 1985).

Boylan, Thomas A., and Timothy P. Foley, *Political Economy and Colonial Ireland: The Propagation and Ideological Function of Economic Discourse in the Nineteenth Century* (London: Routledge, 1992).

Brantlinger, Patrick *Fictions of State: Culture and Credit in Britain, 1694–1994* (Ithaca: Cornell University Press, 1996).

—— *The Reading Lesson: The Threat of Mass Literacy in Nineteenth Century British Fiction* (Bloomington: Indiana University Press, 1998).

Brewer, John, and Roy Porter (eds), *Consumption and the World of Goods* (London: Routledge, 1993).

Cain, P. J. and A. G. Hopkins, *British Imperialism: Innovation and Expansion* (London: Longman, 1993)

Carey, John, *The Intellectuals and the Masses: Pride and Prejudice among the Literary Intelligentsia, 1880–1939* (London: Faber, 1992).

Carson, Cary, Ronald Hoffman, and Peter J. Albert (eds), *Of Consuming Interests: The Style of Life in the Eighteenth Century* (Charlottesville: University Press of Virginia, for the United States Capitol Historical Society, 1994).

Chase, Karen, and Michael Levenson, *The Spectacle of Intimacy: A Public Life for the Victorian Family* (Princeton, NJ: Princeton University Press, 2000).

Church, R. A., *The Great Victorian Boom, 1850–1873* (London: Macmillan, 1975).

Copeland, Edward, *Women Writing about Money* (Cambridge: Cambridge University Press, 1995).

Crary, Jonathan, *Techniques of the Observer: On Vision and Modernity in the Nineteenth Century* (Cambridge, MA: MIT Press, 1990).

Crossick, Geoffrey, and Serge Jaumain (eds), *Cathedrals of Consumption: The European Department Store, 1850–1939* (Aldershot: Ashgate, 1999).

Davidoff, Leonore, and Catherine Hall, *Family Fortunes: Men and Women of the English Middle Class, 1780–1850* (Chicago: University of Chicago Press, 1987).

Davies, Glyn, *A History of Money* (Cardiff: University of Wales Press, 2002).

Davis, Tracy C., *The Economics of the British Stage, 1800–1914* (Cambridge: Cambridge University Press, 2000).

Delany, Paul, *Literature, Money and the Market from Trollope to Amis* (Basingstoke: Palgrave, 2002).

Derrida, Jacques, *Specters of Marx: The State of the Debt, the Work of Mourning, and the New International*, trans. Peggy Kamuf (London: Routledge, 1994).

Dowling, Linda, *The Vulgarization of Art: The Victorians and Aesthetic Democracy* (Charlottesville: University Press of Virginia, 1996).

Dumett, Ramond E., with an afterword by P. J. Cain and A. G. Hopkins, *Gentlemanly Capitalism and British Imperialism: The New Debate on Empire* (London: Longman, 1999).

D. Morier Evans, *Facts, Failures, and Frauds: Revelations Financial Mercantile Criminal* (1859; Newton Abbot: David and Charles, 1968).

—— *The History of the Commercial Crisis, 1857–1858: and the Stock Exchange Panic of 1859* (1859; reprint of Economic Classics, New York: Kelley, 1969; also Newton Abbot: David and Charles, [1970]).

—— *Speculative Notes and Notes on Speculation: Ideal and Real* (1864; reprint of Economic Classics, New York: Kelley, 1969).

Erickson, Lee, *The Economy of Literary Form: English Literature and the Industrialization of Publishing, 1800–1850* (Baltimore: Johns Hopkins, 1996).

Fegan, Melissa, *Literature and the Irish Famine, 1845–1919* (Oxford: Clarendon Press, 2002).

Feltes, N. N., *Modes of Production of the Late Victorian Novel* (Chicago: University of Chicago Press, 1986).

——— *Literary Capital and the Late Victorian Novel* (Madison: University of Wisconsin Press, 1993).

Ferguson, Niall, *The Cash Nexus: Money and Power in the Modern World, 1700–2000* (New York: Lane, 2002).

Flandreau, Marc, *The Glitter of Gold: France, Bimetallism and the Emergence of the International Gold Standard, 1848–1873* (Oxford: Oxford University Press, 2004).

Freedgood, Elaine, *Victorian Writing About Risk: Imagining a Safe England in a Dangerous World*, Cambridge Studies in Nineteenth-century Literature and Culture, 28 (Cambridge: Cambridge University Press, 2000).

Gagnier, Regenia, *Idylls of the Marketplace: Oscar Wilde and the Victorian Public* (Stanford, CA: Stanford University Press, 1986).

——— 'Culture and Economics', *Victorian Literature and Culture*, 26 (1998), 477–84

——— *The Insatiability of Human Wants: Economics and Aesthetics in Market Society* (Chicago: University of Chicago Press, 2000).

Giddens, Anthony, *Modernity and Self-Identity: Self and Society in the Late Modern Age* (Cambridge: Polity, 1991).

——— *Runaway World: How Globalization is Reshaping our Lives* (London: Profile, 2002).

Guillory, John, *Cultural Capital: The Problem of Literary Canon Formation* (Chicago: University of Chicago Press, 1993).

Guy, Josephine M., ' "The Soul of Man Under Socialism": A Con-Textual History', in Joseph Bristow (ed), *Wilde Writings: Contextual Conditions* (London: University of Toronto Press, 2003), 59–85.

——— and Ian Small, *Oscar Wilde's Profession: Writing and the Culture Industry in the Late Nineteenth Century* (Oxford: Oxford University Press, 2000).

Hack, Daniel, *The Material Interests of the Victorian Novel* (Charlottesville and London: University of Virginia Press, 2005).

Heinzelman, Kurt, *The Economics of the Imagination* (Amherst: University of Massachusetts Press, 1980).

Henderson, Willie, *Economics as Literature* (London: Routledge, 1995)

Hobsbawm, Eric, *The Age of Capital, 1848–1875* (London: Weidenfeld & Nicolson, 1975)

Hoeckley, Cheri Larsen, 'Anomalous Ownership: Copyright, Coverture, and *Aurora Leigh*', *Victorian Poetry*, 36 (1998), 135–61.

Hume, David, *Essays and Treatises on Several Subjects*, 2 vols (London: Cadell, 1793).

Ingham, Geoffrey, *The Nature of Money* (Cambridge: Polity, 2004).

Ingrassia, Catherine, *Authorship, Commerce, and Gender in Early Eighteenth-century England* (Cambridge: Cambridge University Press, 1998).

James, Elizabeth, (ed), *Macmillan: A Publishing Tradition* (Basingstoke: Palgrave, 2002).

Jardine, Lisa, *Worldly Goods: A New History of the Renaissance* (London: Macmillan, 1996).

Jevons, W. Stanley, *The Theory of Political Economy* (London: Macmillan, 1871).

——— *Money and the Mechanism of Exchange* (2nd edn, London: King, 1876).

Joseph, Gerhard, 'Producing the "Far-Off Interest of Tears": Tennyson, Freud, and the Economics of Mourning', *Victorian Poetry*, 36 (1998), 123–33.

Kindleberger, Charles P., *A Financial History of Western Europe* (London: Allen & Unwin, 1984).

——— *Manias, Panics, and Crashes: A History of Financial Crises*, rev. edn (New York: Basic Books, 1989).

Knezevic, Borislav, *Figures of Finance Capitalism: Writing, Class, and Capital in the Age of Dickens* (London: Routledge, 2003).

Ledbetter, Katherine, 'Protesting Success: Tennyson's "Indecent Exposure" in the Periodicals', *Victorian Poetry*, 43 (2005), 53–73

Ledger, Sally, and Scott McCracken (eds), *Cultural Politics at the Fin de Siècle* (Cambridge: Cambridge University Press, 1995).

Lester, V. Markham, *Victorian Insolvency: Bankruptcy, Imprisonment for Debt, and Company Winding-up in Nineteenth-century England* (Oxford: Clarendon Press, 1995).

Levine, George, *The Realistic Imagination: English Fiction from* Frankenstein *to* Lady Chatterley (Chicago: University of Chicago Press, 1981)

Luhmann, Niklas, *Risk: A Sociological Theory* (Berlin: De Gruyter, 1993)

McLaughlin, Kevin, *Writing in Parts: Imitation and Exchange in Nineteenth-century Literature* (Stanford, CA: Stanford University Press, 1995).

McVeagh, John, *Tradeful Merchants: The Portrayal of the Capitalist in Literature* (London: Routledge & Kegan Paul, 1981).

Macherey, Pierre, *A Theory of Literary Production*, trans. G. Wall (London: Routledge & Kegan Paul, 1978)

McCloskey, Donald [now Deirdre] N., *The Rhetoric of Economics* (Madison: University of Wisconsin Press, 1985).

——— *If You're So Smart: The Narratives of Economic Expertise* (Chicago: University of Chicago Press, 1990).

——— *Knowledge and Persuasion in Economics* (Cambridge: Cambridge University Press, 1994).

McDonagh, Josephine, *De Quincey's Disciplines* (Oxford: Clarendon Press, 1994).

McDonald, Peter D., *British Literary Culture and Publishing Practice: 1880–1914* (Cambridge: Cambridge University Press, 1997).

Marx, Karl, *Capital: A Critique of Political Economy*, trans. from 3rd German edn by Samuel Moore and Edward Aveling; ed. by Frederick Engels, 3 vols (London: Lawrence & Wishart, 1956–59).

——— and Friedrich Engels, *Manifesto of the Communist Party*, trans. Samuel Moore (Moscow: Progress, 1967).

Michie, Elsie B., 'Buying Brains: Trollope, Oliphant, and Vulgar Victorian Commerce', *Victorian Studies*, 44 (2001), 77–97.

Michie, Ranald C. *The London Stock Exchange: A History* (Oxford: Oxford University Press, 1999).

Miller, Andrew H., *Novels Behind Glass: Commodity Culture and Victorian Narrative* (Cambridge: Cambridge University Press, 1995).

Moss, Laurence S., *Mountifort Longfield: Ireland's First Professor of Political Economy* (Ottawa, IL: Green Hill, 1976).

Nicholson, Colin, *Writing and the Rise of Finance: Capital Satires of the Early Eighteenth Century* (Cambridge: Cambridge University Press, 1994).

Nunokawa, Jeff, *The Afterlife of Property: Domestic Security and the Victorian Novel* (Princeton, NJ: Princeton University Press, 1994).

O'Brien, D. P., *The Classical Economists* (Oxford: Clarendon Press, 1975).

O'Gorman, Francis, (ed.), *A Concise Companion to the Victorian Novel* (Oxford: Blackwell, 2005).

_____ and Katherine Turner (eds), *The Victorians and the Eighteenth Century: Reassessing the Tradition* (Aldershot and Burlington, VT: Ashgate, 2004).

Pettitt, Clare, *Patent Inventions: Intellectual Property and the Victorian Novel* (Oxford: Oxford University Press 2004).

Pollard, Arthur, (ed.), *The Representation of Business in Literature,* (London: Institute of Economic Affairs, 2000).

Poovey, Mary, *A History of the Modern Fact: Problems of Knowledge in the Sciences of Wealth and Society* (Chicago: University of Chicago Press, 1998).

_____ (ed.), *The Financial System in Nineteenth-century Britain* (New York; Oxford: Oxford University Press, 2003).

Purdy, Anthony, (ed.), *Literature and Money* (Amsterdam: Rodopi, 1993).

Rappaport, Erika Diane, *Shopping for Pleasure: Women in the Making of London's West End* (Princeton, NJ: Princeton University Press, 2000).

Raven, James, *The Commercialization of the Book: Booksellers and the Commodification of Literature in Britain, 1450–1900* (Cambridge: Cambridge University Press, 2005).

_____ 'The Promotion and Constraints of Knowledge: The Changing Structure of Publishing in Victorian Britain', in Martin Daunton (ed.), *The Organisation of Knowledge in Victorian Britain* (Oxford: Oxford University Press, 2005), 263–86.

Reed, John, 'A Friend to Mammon: Speculation in Victorian Literature,' *Victorian Studies*, 27 (1984), 179–202.

Richards, Thomas, *The Commodity Culture of Victorian England* (Stanford, CA: Stanford University Press, 1990).

Robb, George, *White Collar Crime in Modern England: Financial Fraud and Business Morality, 1845–1929* (Cambridge: Cambridge University Press, 1992).

Rose, Jonathan, *The Intellectual Life of the British Working Classes* (New Haven: Yale University Press, 2001).

_____ 'Was Capitalism Good for Victorian Literature', *Victorian Studies*, 46 (2004), 489–501.

Rostow, W. W., *British Economy of the Nineteenth Century* (Oxford: Clarendon Press, 1948).

Russell, Norman, *The Novelist and Mammon: Literary Responses to the World of Commerce in the Nineteenth Century* (Oxford: Clarendon Press, 1986).

Schmitt, Cannon, Nancy Henry, and Anjali Arondekar (eds), *Victorian Studies,* 45 (2002), Special Issue on Victorian Investments

Schumpeter, Joseph A., *History of Economic Analysis*, ed. Elizabeth Boody Schumpeter (New York: Oxford University Press, 1954).

Searle, G. R., *Morality and the Market in Victorian Britain* (Oxford: Clarendon Press, 1998).

Seville, Catherine, *Literary Copyright Reform in Early Victorian England* (Cambridge: Cambridge University Press, 1999).

_____ *The Internationalisation of Copyright Law: Books, Buccaneers and the Black Flag in the Nineteenth Century* (Cambridge: Cambridge University Press, 2006).

Shell, Marc, *The Economy of Literature* (Baltimore: The Johns Hopkins University Press, 1978).

Shell, Marc, *Art and Money* (Chicago: Chicago University Press, 1995).

Shillingsburg, P. L., *Pegasus in Harness: Victorian Publishing and W. M. Thackeray* (Charlottesville and London: University Press of Virginia, 1992).

Shrimpton, Nicholas, 'Economic, Social and Literary Influences upon the Development of Ruskin's Ideas to *Unto this Last* (1860)' unpublished DPhil thesis, University of Oxford, 1976.

Simmel, Georg, *The Philosophy of Money* (2nd edn, 1900; London: Routledge, 1990)

Smith, Andrew (guest ed.), *Victorian Review* (31.2 (2005), Special edition on Literature and Money.

Still, Judith, *Feminine Economies: Thinking Against the Market in the Enlightenment and the Late Twentieth Century* (Manchester: Manchester University Press, 1997).

Sutherland, John, *Victorian Novelists and Publishers* (Chicago: University of Chicago Press, 1976).

Taylor, James, *The Joint Stock Company in Law, Politics and Culture in Nineteenth Century Britain* (London: Royal Historical Society, 2005).

Thurschwell, Pamela, *Literature, Technology and Magical Thinking, 1880–1920* (Cambridge: Cambridge University Press, 2001).

Tucker, Herbert (ed.), *A Companion to Victorian Literature and Culture* (Oxford: Blackwell, 1999).

Vernon, John, *Money and Fiction: Literary Realism in the Nineteenth and Early Twentieth Centuries* (Ithaca: Cornell University Press, 1984).

Wagner-Lawlor, Jennifer A., '"Who Acts John Bull?": Speculating on English National Character and Modern Morality', *Victorian Review*, 23 (2003), 64–96.

Watts, Cedric, *Literature and Money: Financial Myth and Literary Truth* (Hemel Hempstead: Harvester Wheatsheaf, 1990).

Weatherill, Lorna, *Consumer Behaviour and Material Culture in Britain, 1660–1760*, (2nd edn, London: Routledge, 1996).

Weber, Max, *Economy and Society* (1922; Berkeley: University of California Press, 1978).

Weiss, Barbara, *The Hell of the English: Bankruptcy and the Victorian Novel* (Lewisburg: Bucknell University Press, 1986).

Williams, Raymond, *The English Novel from Dickens to Lawrence* (London: Chatto & Windus, 1970).

—— *Keywords: A Vocabulary of Culture and Society* (London: Fontana, 1976).

Woodmansee, Martha, and Mark Osteen (eds), *The New Economic Criticism: Studies at the Intersection of Literature and Economics* (London: Routledge, 1999).

Index

NB. References to critics are to those *discussed* in this book.